Imagining the Victim
of Crime

Imagining the Victim of Crime

Sandra Walklate

 Open University Press

Open University Press
McGraw-Hill Education
McGraw-Hill House
Shoppenhangers Road
Maidenhead
Berkshire
England
SL6 2QL

email: enquiries@openup.co.uk
world wide web: www.openup.co.uk

and Two Penn Plaza, New York, NY 10121–2289, USA

First published 2007

Copyright © Sandra Walklate 2007

A catalogue record of this book is available from the British Library

ISBN–10: 0 335 21727 3 (pb)   0 335 21728 1 (hb))
ISBN–13: 978 0 335 21727 4 (pb)   978 0 335 21728 1 (hb)

Library of Congress Cataloging-in-Publication Data
CIP data applied for

Typeset by YHT Ltd, London
Printed in Poland by OZ Graf. S.A.
www.polskabook.pl

The *McGraw·Hill* Companies

For Kenneth Joseph Walklate

Contents

Preface and Acknowledgements

This book brings together a range of writing about criminal victimization that I have been involved in over recent years. Since my first foray into researching and writing about criminal victimization and its impact in the early 1980s, interest in the victim of crime has grown apace. Then it was relatively easy to direct students to the key literature in the area. Now that task is neither easy nor straightforward as the stream of academic literature, policy and political documentation on crime and its impact is added to on a month-by-month basis. This mushrooming concern about the crime victim is nowhere more evident that in the political domain, as each successive Home Secretary seeks to justify criminal justice policies of all kinds by reference to the perceived contemporary need to ensure a victim-oriented criminal justice system. This book charts that changing policy landscape from the early 1980s to its contemporary preoccupations and imaginings of the victim of crime. In so doing, it does not claim to be exhaustive – that would be an almost impossible task in a volume of this kind – but it does claim to have a view about where we have been and where we are going with our contemporary concerns, a view that has grown out of the opportunities I have been given to think and write critically about criminal victimization in recent years.

In the latter respect there are many people to whom acknowledgement is due, but I would like to offer particular thanks to Ronnie Lippens and Tony Kearon, both at the University of Keele, for inviting me to write something for their Special Issue of *Social Justice* published in 2005. I would also like to thank Brian Williams for inviting me to contribute to the inaugural publication of the *British Journal of Community Justice* in 2002; Nony Ardill of the Legal Action Group for inviting me to speak at their series of events debating the government's White Paper, *Justice for All*, in 2003; and Maureen Cain and Adrienne Howe for inviting me to speak about criminal victimization surveys at their international feminist network workshop held in Onati, Spain in 2003. Updated versions of these various contributions can be found on the pages here. I would also like to acknowledge the work that I have been involved with at Manchester Metropolitan University with Gabe Mythen on terrorism and fear which has influenced some of my thinking in relation to criminal victimization and is also reflected in Chapter 4.

I took up the Eleanor Rathbone Chair of Sociology at Liverpool University in January 2006, and it seems fitting that I have been involved in writing my third book about criminal victimization while occupying that position, in a city in which I did my first work with crime victims in the early 1980s. I would like to thank my new colleagues there for their very friendly welcome, especially Gerard Delanty who made it easy for me to join the department and finish the work I had in hand. In the latter respect, particular thanks go to Henrik Tham, at the Institute of Criminology at the University of Stockholm, who offered me such good hospitality and warm comradeship during April 2006 and gave me the space to complete the final draft of this book. My partner, Ron Wardale, who read, reread, and commented on much of this work during that month, with his unerring ability not to let me lose sight of maintaining a critical edge, has been, and is always, appreciated. Last, but by no means least, this book is dedicated to my father, Kenneth Joseph Walklate, who, all those years ago, resisted the family pressures to send me out to work rather than stay on at school, a decision that has rewarded me thousands of times over and one that I hope he is still proud of.

Sandra Walklate
Eleanor Rathbone Chair of Sociology, University of Liverpool
Stockholm, April 2006

Introduction

> The good news is that the number of people who are victims of crime has fallen by 40% compared to ten years ago. And if people are the victims of crime, their experience of the criminal justice system is vastly improved. For example, the Code of Practice for Victims of Crime means that victims will be regularly updated about the progress of their case. When victims, or witnesses, have to go to court, they are helped throughout the process by Witness Care Units, the Witness Service, and new measures in court which make giving evidence less traumatic. Victims now have the opportunity to make a personal statement of how the crime has had an impact on them, and there has been a radical reform of sentencing. Many more victims are now receiving support from Victim Support and other organisations than in the past. (Home Office 2005)

The statement above is taken from the ministerial foreword to a Home Office consultation document published in December 2005. That document lists the achievements that have been made in delivering improved services to victims of crime and is concerned to explore where further work needs to be done. One of its main concerns is with improving the operation and delivery of the work of the Criminal Injuries Compensation Authority (CICA), especially with respect to the speed with which it operates. Arguably this particular focus of concern emerged in the aftermath of the London bombings on 7 July 2005 that pointed to not only the efficiency with which the CICA operated but also what it understood, and was permitted to understand, were appropriate levels of compensation, for what kind of injury and for whom. At the time of writing, this process of consultation is yet to draw to a close, but the nature of it, and the spirit of the document, epitomized by the tone of the ministerial foreword quoted above, say much about how understandings of, and responses to, criminal victimization have changed since the first establishment in 1964 of what was then called the Criminal Injuries Compensation Board. The intention of this book is to trace those changing understandings in order to offer a critical documentation and contextualization of the policy responses that are contemporarily in play. However, it is difficult to offer a full appreciation of the changes that have occurred in the local context of England and Wales, in which the Home Office might produce a document like *Rebuilding Lives*, without situating an understanding of those changes within the wider changing global context. The central purpose of this Introduction is to map some of those wider, and perhaps all-embracing, global changes.

Then and now: 1964–2005

As will be argued in Chapter 1, the early 1960s in many ways were marked, in policy terms, by consolidation of the achievements of the welfare state in the era after the Second World War. Victims of crime, *per se*, were not part of political or policy rhetoric, neither was there any substantive available or influential research conducted on victims of crime. Much of the early victimological work that might claim that name was largely conducted by émigré lawyers cum criminologists and was done in the United States. These commentators took the Holocaust as their problematic, and the World Society of Victimology, in its early life, shared in those intellectual origins. Indeed, with the exception of the formation of the Criminal Injuries Compensation Board which, as Miers (1978) argued, constituted the first politicization of the crime victim, a lack of interest in the victim of crime and/or the impact of crime was largely sustained until towards the end of the 1960s – largely, it could be argued, as a consequence of relatively stable rates of recorded crime. But then these relatively stable conditions began to change.

The first criminal victimization survey was conducted in the United States in 1967. The development of this research instrument, designed in the first instance so that policy makers could say something about the nature and extent of what was then called the 'dark figure' of crime, marked the beginning of a turning point both for victimology and for policy responses to the victim of crime. It is in the development of this research instrument that we can observe one of the early examples within the domain of victim research of the way in which not only research methodologies travel (in the context of the criminal victimization survey and the problems that this engenders, see Chapter 3), but also policy responses might travel (a theme that recurs throughout this book). However, this research instrument, intimately connected with policy from its inception, like its home discipline of victimology, provided researchers and policy makers with a wealth of information about what concerned people, not only about crime, but also about the criminal justice system, and provided one route through which concern about the victim of crime became possible.

During the 1970s and early 1980s crime rates grew, especially in the USA and the UK, and in the first instance, in England and Wales, concern for the victim of crime emerged in a rather informal and patchy way within the voluntary sector. Parallel with these developments, the pilot criminal victimization survey done by Sparks *et al.* 1977 was the forerunner of the development of the British Crime Survey that was first conducted in 1982. Faced with rising crime rates, and a criminal justice system in which, it would appear, nothing worked, the data from that first survey were deliberately used politically to underplay the nature and extent of crime (see Mayhew and Hough 1988) as a way of not only allaying public concerns about crime but also justifying the demands for economy and efficiency that were to be increasingly expected of the different branches of the criminal justice system at that time. The links between the further politicization and reconstruction of the crime victim from being a complainant in the criminal justice system to a consumer of criminal justice services evidences the impact of the global recession of the mid-1970s, which was repeated in the early 1990s, on the local service delivery context. Such global processes were also increasingly felt in the nature of service delivery itself, as governments looked for better (that is, more efficient and cost-effective ways) of delivering services of all kinds, including those of the criminal justice system. The increasing presence of these kinds of management strategies has frequently been referred to as a form of 'actuarial justice' (Feeley and Simon 1994) in which the victim became constituted as a central feature of achieving these management processes. Evidence of the impact of these kinds of changes can be traced through the concerns addressed in this book from the reorientation of services to women as victims (consumers) of services (see Chapter 6) through to the more explicitly audit culture driven modernizing agenda of the contemporary government and the policies that have been introduced under that rubric (see, for example, Chapter 5).

During this time research on the impact of crime continued apace, in some respects led by the Home Office sponsored criminal victimization survey and the response that it generated and, in other respects, responsive to the emergent work of the voluntary sector (both feminist and non-feminist) alongside the increasing academic space being given to criminology and victimology. At the beginning of the 1980s the Home Office in England and Wales was the biggest employer of those who called themselves criminologists. In contemporary terms, this is certainly not the case. (These developments, alongside the academic development of the discipline of victimology, are covered in more detail in Chapters 1 and 2.)

By the mid-1990s the academic, political and policy concern for the victim of crime was well established. However, arguably these concerns took a sharper edge in the aftermath of a number of high-profile crimes that were taken by the media, at least, to signify the state of some aspects of society in England and Wales. The murder of James Bulger, in particular, provoked some considerable debate (in a shape and form that the murders committed by Mary Bell in the late 1960s did not) not only politically but also socially. The screaming mob chasing the prison van that contained Jon Venables and John Thompson was an image arguably belonging to a different era. Nevertheless these images marked an (acceptable) expression of emotion in the face of victimization that also had changed from the 1960s.

Put in the context of understanding the nature and impact of criminal victimization, it can be argued that the emergence and development of (mostly voluntary) services, designed to help an individual put their lives back in order both practically and emotionally after such an event, reveal much about how, as a society, changes in emotional management have evolved. Furedi (2002) would argue that these changes are part of wider cultural changes that encourage victimhood in all of us. Whatever the underlying cause of these changes, the management of emotion constitutes an increasingly important feature of criminal justice policy responses to the victim of crime that has changed in its tenor from the 1960s to contemporary times. In some respects, of course, these concerns have become elided and hidden by the political rhetoric and continued politicization of the crime victim, but the perpetual invocation of the image of the victim as a justification for policy, needs to be related to these wider concerns about emotional management, and in this book an attempt has been made to stitch this consideration into the analysis that is offered. Of course emotion is nowhere more rife than in considering the fear of crime as a source of victimization (see Chapter 4) and in the context of a world faced with the threat of 'new' terrorism raises quite fundamental questions concerning victimology's ability to make sense of this feature of the contemporary social condition.

In this latter sense this book endeavours to take account of the questions that are raised by a world in which, since 11 September 2001, things will never be the same again (Worcester 2001). Such events, alongside the events in Madrid in 2004, in London in 2005, and other global disasters such as the tsumani of December 2004, other natural disasters, and continued interethnic conflicts throughout the world, raise all kinds of questions about what can be considered as legal or illegal, criminal or not criminal, and who as a consequence is considered to be a victim or otherwise of crime (issues around the cultural processes associated with victimhood notwithstanding). In the social sciences over the last 40 years increasing space has been given to the risk society thesis, most famously explicated by Beck (1992) as a way of making sense of the precariousness of contemporary social life. Victimology, as a discipline, demands a theoretical framework that can work with the questions that the events listed above pose as well as those events and issues more conventionally understood as criminal or problematic for the victim of crime in their relationship with the criminal justice system. Efforts have been made throughout this book to stitch these kinds of concerns into its agenda, and the concerns posed by a 'post terroristic world society' (Beck 2002), and point to areas where policies and debates could be differently shaped if such concerns had a more central place on the victimological agenda.

Elsewhere (Walklate 1990) I have argued for the adoption within victimology of a theoretical position that recognizes that human beings actively construct and reconstruct their daily lives; that these constructions reflect both practices of resistance and acceptance of their social reality, and are made in a context of observable and unobservable generative mechanisms that have a real impact on people's lives, whether or not they are aware of them; and that these processes have both intended and unintended consequences that further feed the knowledgeability of human beings and set the scene for future action. As Sayer (2000: 19), quoted by Flynn (2006: 89), adds: 'Much of what happens does not depend or correspond to actors' understandings; there are unintended consequences and unacknowledged conditions and things can happen to people regardless of their understandings.' Moreover, Flynn (2006: 89) adds to this by suggesting that: 'What is *critical* about this approach is that it assumes the possibility of alternative conditions. It asks what must and what might happen, and it is critical of existing structures and processes – critical realism aspires to offer a potentially emancipatory analysis associated with normative choices.' This is the critical edge to the critical victimology with which this book endeavours to work and is discussed in more detail in Chapter 2. Put rather simply this posits a meaningful, if not straightforward, relationship between individual action and the social conditions of and for action. This is a position that is not far from that posited by Giddens (1984), and in the context of understanding some important features of the contemporary social condition it means recognizing that there are real risks of victimization, independent of people's knowledge of them, there are actual risks (what happens when people encounter victimizing situations) and there are the risks and victimizations that people experience for themselves. For example, those in positions of power long knew about the real risks of terrorist attack in London, which are distinct from the actual risks for those people who encountered those attacks, and how those who survived dealt with them. Then, in addition, there is the empirical reality of what people may choose to do or not to do in the aftermath of such an event. The latter two types of choice bear very little, if any, relationship with the real chance of further victimization. However, a critical realist approach, with its intrinsic commitment to the possibility of change, offers up the opportunity of being critical of structures and processes that engender or prevent victimization, and is set within the realm of the normative: what should and should not be the case. In other words, it meets head on the political, structural and moral processes that lie embedded within the delivery of criminal justice policy and the drive to use criminal justice policy as a vehicle for change. It leads us to ask who gets what and why.

Hudson (2003) has cogently argued that, over the last decade, decisions about the nature of criminal justice policy have also become entwined with questions of responsibility. As she says (2003: 52): 'although there may be nothing new about fearful consciousness of risk [of crime], there is something

new about the placing of responsibility for risk so unequivocally on individuals'. Moreover, she goes on to suggest that 'What is new, perhaps, is the
joining together of the actuarial, probabilistic language of risk and the moral
language of blame' (2003: 53). Such intertwining can be found across the
social science disciplines that have concerned themselves with issues of risk,
from health to sexuality, the workplace and crime. The one question that
they all subsume is captured in Hudson's (2003: 40) question: how much
liberty should be traded in the interests of security? Or perhaps, put another
way, and foregrounding a concern that can be traced through this book:
whatever happened to the criminal justice system as a public (social) good?
Thus the critical victimology embraced by the analysis offered by this book is
hopefully the means by which critical documentation, contextualization and
appreciation of the processes underpinning contemporary policy options can
be better understood.

Structure and outline of this book

Having set the concerns of this book within the wider changing landscape of
the processes of globalization, the problems of policy transfer, the processes of
emotional management, and the nature of the contemporary social condition
and its associated risks, the chapters that follow take up each of these themes
to a greater or lesser degree. Chapter 1 concerns itself with a historical overview of the way in which concerns about the victim of crime emerged and
what influenced the shape and form of those concerns. Chapter 2 assesses the
various theoretical perspectives available within the discipline of victimology
and their ability to make sense of the issues relating to criminal victimization.
Chapter 3 documents the nature of the criminal victimization survey instrument, its impact, and the way in which it has facilitated an understanding
of how crime impacts upon people's lives. Chapter 4 deals with the fear of
crime as a major source of that impact. Chapters 5 and 6 examine the question of policy from two different angles. The first takes the structurally neutral
image of the crime victim and explores the problems and possibilities of
policy intervention that derive from this position. The second takes a structurally informed view of the crime victim (looking particularly at women and
people from ethnic minorities) and engages in a similar policy exploration
process. Whilst the central focus of this discussion is England and Wales,
wherever possible research findings and policy possibilities are discussed with
reference to work done and relevant initiatives that have taken place in other
countries. The concluding chapter revisits some of the themes that have been
flagged up for consideration in this Introduction with a view to asking the
reader to consider whether or not the current government's preoccupation
with the victim of crime is reasonable, justified, or just politically expedient.

1   Are we all victims now?

Introduction

It is now commonplace to discuss the contemporary social condition in relation to the risk society thesis. Put simply, this thesis posits that we now live
in a society that is preoccupied with the future: the desire to be free from risk.
Furedi (1997, 2002) has referred to this desire as a 'culture of fear'. Indeed in a
global society that has clearly been affected not only by the attacks on the
United States (11 September 2001), Madrid (11 March 2004) and London (7
July 2005), but also by a number of recent natural disasters (notably the
tsunami in December 2004), it is hard not to escape the significance of
Furedi's analysis. The processes associated with a preoccupation with safety in
the light of a world of instantaneous communication manifest themselves in
diverse ways. Young (1999) identifies some of them in the shift from the
inclusive society of the period after the Second World War to what he calls
the contemporary exclusive society, and Garland (2001) identifies such processes in criminal justice policy in the manifestation of what he calls a 'culture of control'. A concern common to these commentators is the rapidly
changing social context in which we now all live. In such a rapidly changing
context, even the government's own futurologists in the UK admit that we
are 'leaving behind a social order that we know well and are entering a world
the contours of which are dim' (Foresight 2000).

   In this socio-cultural context a number of features in relation to crime
have come to be taken for granted, especially in the UK and the USA. Garland
and Sparks (2000) list these in the following way. First, high crime rates have
become a normal feature of everyday life, along with avoiding victimization.
Second, the fear of crime has become a highly emotive political reference
point. Third, there has been an acceptance of a growing private sector of
criminal justice provision and an increasingly individualized involvement in
crime management. Fourth, crime and the awareness of crime have become
institutionalized in the media and within popular culture. Fifth, a concern
with and for the victim of crime has become not just a symbolic reference
point in government policy but the dominant one. Taken together, all of
these presume some idea and understanding of the harm done by criminal
victimization, an understanding that has increasingly informed the policy-
making process.

   In this kind of social and policy context others have suggested that we now live in a society marked by victimization prevention policy rather than crime prevention policy (Karmen 1990), a view that is expressed a little more subtly by Garland (1996) as a process of 'responsibilization'. The processes that all of these writers are referring to are not necessarily simple nor straightforward but reflect, at a minimum, what Garland (2001) has called the criminal justice system's adaptation to failure: an admission that the crime problem cannot be solved, only managed. Against this background, current criminal justice policy is being formulated such that, as Zedner (2002: 419) has observed:

> Victims, once on the margins of criminological research, are now a central focus of academic research. Crime surveys, both national and local, and qualitative studies of the impact of crime, of victim needs and services have furnished a wealth of information which has permanently altered the criminological agenda. . . . As a result the victim has moved from being the 'forgotten actor' to key player in the criminal justice process.

This is a move that is clearly evident in the Home Office (2005) consultation document referred to in the Introduction. The central purpose of this chapter is to trace the ways in which the victim of crime has been transformed from being the forgotten party of the criminal justice system (Schafer 1968) to now occupying the centre of the stage of criminal justice policy initiatives (Zedner 2002), especially in the UK. Whether or not this contemporary policy position of the victim of crime constitutes a symbolic or a real shift of concern is a moot point, and this chapter will be concerned to explore some of the tensions that are posed between this symbolism and reality. However, in order to explore some of these tensions, it will be useful to begin by considering the historical role afforded to the victim in the criminal justice system in England and Wales. From this starting point we shall consider some of the key moments in the transformation of the role of the crime victim, and move on to consider how these moments of change might be understood by reference to the kinds of wider socio-cultural changes mentioned above. Much of the discussion in this chapter will be situated in England and Wales. However, as this book unfolds these developments and transformations will be placed within a wider global context. But before it is possible to move on to that wider global scene, a little local victim history.

A victim history: England and Wales to 1979

Schafer (1968) argued that Anglo-Saxon times constituted the 'Golden Age of the victim' in England and Wales. This view was predicated on a particular understanding of the role that the victim then had both in the process of prosecution and in their right to compensation. However, during the Middle Ages, as the state became increasingly centralized, this 'Golden Age' came to an end and the right to either of these roles receded somewhat. Moreover, by the 1870s the victim's role in the process of prosecution was rendered almost extinct as the emergent (new) police forces in England and Wales increasingly took over this role. Neither of these elements of victim participation in the criminal justice system was completely eroded, as Mawby and Gill (1987) observed, since even in the late 1870s there was still legal provision for the victim of crime to claim compensation from the offender. However, such 'rights' were rather minimal and, apart from their obvious role in reporting crime to the police, by the beginning of the twentieth century the crime victim hardly featured in criminal justice policy, criminal justice practice, or even less in political rhetoric. Nevertheless there appears to be a consensus of opinion that the campaigning work of Margery Fry in the mid-1950s constituted a moment of change in all of this. Margery Fry's book, *Arms of the Law* (1951), opened a debate concerning whether or not the state was obliged to compensate the (innocent) victim of crime. This debate lasted through the 1950s and culminated in the establishment in 1964 of the Criminal Injuries Compensation Board (CICB) for England and Wales, now called the Criminal Injuries Compensation Authority.

Waller (1988) has argued that the establishment of this board 'trail blazed' the way for other countries to follow. Moreover, as Mawby and Walklate (1994) have also suggested, its implementation could be seen as the last brick in the wall of the postwar welfare state – a brick that was cemented by the principle of insurance that proffered a contractual relationship between the individual and the state. It was arguably the commitment to this principle of insurance, which was found in the campaigning voice of Margery Fry, which informed the formation of the CICB. Rock (1990: 66) offers this analysis of her argument:

> In her last formulation of the problem, compensation would represent a collective insurance provided by society. All taxpayers would be regarded as subscribers. All taxpayers were at risk of becoming victims. Since the state forbade citizens arming themselves, it should assume responsibility for its failure to provide protection.

This understanding of the importance of the principle of insurance, and the relationship between the citizen and the state that it presupposed, is a theme that we shall revisit; however, it must be remembered at this juncture that this 'trail blazing' policy initiative was established to address the *perceived* needs of the *innocent* victim of violent crime and thus was not rooted in *evidence* at all. Moreover, as Mawby and Gill (1987) were to argue later, this narrow remit was justified on the grounds that many other 'rights' that victims of violence might want access to, such as health care, were already in place as part of other packages in the postwar welfare state.

So, embedded within the CICB was the notion of the 'innocent' victim of crime that was derived from earlier distinctions between 'the deserving' and 'the undeserving', and as we shall see this kind of distinction in relation to criminal victimization has persisted to a greater or lesser extent in a variety of forms within criminal justice policy. Despite the problems inherent in such distinctions (not least of which is the implied regulatory power of the state to distinguish the deserving from the undeserving), there was a sense in which, with the formation of the CICB, the welfare state was at that point in time considered complete. So the establishment of the CICB in the 1960s is arguably one of the first significant moments in the transformation and movement of the victim of crime from the periphery towards the centre of criminal justice policy. Along with this moment, however, as Miers (1978) has cogently argued, the victim of crime also became politicized. Put simply, in the 1960s no one asked what it was that a crime victim in England and Wales might want or need from the criminal justice system. Politicians, in evoking the image of the victim of crime, presumed that they knew, as did of course those professionals working within the criminal justice system. Moreover, from this point in time this process of politicization continued apace. The next impetus in the transformation of the victim of crime came, however, not from formal political and policy processes, but from the voluntary sector.

During the 1970s two distinct but important groups each made their own contribution to widening the appreciation and understanding of the impact that crime had on the victim. These were the feminist movement and what was then (in the late 1970s) called the National Association of Victim Support Schemes. The feminist movement then and now, whilst not concerned with criminal victimization *per se*, in focusing attention on the nature and extent of rape and domestic violence through the establishment of rape crisis centres and women's refuges, undoubtedly played its part in transforming understandings of the nature and extent of criminal victimization. As I have argued elsewhere (Walklate 2003a, 2004) the feminist focus of concern reflected a tendency to construct an image of the crime victim as predominantly female, to the exclusion of male victimization, but nevertheless this focus usefully demanded that policy makers think about the gendered dimensions to the experience of being a victim of crime.

Victim Support (as it is now called) operated with a much more structurally neutral image of the crime victim (Rock 1990). Yet in a similar way, as the fastest-growing voluntary organization in England and Wales from the late 1970s to the early 1990s it too had an enormous impact in acting as a voice for the crime victim. This voice was, in the 1970s and early 1980s, concerned with the rather more 'mundane' impact of crimes such as burglary and theft. These crimes, it was assumed at that point in time by this voluntary group, were committed on ordinary people by others unknown to them. It is only more recently that Victim Support has also concerned itself with the more 'contentious' issues of crimes in which the victim often knows the offender, as in cases of racial harassment or domestic violence.

The presence and efforts of these two different voices from within the voluntary sector have been analysed in greater detail by Mawby and Walklate (1994; see also Spalek 2006) but their presence during the 1980s, a decade that was marked by the increasing importance and impact of public expenditure cuts in England and Wales under the creeping influence of neo-liberal economic policies, ensured that in their different ways they played a part in another dimension of the transfer of the victim from the periphery to the centre. This, Mawby and Walklate (1994) have argued, transformed the victim of crime from a victim *per se* into a *consumer* of the criminal justice process. This transformation began in 1979 and arguably culminated in 1990 in the publication of the first Victim's Charter. Given the historical importance of the election of the Conservative Party to power in 1979 and the subsequent impact this had on public service delivery, it will be useful to consider the impact of those intervening years in a little more detail.

A victim history: England and Wales 1979 to date

Different writers have attempted to explain how and why the years since 1979 have had such an impact on the presence and visibility of the victim of crime. Dignan's (2005) analysis focuses on the importance of the work of Margery Fry in putting the groundwork in place; the role of the media (especially during the 1960s in their coverage of the Moors murders) in the nature and extent of their coverage of crime; the increasing awareness of who was vulnerable in relation to crime (especially women, children and the elderly); the impact of terrorist activity before September 2001, on the one hand, and the rising crime rate, on the other; the wider use of the criminal victimization survey; and the increasing interest of criminologists in victimization. Goodey (2005) lists ten factors, some of which are coterminous with those of Dignan, but others include factors such as changing levels of public tolerance and the increasing use of victims as vote winners by politicians. In reality, then, the picture is likely to be a rather complex one, and it will be difficult to do justice to all of the developments that have taken place from 1979 onwards. However, attention will be paid here to three ingredients to this process: the development and application of the criminal victimization survey; research on gender and victimization; and the increasingly widespread understanding of the impact of crime.

Sparks *et al.* (1977) did the groundwork for the development and application of the criminal victimization survey in the UK. The first British Crime Survey was conducted in 1982, and gathered data from over 10,000 people that included information on their experiences of crime, their expressed fear of crime, the impact that it had had on them and their attitudes towards the police, amongst other issues. Its findings were reported in Hough and Mayhew (1983) and the survey, refined and developed, has been repeated on a number of occasions since then (see Hough and Mayhew 1985; Mayhew *et al.* 1989, 1994; Mayhew 1993; Mirrlees-Black *et al.* 1996, 1998; Kershaw *et al.* 2001; Simmons and Dodd 2003). In addition, similar surveys have been conducted in Scotland (see Chambers and Tombs 1984; MVA Consultancy 2000). Moreover, as Chapter 3 illustrates, the reach of this survey methodology is now global.

These surveys provide a rich source of data about criminal victimization. They not only offer a more complete picture of the nature and extent of criminal victimization, but can now also provide an important source of information about the way in which criminal victimization may or may not be changing over time. For example, Simmons and Dodd (2003: 1) report that 'The risk of becoming a victim of crime remains at an historic low (around 27%) according to [the British Crime Survey], one third lower than the risk in 1995 (40%)'; yet interestingly, 'three quarters of the general public still believe that the national crime rate is rising'. This kind of anomaly, amongst others, afforded the opportunity for the development of further research questions, not least of which has been the findings that the British Crime Survey has generated with respect to the impact of crime (see below and Chapters 3 and 4).

The findings of the first British Crime Survey, in and of themselves, acted as an impetus for the development of this survey technique in other settings. These initial findings were presented to convey the clear message that the public's concern about crime was out of proportion to the actual risk from crime (see Hough and Mayhew 1983; Mayhew and Hough 1988). Whilst this was designed to meet with government policy it also masked a deeper problem with national victimization surveys: the tendency towards using statistical evidence as a way of generalizing to local experiences. This is an important problem, since during the 1980s it was also clear that some sections of the population were experiencing criminal victimization at a much higher level than others. Sparked by Young's (1986) demand for an 'accurate victimology', a number of local, geographically focused survey were conducted, notably in Islington, Edinburgh and Merseyside, as a way of trying to establish the extent to which criminal victimization was largely an urban, intra-ethnic and intra-class experience. Constructed as a part of what came to be called a 'left realist criminology' (see Matthews and Young 1992) these surveys significantly added to the wider appreciation of the structural dimensions of criminal victimization in the UK, and, as Percy and Mayhew (1997) report, led to changes in the British Crime Survey itself.

In addition, the more sophisticated development of this victimization survey methodology has led to further refinement and understanding of what might be called 'differential victimization', with work being conducted not only in locally geographically and socially focused areas but also to take account of the way in which certain 'structural locations' interact with one another. For example, survey work has been conducted on women's experiences of domestic violence within ethnic minority communities (Choudry 1996); other work has focused on experiences of rural crime (Dingwall and Moody 1999); yet other work has looked at the question of victimization in prison (O'Donnell and Edgar 1998). As was suggested earlier and is discussed in Chapter 3, this kind of work using this kind of methodology now has a global reach.

This is just a brief overview of the kind and range of victimological research that has been conducted over the last 25 years that had its origins within the development of the criminal victimization survey. It clearly illustrates that there is now a wealth of data available about levels and rates of victimization covering a wide range of topics. Indeed, establishing levels and rates of criminal victimization is now almost taken for granted in both local and national policy formation processes in England and Wales in the context of crime; at the local level this has been particularly determined by the Crime and Disorder Act of 1998. This rise and rise of the criminal victimization survey has had a number of telling effects: first, in the further work it has facilitated with respect to the impact of crime; and second, in the way in which it has contributed to the parameters of our understanding of what constitutes criminal victimization. Each of these issues is addressed more fully below, but first we shall consider the second ingredient that was highlighted for the discussion here: the relationship between gender and victimization.

The marginalization of the feminist movement from those committed to a more mainstream victimological research agenda has been well documented (see, for example, Rock 1986; see also Chapter 2 below). Rock implied that this occurred to a certain extent as a result of the choices made by feminists themselves who regarded the concept of victim precipitation as equivalent to victim blaming. (Though it has to be said that the concerns of feminism run much deeper than those proposed by Rock: see Walklate 2003a; and Chapter 2 below). Nevertheless the influence of research emanating from the feminist movement that documents women's 'victimization' from male violence should not be underestimated. Whilst there have always been problems in comparing what is being measured in relation to violence against women (incidence or prevalence), in the UK the work of Hamner and Saunders (1984) in Leeds, Hall (1985) in London and Radford (1987) again in

London all reported a remarkable level of sexual violence perpetrated by men towards women (59%, 33% and 76%, respectively). One of the problems with these studies, however, whilst indicating the potentially poor level of such crime reporting to the police, was that they all used different definitions of what constituted sexual violence, and these definitions did not necessarily resonate with the legal definition. This, as a result, added a further difficulty to the question of measurable comparison. (The legal definition has, of course, been a source of contention for some time for those committed to seeing the world through the eyes and experiences of women – an issue that shall be returned to later in this book.)

Nevertheless these kinds of findings stood in stark contrast to the absence of incidents of rape from the first British Crime Survey of 1982 (with only 18 incidents of attempted sexual assault being reported). Moreover, the findings based on data gathered for the British Crime Survey conducted in 1984 did little better. Similar disparities in findings could be found in respect of domestic violence. Indeed, the absence of a crime called 'domestic' violence meant that in the early criminal victimization studies it just was not counted at all. Yet at the same time the work of Dobash and Dobash (1979, 1998), Hamner and Saunders (1984), Painter (1991) and Mooney (1993) all pointed to high levels of violence 'behind closed doors'.

Increasingly the kinds of crimes highlighted in the findings of this work, despite the empirical and operational problems associated with them, have been given a much more prominent position in the more methodologically conventional criminal victimization survey work conducted by the Home Office. For example, the work of Myhill and Allen (2002) based on reporting to the British Crime Survey suggests an incidence of rape for the year 2000 of 61,000 women and a prevalence rate (i.e. number of incidents experienced by women since) of 754,000. They also report that 'current partners' were responsible for 45% of alleged rapes reported to the British Crime Survey. In addition, a recent report on the nature and extent of violence sponsored by the Economic and Social Research Council (ESRC 2002) using a range of data sources, suggests that there were 600,873 recorded incidents of violence against the person in England and Wales for the year ending March 2001, 25% of which are estimated to be domestic assaults, and that in the UK the police receive the equivalent of one call every minute asking for assistance with domestic violence. Only 5% of these incidents involve the man as a victim.

Thus, even from this brief overview (these issues are given much thorough coverage in Chapter 6), it can be seen that the issues that were of central concern to women committed to feminism in the early 1980s, namely male violence against women, have moved from being either non-existent or marginal with respect to mainstream victim-oriented research to being much more at the centre of that work, especially in relation to policy. This has resulted in not only the British Crime Survey acknowledging the importance of taking account of such victimization but also a widening of the academic agenda of criminology in the UK, as well as the policy agenda. One example of the latter effect is that the 2003 Sexual Offences Act, which came into force in May 2004, incorporates a definition of rape that includes oral, anal and vaginal penetration, constituting an important extension of the legal under-standing of how rape is experienced that has been a long-standing focus of feminist campaigns. A further example can be found in the amount of effort that has gone into ensuring that 'domestic' violence is responded to more appropriately by all the relevant agencies. (Both of these issues are discussed much more fully in Chapter 6.) However, the extent to which these policy changes have occurred as a consequence of the research findings highlighted above or as a result of other processes is difficult to discern – something that we shall explore again later. In addition, it is also important to note that victim-oriented research in and around sexual violence has latterly begun to take more seriously such violence perpetrated on men. McMullen (1990), Mezey and King (1992), Lees (1997), Coxell *et al.* (1999) and Allen (2002) all point to the extent and hidden nature of such violence against men and its impact. The study by Coxell *et al.* suggests that almost 3% of men in England report non-consensual sexual experiences with other men as adults. In ad-dition, there is now an increasing awareness of the impact that such violence has on men as its victims, with the concomitant emergence of support ser-vices for men who have been so victimized.

In summary, then, the impact of feminism on victim-oriented studies has been quite profound. Such research has not only put the nature and extent of (sexual) violence against women clearly on the research agenda, but also been a key factor in the growing recognition of the nature and extent of such violence on men. Thus, contemporarily, the gap between more con-ventionally oriented work sponsored by central and local governments and that of a more radical persuasion is much narrower than it was. In addition, there have been some significant shifts in the policy arena that parallel this narrowing gap and a clear widening of what might be considered to be the legitimate concerns of a victim-oriented research agenda. However, before offering an overall evaluation of the impact of such victim-oriented research, it is useful to consider what has been generated concerning the impact of crime from these different data sources – the third of the ingredients to policy change to be discussed here.

The development and application of the criminal victimization survey and the related work discussed above have afforded the opportunity of a much more sensitive and in-depth appreciation of the impact of criminal victimi-zation and the subsequent experience that people who have been criminally victimized have of the criminal justice system. This has led to a wealth of research on issues from the 'fear' of crime (for a recent overview of how this has been developed and refined, see Hope and Sparks 2000) to the impact of particular kinds of crimes on particular groups of people. For example, work on burglary victims has been done by Maguire (1982); on victims of violent crime by Shapland *et al.* (1985) and Stanko (1988); on child victims by Morgan and Zedner (1992); on the secondary victimization of the families of murder victims by Rock (1998); on rape victims by Chambers and Millar (1983) and Allen (2002); and on the elderly as victims by Brogden and Nijhar (2000). This work has variously concerned itself with the short- and long-term emotional and physical effects of victimization alongside the different kinds of support that might be needed to offset the worst effects. Some of the earlier work has also contributed to an appreciation of different levels of vulnerability to victimization, an issue that has spawned a research agenda of its own in the form of the phenomenon of 'repeat victimization'.

Targeting repeat victimization became a key part of crime prevention policy during the 1990s in the UK. Of course, the phenomenon of repeat or multiple victimization has a history of its own (see Farrell 1992). It is also commented on in the study by Sparks *et al.* (1977) and, of course, the feminist work cited above had been aware of repeat victimization in the context of domestic violence for some time. Borrowing from this work, Hope and Walklate (1995) argued for a more sensitive understanding of these experiences in terms of victimizing relationships over time and space. Nevertheless, work on repeat victimization proceeded apace (see, for example, British Journal of Criminology 1995; Pease 1998), and some of this focus has led to a more finely tuned appreciation of the nature and extent of racial harassment (Bowling 1998). The phenomenon of repeat victimization is discussed in more detail in Chapter 3.

One final area in which the impact of crime has been demonstrated is with respect to people's experiences of the criminal justice system. Here Shapland *et al.* (1985), Mawby and Gill (1987), Raine and Smith (1991) and Maguire and Kynch (2000) all point in their different ways to the different kinds of information and support that victims of crime report would improve their experience of the criminal justice process. This work has differently centred the need to be kept informed about what is happening in 'their' case, the availability of information about compensation in its various forms, and the need for support when acting as witnesses in court, to list a few of the main findings that have resulted from it. Indeed, it is within the criminal justice system that many policy initiatives have occurred, especially since the introduction of the first Victim's Charter in 1990.

Since the introduction of the first charter in 1990 there have been two other charters in 1996 and 2002; the victim personal statement scheme has been introduced, much of the work of the Probation Service has been re-oriented towards concern for the victim of crime, police forces throughout England and Wales have dedicated domestic violence units, with many also having racial harassment units, and latterly much policy and research energy has been devoted to the development of restorative justice initiatives following on from the 1998 Crime and Disorder Act. As a consequence it is probably self-evident, as Zedner (2002) stated and as quoted earlier, the victim is no longer the forgotten party of the criminal justice system. It is, however, still a moot point, as Sebba (2001) suggests, how far this is a result of the research outlined above or the further politicization of the victim of crime. Nevertheless it is the case that, in contemporary terms, the victim of crime is central to the *expressed* concerns of criminal justice policy and government, exemplified perhaps by the contemporary existence of the Home Office's own Victims Unit.

This brief presentation of a 'victim history' has introduced a number of themes that will be taken up in greater detail in later chapters of this book, but it has suggested that there have been a number of key moments and processes that have contributed to the transformation of the role of the victim of crime. As was suggested above, different commentators have highlighted different features of the changing nature of the political and policy context since the end of the Second World War, though there appears to be some common agreement on the heightened nature of these changing processes since 1979. The three ingredients discussed above point in themselves to the rapid growth and development of the sheer amount of information about victims of crime. However, as Sebba (2001) has pointed out, there is no necessary correlation between this kind of information and its appropriate use within the policy-making process, despite the fact that much of the funding for the gathering of the information has come from government departments. Moreover, as was implied at the beginning of this chapter, and as Goodey (2005) observes, the contemporary preoccupation with risk and insecurity offers a cultural resonance with being a victim. As a consequence, our understanding of the increasingly acute presence of the crime victim, especially since 1979, needs to go beyond the ingredients that have been discussed so far and towards offering a more complete understanding of the sociocultural and policy changes with which we are concerned. So perhaps, by implication, the movement of the victim from the periphery to the centre of criminal justice issues needs to be understood by reference to the ways in which governments have sought to manage the impact of risk and insecurity since the 1950s and what shifts in emphasis those management processes suggest.

A victim history in policy context

In the context of the UK there have been several interconnected shifts to the political, economic and democratic processes that constitute a significant part of the wider setting in which to understand the way in which responses to the victim of crime have evolved. In contemporary political terms, that is, since the election of the Labour Party to government in 1997, it is usual to contrast the social democratic commitment of Old Labour party policies of the 1950s and 1960s with the neo-liberal democratic policies of New Labour at the end of the 1990s and into the twenty-first century. This shift in policy position reflects the power and success of Conservative politics and policies in the intervening years (commented upon earlier in this chapter) and the consequent desire to be elected on the part of the Labour Party; hence the need for the party to reconsider its policy position. However, this shifting political position belies more fundamental economic processes also associated with neo-liberal democracies that are not solely confined to the UK. The global recession of the mid- to late 1970s, revisited in the early 1990s, took its toll economically in the UK, the USA and elsewhere and resulted in a radical reconsideration of what it could be considered that the state might deliver for its citizens. Referred to earlier in this chapter as a shift in responsibility from the state to the citizen, this economic reorientation was marked by a change of emphasis in which, rather than the state defining and enhancing what might be considered to be in the public interest, market forces were given the priority in this defining process. The space given to free market policies had an effect on a whole range of public services, including the delivery of the criminal justice system, and it is within this space that the privatization of such delivery again sets the framework for the reorientation of the criminal justice system towards the victim as a consumer of those services. It is also as a result of the space given to the market within this sphere, with its global characteristics, that criminal justice policies begin to travel globally. In particular, in the UK politicians increasingly looked across the Atlantic for policy initiatives that might work (hopefully more economically) in the UK. Victim policies in the contemporary context in the UK have made the journey across the Atlantic and have also travelled from the Antipodes to the UK (some of which are discussed in Chapter 5). In addition, these globalizing trends can be found within the work of victimology itself with the development of the International Criminal Victimization Survey discussed in detail in Chapter 3. In the local context of the UK these global processes have had an impact on the nature of the democratic process, so that commentators now no longer talk in terms of parliamentary democracy but rather the process of governance.

Taken together these processes raise questions about who now decides what is in the public interest and what constitutes a public good. How those questions are managed also reflects a more fundamental change in the role of the state from what Jessop (2002) has called the determined state to the hegemonic state. However, before we go on the consider this, it will be of value to spend some time discussing in a little more detail the relevance of two of the features highlighted above: the shift from Government to governance, and the question of the public good.

The shift from parliamentary democracy (or Government with a capital G) to governance is also discussed by Goodey (2005). In order to fully understand the importance of this shift, it is also important to understand the principles that lay behind policy making in the era after the Second World War. Put fairly simply, the idea of Government alludes to a set of principles sometimes referred to as the 'Westminster model'. This model assumed a strong cabinet, parliamentary democracy, electoral accountability and so on. However, as Rhodes (1997: 4) states:

> Since 1945 the institutions of British government have experienced at least two revolutions. The post war Labour government built the welfare state and its institutions, but these barely survived three decades before a reforming Conservative government sought to redefine most and abolish many. Allegedly the Westminster model no longer works.

The revolutions of which Rhodes (1997) speaks have been felt in all aspects of the policy-making process, including criminal justice policy. One key to understanding the radical nature of these changes is captured by the notion of governance. Rhodes (1997) argues that governance is broader than Government: 'governance refers to self-organising intra-organisational networks' in which the boundaries between the public sector, the private sector and the voluntary sector are constantly shifting and opaque. Nowhere is this diffusion of influence in the policy-making process more evident than in the context of responses to the victims of crime.

For example, the CICB, discussed earlier, was implemented without reference to the victim of crime *per se*. In other words, there was no empirical evidence to support the establishment of such a body, nor was there a voice speaking for the victim of crime in the policy process. The policy behind the formation of the CICB did have a champion (Elizabeth Fry), but as a policy it was formulated within the principles and framework of the welfare state of the 1950s; that is, informed by a principle of what it was reasonable to expect the state to put in place for its citizens. The same cannot be said today. Not only has Victim Support become one of the most successful voluntary organizations over the last 25 years, now having a central place in informing the policy process in relation to crime victims, but there is also a massive Home Office database in the form of the British Crime Survey that maps the impact of crime and the views of crime victims on a large number of matters, as illustrated in the discussion above. In addition, there has been a proliferation of organizations purporting to speak for the victim of crime – not as powerful in their influence as Victim Support, but none the less vociferous in their claims (for a fuller analysis of these groups in relation to homicide, see Rock 1998). In addition, high-profile crimes, such as the abduction and murder of Sarah Payne in 2000, have led to particular individuals, among them Sarah Payne's parents, claiming the ear of government ministers. It is important to remember that none of the aforementioned groups are elected representatives and none are necessarily accountable to anyone other than their own interests or the interests of their organizations. This articulates very clearly the blurring of the boundaries and the shifting nature of the influences on the policy process as conceptualized by Rhodes. There is, however, another layer to these changes.

The existence and proliferation of victims groups demonstrates the continuing 'powerful motif' of the victim (Bottoms 1983) and the continued 'politicisation of the victim' (Miers 1978). However, in the intervening years since the inception of the CICB, the policy-making process has not only become more differentiated and diffuse but also simultaneously less partisan and more political. In other words, whose voice is listened to, how, why, when and what about, are all key questions that need to be asked in the current policy climate. This leads to a consideration of the second, though related, theme in understanding the contemporary political and policy climate: the changing role of public services and what they are expected to deliver, frequently discussed in the context of 'new managerialism'.

New Labour, the political party that took the reins of power in 1997 in the UK, tasked the criminal justice system with deploying early effective interventions to divert those thought likely to offend from a life of crime; implementing fast-track, efficient procedures from arrest to sentence; improving services to victims and witnesses; enforcing court sentences more effectively; and ensuring that the component parts of the system are performing to their maximum potential. These tasks articulated the government's vision of how a modern criminal justice system might work. This is not the place to debate the impact or otherwise of new managerialism or the audit culture on the criminal justice system *per se* (though see, for example, McLaughlin *et al.* 2001), other than to observe that notions of the public interest or what constitutes a public good have changed as these processes have unfolded.

Since 1979, articulations of the 'public interest' have taken a number of forms. Clarke *et al.* (2000) suggest a number of representations of this. The first is a view of the public as taxpayers with their interests being equated with economy, efficiency and effectiveness, and who it is presumed have an antagonistic relationship with non-taxpayers. The second is a view of the public as consumers, as active choice makers within the public services (see Mawby and Walklate 1994, cited above). Hence the various charters of the late 1980s and early 1990s and contemporarily with the Victims' Code of Practice. The last view of the public identified by Clarke *et al.* is one of a community of diverse interests, a community which nevertheless is now 'responsibilized' (Clarke 2005) in the whole range of relationships it has with the state.

There are specific difficulties with all of these visions of the public interest. Yet despite the differences between them, they are all surface manifestations of a more fundamental and deeper changing relationship between the citizen and the state. What they share is a common view of the citizen who has rights to call upon the state, but rights that are contingent upon their willingness and ability as citizens to fulfil their obligations to the state. This is a significant shift from the relationship of the 1950s in which the citizen had rights and the state had obligations. In this fundamental shift, managed as it is in contemporary policy terms through a modernization agenda, there is considerable confusion as to what is in the public interest or what counts as a public good. Waldron (1993: 358) argues that a public good is 'something which is said to be valuable for human society without its value being adequately characterisable in terms of its worth to any or all of the members of the society considered one by one'. In this view the value of public goods, then, is not reducible to their aggregate value for each member of society but what they are worth to everyone together. In other words, they are irreducibly *social*. Public goods represent something more than their economic worth. Yet what it is that public goods represent contemporarily seems to be both uncertain and unclear. What is clear and certain, however, in the context of contemporary criminal justice policy, is that sight has been lost of the *social* value of the criminal justice system. Put more generally, there is an absence of a debate concerning what we understand by justice in general, and social justice in particular. In the absence of such a debate concerning the social value of justice, policy makers and politicians can make claims about 'Justice for All', the title of a government white paper (Home Office 2002) in which the victim of crime was placed at the centre of the criminal justice policy agenda.

Of course, what has been assumed in these processes, especially in the claims made on behalf of the crime victim, is that the victim of crime equates with 'us all'. As Alison Young (1996) has argued, victimhood has become elided with citizenship. Yet, as we have observed above, the proliferation of victims' groups, all with differential access to the policy process, along with the differential fragmentation of articulations of the public interest militate against any meaningful understanding of what is to be understood as 'all of us'. This is a hugely contested arena that, as we shall see, especially in Chapters 5 and 6, takes the policy agenda in quite different directions depending upon who is included and/or excluded in our understanding of 'all'.

This analysis of the transformative processes associated with the victim of crime clearly points to the way in which successive governments, in their desire to manage the problem of crime in changing economic circumstances and in the light of an increasing awareness of the nature and extent of criminal victimization, have looked to the victim of crime as a 'solution' to the questions that have been posed for them. However, this 'solution' has to be set in the wider cultural context of the risk society thesis on the one hand, that in the context of criminal justice policy has manifested itself as a 'culture of control' (Garland 2001) and the shift from a determined state to a hegemonic state (Jessop 2002) on the other. These two processes are the last ingredients in understanding the transformation of the victim of crime from the periphery to the centre of criminal justice policy, and each will be discussed in turn.

Crime, victims and the culture of control

Garland's book, *The Culture of Control* (2001), is part of a trilogy that reflects his concern with penal policy. In it he lays out the problem of how to account for the social and historical processes that have given rise to the current way of responding to crime, which, for the purposes here, focuses on the victim of crime. In his terms, he attempts to offer us a 'history of the present'. In other words, his analysis is rooted in trying to make sense of what has contributed to the current increasing prison population, the processes of social exclusion that can be observed between ethnic groups and social classes, the multiplicity of agencies that are now involved in delivering criminal justice policy (public, private, voluntary), and the co-existence of the increasing punitiveness of policy stances to be found especially in the UK and the USA, on the one hand, and the favourable response given to 'softer' restorative justice initiatives, on the other. In the background of his analysis of the changing nature of criminal justice policy he includes a consideration of the influence of the 'enterprise culture' so valued in the 1980s, the changes in the labour market, increasing spatial mobility, changing family structures, and the rise of individualism. In the foreground of his analysis his conceptual apparatus includes responsibilization, new managerialism, and what he calls the criminal justice system's adaptation to failure, that taken together comprise his vision of the 'culture of control'. Put simply, if we can't solve it, we'll control it. The cumulative effect of these processes is that crime is normalized (therefore being a victim of crime is normalized) and, moreover, there are quite distinct limits on the state's ability to solve the problem of crime.

Much of Garland's analysis is concerned to map the similarities in the developments that have taken place in the UK and the USA in the emergence of this culture of control. This analysis has been subjected to solid critique that need not concern us at this juncture (but see, for example, Braithwaite 2003; Feeley 2003; Young 2003a; Walklate 2005a), but an awareness of this culture of control facilitates an understanding of how and why the victim of crime features so much more now in political and policy terms than they did in the 1950s and 1960s. That understanding lies within an appreciation of the processes of *normalization* associated with being a victim of crime. These processes require more than being aware of the nature and extent of criminal victimization and the symbolic use of the crime victim, including understanding how these processes come together to meet political needs, on the one hand, and the underlying needs of the state, on the other. So the cultural processes of normalization of which Garland speaks reflect underlying structural processes. This returns us to the question of the changing role of the state in general, but also in relation to the victim of crime in particular.

Crime, victims and the state

Some time ago, Jefferson *et al.* (1992: 15) said that 'what is needed is an understanding of the role of the state which does more that reassert its ideological purpose and project, but neither assigns the 1980s [read here the 1990s onwards] to an economic nor a political determinism'. Quoting Jessop (1991), they then argued that criminology needed not only to bring the state back in but also to put the state in its place. Revisiting some of these questions contemporarily, including revisiting Jessop (2002), it is possible to consider that whilst '[i]nstitutions matter' (2002: 34) – and in this context this can be used to refer to the institutions of the criminal justice system – they matter in a context in which

> the state can be defined as a relatively unified ensemble of socially embedded, socially regularized, and strategically selective institutions, organizations, social forces and activities organized around (or at least involved in) making collective binding decisions for an imagined political community (2002: 40)

and of

> hegemonic projects that seek to reconcile the particular and the universal by linking the nature and purposes of the state into a broader – but always selective – political, intellectual and moral vision of the public interest, the good society, the commonweal, or some analogous principle of societalization. (2002: 42)

Through this kind of lens we can get a sense of the deeper structural processes that may be in play and that have resulted in the surface manifestation of the 'culture of control' (Garland 2001) in which the crime victim features so prominently, not only as a rhetorical and real policy device, but also as a claim to citizenship. The resultant effect: I am a victim, therefore I am (hence the title of this chapter).

Jessop's (2002) analysis of the state, whilst clearly retaining its Marxist orientation, is a subtle analysis that does not demand determinism, co-ordination, evenness of distribution of processes, or uniformity in understanding the nature of the state and its activities but does remind us of the importance of the possible relationship between 'deep' structure and 'surface' structure. There are two important clues that connect Jessop's analysis of the current form of the capitalist state to contemporary criminal justice policy and the victim of crime: the imagined political community, and the moral vision of the good society. So a more complete understanding of the processes relating to criminal justice policy in England and Wales over the last 25 years would also include an analysis of the shift from what might be called the 'determined state' to the 'hegemonic state' in which 'victimhood' has become a key strategy for the continued maintenance of the (capitalist) hegemonic state – a strategy that facilitates an appeal to an 'imagined political community' that simultaneously offers a vehicle for envisaging a 'good society'.

The development of victim-centred policy, then, has clearly not proceeded in a vacuum. Goodey (2005) situates many of the processes discussed above within the wider framework of understanding the impact of globalization that, as she says, 'has brought with it both promise and pitfalls' (2005: 18), in the form of wider consumer choice (albeit predicated on the decision of a few powerful corporations) and greater economic instability (predicated on those same decision-making processes). These processes, along with the advent of global terrorism and migrant (economic) populations, all add to the feelings of risk and insecurity: the idea of victimhood. As Young (2003a) has asserted, in a world that has experienced the events of 11 September 2001, the problems and possibilities of rising ontological insecurity need to be much more carefully understood. However, it is difficult to deny the increasing importance of victimhood, not just as a cultural process (Furedi 1997, 2002) but also as a claim to status. In this sense victimhood is the status whereby the state, through increasingly subtle and not so subtle global and local processes, is reasserting its power over citizenship. In this sense victimhood is harnessed as a source of oppression in the interests of the increasingly diverse and hegemonic (capitalist) state. How this permeates a policy agenda is neither simple nor straightforward, but the global influence of restorative justice is a good example to think about (see also Chapter 5). So it is against the backcloth of these kinds of socio-political developments that we can begin to construct a more complete picture of the historical emergence and increasing concern with the victim of crime in particular and the question of victimization in general. It is also against this kind of way of thinking about or imagining the victim of crime that the rest of this book unfolds.

Conclusion

In this chapter we have placed the contemporary focus on criminal victimization within a historical framework. In so doing, attention has been drawn to a number of important features of that contemporary focus. In particular, it is important to note the extent to which historical distinctions between 'deserving' and 'undeserving' that belonged to the nineteenth century became embedded within twentieth-century policy and have arguably been perpetuated into the twenty-first century, as we shall see especially when we discuss more challenging and contested images of the victim as presented in Chapter 6. In addition, this chapter has alluded to the relationship between local/national policies that have been influenced and shaped by global processes. This theme will be revisited in the chapters that follow, and in that revisiting our victimological gaze will also attain a wider lens as we shall draw increasingly on material from different socio-cultural contexts as a way of adding a further dimension to understanding the local context and construction of the victim of crime in England and Wales. In addition, this chapter has suggested the idea that victimhood equips us as individuals not only with claims to citizenship but also with a sense of identity. Again these are themes that will be revisited in the chapters that follow and carry with them questions about not only the changing relationship between the citizen and the state that has been discussed here but also how we might understand the issue of difference. In other words, how, if at all, can policy processes designed to appeal to 'all of us' accommodate those whose sense of identity might be informed by ideas and ideals that lie beyond the 'all of us' presumed by the nation state?

There is a further theme to this chapter that has remained somewhat implicit to the material and ideas that it has covered. Much has been made in this chapter of the symbolic power of the victim both as a rhetorical and a real device in appealing to a wide range of groups (including the electorate) in seeking support and justification for policy initiatives. That rhetoric, and the 'reality' it presumes, has increasingly called upon and excavated emotion in seeking to harness support. The emotionality associated with these processes is multi-layered. It is not solely the vindictiveness of which Young (2003b) speaks (although that is an important element of the contemporary policy scene, especially in the UK) but also the use of abjection, horror and fear, which we pick up on in Chapter 4, that potentially fuel understandings of victimhood. Interestingly, tensions around emotionality have always been present within victimology as an area of analysis, comprised as it is of activists and academics, and it is to an appreciation of the theoretical and practical diversity of this area of work that we shall turn in the next chapter.

2   Ways of thinking about victims and victimology

Introduction

The purpose of this chapter is to set the growing interest in, and awareness of, the victim of crime discussed in Chapter 1 against the kinds of theoretical frameworks available to those interested in making sense of the nature of criminal victimization. In so doing, it will be possible to establish the links between that emergent victim history and the academic agenda of victimology. It must be remembered that victimology, like criminology, is an area of interest inhabited by people from a diverse range of disciplines who on occasion do not even agree on the relative validity of the term 'victim' itself. So, before we proceed with that more general theoretical discussion, it will be useful to consider what different interpretations might be placed on that term.

What does the term 'victim' mean?

> Observers on both sides of the Atlantic have commented on the growth of the culture of victimhood. They have pointed to the frequency with which a wide variety of interests seem to be playing the victim card. (Furedi 1997: 95)

Of course, in making this observation Furedi is encouraging us to consider the not inconsiderable connections to be made between acquiring the status of victim and making a subsequent claim for compensation. However, he is also encouraging us to consider what cultural changes have facilitated this connection. Put simply, how are we to understand the popularity of personal testimony (Salecl 2004), stories of victimhood survival, that nevertheless have left a permanent stain upon the teller's identity? Part of the answer to this question lies in understanding the ways in which the term 'victim' is itself socially constructed. As a term it has a history, and as a term it also has a history of application. For Furedi (1997: 101), 'The consciousness of being "at risk" readily translates itself into the victim identity.' Some of the implications of Furedi's view have much wider ramifications than can be discussed here. However, the connections between victimhood and risk were elided in the context of crime specifically in the development of the criminal victimization survey both in the USA in the late 1960s and in England and Wales during the late 1970s. So, as Dignan (2005) observes, it is only relatively recently that the term 'victim' has become intertwined with crime. Yet even in this context the term is open to interpretation.

As Spalek (2006: 9) points out, the *Oxford English Dictionary* suggests four definitions:

- A person who is injured or killed as a result of an event or circumstance
- A person or thing injured or destroyed in pursuit of an object or in gratification of a passion
- A prey, a dupe
- A living creature sacrificed to a deity or in a religious rite

Despite these rather specific definitions, the common usage of the word connotes an individual who has suffered some kind of misfortune. However, its link with crime is now well made even though for many people working with victims of crime, either as practitioners or academics, the term 'victim' is highly problematic and can be invoked in the criminal justice process as a term equally applicable to complainants or defendants (see, for example, Farrall and Maltby 2003). Moreover, it is a term that has been particularly problematic for those working within the feminist movement. So, before we go on to consider the different theoretical frameworks that inform victimological work, it will be useful to reflect upon some of these difficulties.

When the word 'victim' is gendered – as in French, for example, being *la victime* – it is denoted as female. If the genealogy of the word 'victim' is examined, it is connected to processes of sacrifice in which again the victim was more often than not female. The links between this word and being female imply that the passivity and powerlessness associated with being a victim are also associated with being female. It is this link that is problematic for those working within the feminist movement who prefer to use the term 'survivor' to try to capture women's resistance to their structural powerlessness and consequent potential victimization. At the same time the tensions between being labelled a victim and being labelled a survivor are also problematic for others interested in criminal victimization since the either/or distinction fails to capture the *processes* of victimization. In other words, it is possible that an individual at different points in time in relation to different events could be an active victim, a passive victim, an active survivor, a passive survivor, and all the experiential possibilities in between these. From this viewpoint the label 'victim' seems quite sterile.

There is, however, another problem associated with the word 'victim'

that is derived from appreciating the processes whereby an individual acquires the label 'victim'. This problem is connected to the presence of that
which Christie (1986) called the 'ideal victim'. For Christie the 'ideal victim' is
the Little Red Riding Hood fairy tale victim: a young, innocent female out
doing good deeds who is attacked by an unknown stranger. Indeed, this 'ideal
victim' fits all the common-sense stereotypes of the 'legitimate' victim of
rape. The power of such 'ideal' images results in some people being viewed as
deserving victims, that is, acquiring the label 'victim' very readily and easily,
and other people being viewed as undeserving victims who may never be
labelled as victims. In addition, theoretically, as Rock (2002) has argued, the
process of who acquires or fails to acquire victim status, and the subsequent
impact that this has upon their sense of identity, has been relatively under-
explored at the level of the individual, though the presence of a culture of
victimhood at a social level, which Furedi (1997) comments on, has been
better documented. Despite this theoretical lacuna, the distinction between
deserving and undeserving victims and how it impacts upon people's experiences of the criminal justice process is one of the issues that has preoccupied criminologists interested in the victim of crime. It is a distinction
that is very powerful, as was observed in the previous chapter, in the early
formulation of policy responses to victims of violent crime in enshrining the
importance that the victim be evidenced as the 'innocent' victim. Moreover,
this is a distinction that arguably still carries considerable weight with practitioners, especially in the context of sexual violence (see Chapter 6).

It is clear, then, that becoming a victim is neither simple nor straightforward. Victim status is something that has to be achieved and involves a
process from the individual recognizing that they have been victimized and
thus may claim the label, through to being socially and/or in policy terms
being recognized as a victim. Awareness of these processes of victim status
acquisition has led Carrabine *et al.* (2004: 117) to talk of a 'hierarchy of victimisation'. At the bottom of this hierarchy would be the homeless, the drug
addict, the street prostitute – all those groups of people for whom it is presumed that victimization is endemic to their lifestyle, thus rendering any
claim to victim status a highly problematic one. At the top of this hierarchy
might be the elderly female, most readily identified in the media as the victim
of violent crime, and often consequently given full and graphic coverage. This
is despite the evidence that the group of people most likely to be the victims
of violent crime are young males who go out drinking two or three times a
week (see Chapter 3). Of course, positions in this hierarchy can change, as
evidenced by the greater seriousness contemporarily given to hate crime, for
example, discussed in the next chapter. However, the notion of a hierarchy
draws attention not only to the legitimacy or otherwise of an individual's
victimhood but also to the politics of victimhood. Those politics are part of
what Miers (1978) and Williams (1999) have discussed in relation to the

politicization of the victim referred to in the previous chapter, but acquire a distinctive and personal impact for particular kinds of victims and victimization that we shall discuss more fully as this book unfolds. It is, of course, within those politics, and the policies that have flowed from them, that we have also seen the increasingly visible presence of the space that is given contemporarily to the emotionality of criminal justice (Karstedt 2002), another theme that we shall return to.

Despite the problems associated with the label 'victim', efforts have been made to define the term in different ways. For example, the 1985 United Nations Declaration of Basic Principles of Justice for Victims of Crime and Abuse of Power defines victims broadly as

> persons who, individually or collectively, have suffered harm, including physical or mental injury, emotional suffering, economic loss or substantial impairment of their fundamental rights, through acts or omissions that are in violation of criminal laws operative within Member States,

and goes on to include the families of people so harmed. So victim status, from this definition, can be offered to a wide range of individuals and introduces a further dimension to the victimization experience, that of secondary or even tertiary victimization (this is something that we shall discuss in greater detail when we consider the impact of crime in the next chapter). Yet, despite this wide-ranging definition, some issues are still glossed over by it that have been alluded to in this discussion. For example, how does an individual embrace a victim identity (if they do); what does the dynamic of the victim-survivor process look like; how does the hierarchy of victimization change its shape and form; how might experience of this hierarchy be differently mediated not only in relation to socio-economic position but also in relation to what Spalek (2006) calls 'spirit injury'; where do collective and individual feelings fit into this equation; and can victimhood only be defined in relation to the respective legal codes of 'member states' who sign up to various agreements? Some of these issues will reappear in subsequent chapters; however, this broad and all-inclusive definition of the victim has not necessarily been matched by a similarly broad academic study of the victim from within victimology, and it is to a consideration of that subdiscipline of criminology that we shall now turn.

What is victimology?

Victimology is regarded as a subdisciplinary area of criminology that is peopled by a wide variety of groups and interests. As an area of debate and analysis it draws together academics, activists and policy makers, and within this heady brew there exist a number of tensions. Miers (1989: 17) observes that 'victimology has too many voices to allow any coherence in its reported understanding of the world', and Rock (1986) has commented upon its 'catholic' nature. Moreover, in alluding to deeper issues within the discipline, Fattah (1992) called for the separation of what he called 'humanistic victimology' from 'scientific victimology'. In making this distinction, Fattah was foregrounding the issues that arise from the competing claims on victimization made by those associated with victims' movements and those for whom a concern with victimization might be characterized as being more dispassionate, academic and, as a consequence, more scientific. The need to separate these competing claims was at the time of his writing particularly pertinent, given the strong conservative political overtones associated with many of the victims' movements in North America and their capacity to gain the ear of government. However, this meshing of activism and political influence on the part of victims' voices is something that has also become increasingly apparent in England and Wales, the relatively neutral stance of Victim Support notwithstanding. Since the early 1990s there has been an increase in both the number and the diversity of groups and individuals making claims on behalf of victims of crime in England and Wales, and the political centring of victim interests appears to have proceeded apace during that time (as will be discussed in Chapter 5), in such a way that lends a sympathetic hearing to Fattah's plea, and reminding us of the fact that the intertwining of the emotional demands of speaking and working for and with victims with academic study has always been present within victimology. In a sense, victimology has always been associated with the emotional (the activist voice), hence some of the problems it has had as an academic discipline. More recently, both Dignan (2005) and Goodey (2005) have commented on the complex intermeshing of the academic, policy and activist concerns within the discipline, with Goodey in particular suggesting that the only way the discipline might move forward would be to forge a much more constructive relationship between its constituent parts in which 'academic research needs to critically inform victim advocacy and policy initiatives, that, in due course, can feed back into new research avenues' (2005: 120). So this heady mix of people has the potential to produce quite different agendas for those who call themselves victimologists. These agendas are often quite difficult to disentangle from the processes of politicization and emotionality. In this chapter attention will be paid in the first instance to the academic elements of victimology and, where possible, appropriate links will be made with the kinds of policies and activism supported by the different strands of that academic work.

The origins of victimology have been variously ascribed to Mendelsohn (1956, 1974), von Hentig (1948) and Wertham (1949). Arguably, however, it was the work of von Hentig's (1948) book, *The Criminal and His Victim*, that really focused attention on the relationship between the victim and the offender in contributing to an understanding of the perpetration of a crime. The early conceptual work of both Mendelsohn and von Hentig was concerned to develop ways of thinking about the victim that would enable the victim to be differentiated from the non-victim. In other words, both were clearly suggesting that there is a normal person such that, when the victim is measured against them, the victim falls short. In order to achieve this kind of understanding they each developed victim typologies. (This way of thinking about victims clearly mirrored earlier work of criminologists who tried to develop ways of thinking about offenders that would differentiate them from non-offenders.) Von Hentig's typology worked with a notion of 'victim proneness'. He argued that there were some people, by virtue of their structural characteristics, who were much more likely to be victims of crime than other people. Among those he identified were women, children, the elderly and the mentally subnormal (he had 13 categories in all). In thinking critically about this categorization concerning who is being differentiated from whom in these criteria, it is possible to see that von Hentig thought the normal person was the white, heterosexual male. This presumption, however, has not stood in the way of von Hentig's work being highly influential, and that influence is perhaps most keenly identified in the concept of 'lifestyle' that has informed much criminal victimization survey work.

Mendelsohn adopted a more legalistic framework in developing his typology. His underlying concept was the notion of 'victim culpability'. Using this idea, he developed a sixfold typology, from the victim who could be shown to be completely innocent, to the victim who started as a perpetrator and during the course of an incident became the victim. Arguably his typology is guided by what might be considered a reasonable or rational way of making sense of any particular incident given the nature of the law. Given this starting point, it is possible to suggest that his understanding of what is reasonable also equated with what the white, heterosexual male would consider to be reasonable. This was especially demonstrated in the later work that emanated from Mendelsohn's ideas, in which victim culpability became translated into 'victim precipitation'. From these beginnings the concepts of lifestyle and victim precipitation have formed the core of much traditional victimological work and illustrate what Miers (1989) called a 'positivist' victimology. It is to a discussion of that version of victimology that we shall turn first of all.

Positivist victimology

Miers (1989: 3) defines positivist victimology in the following way:

> The identification of factors which contribute to a non-random pattern of victimization, a focus on interpersonal crimes of violence, and a concern to identify victims who may have contributed to their own victimization.

The grouping of these concerns under the heading 'positivist' parallels Karmen's (1990) identification of a 'conservative' victimology and Walklate's (1989) concern with a 'conventional victimology'. All of these labels capture different, but important, aspects of the kind of work being discussed here. This work focuses on that which is conventionally understood as criminal: the crime that is considered normal or ordinary crime, that which goes on in 'public', such as burglary or street crime. This is the crime of everyday life that neglects the private world of the home and the private world of the business corporation. It is a view of the crime problem that certainly married well with conservative politics, the kinds of crimes that early victims' movements were concerned with, and the emergence of the initial criminal victimization surveys. However, before we go on to discuss this version of victimology in a little more detail, it will be useful to clarify what is meant by 'positivism'.

Wright and Hill (2004) comment that any social theory reflects assumptions about the nature of the social world and how knowledge is produced about that social world. The key assumptions of positivism are twofold. The first is a concern with regularities and the second is a preoccupation with objectivity in the knowledge production process. Regularities, or patterns of behaviour, it is assumed, can be identified objectively through a commitment to a traditional conception of what counts as science. Some time ago Keat and Urry (1975: 3) stated that:

> For the positivist there are no necessary connections in nature; there are only regularities, successions of phenomena which can be systematically represented in the universal laws of scientific theory. Any attempt to go beyond this plunges science into the unverifiable claims of metaphysics and religion, which are at best unscientific, and at worst meaningless.

Given the claims of positivism, it is no wonder that Fattah (1992), referred to earlier, was concerned to separate the scientific victimologist from the humanist, since their claims to knowledge rested on very different assumptions. Yet, of course, what counts as being 'scientific' has become an increasingly contested terrain, especially in the challenge to traditional conceptions of science posed by feminist work (see, for example, Harding 1991) and others (see, for example, MacIntyre 1988). Indeed, it has been argued that the allegiance that positivist victimology has shown to traditional conceptions of science largely accounts for the marginalization, and indeed alienation, of feminist work from victimology (for a fuller discussion of this, see Mawby and Walklate 1994; Walklate 2003a; and below). Nevertheless, this concern with regularities has been immensely influential in victimology and has been manifested in a number of different ways. Initially its influence could be seen in the refinement and development of the criminal victimization survey that was informed by the concept of lifestyle as articulated in the work of Hindelang *et al.* (1978). Given the influence of the concept of lifestyle and the criminal victimization survey, it will be of some value to consider the work of Hindelang *et al.* in some depth as a sound example of the kind of scientific work so valued by victimologists such as Fattah.

Hindelang *et al.* (1978) presented a way of thinking about personal victimization in which 'lifestyle' refers to 'routine daily activities, both vocational activities (work, school, keeping house etc.) and leisure activities' (1978: 241). In this concept of lifestyle, individuals reflect the way in which they are constrained by role expectations and structural characteristics endemic in their demographic position (class, age, sex, ethnicity, etc.). The ways in which individuals adapt to these constraints are reflected in their daily routines, their lifestyles. They argued that there is a direct link between an individual's routine daily activity and their exposure to high-risk victimization situations in which personal victimization occurs. From this starting point they go on to posit eight propositions (1978: 250–66). These are worth reiterating in some detail to get a better feel for this way of thinking about the patterning of criminal victimization:

1. The probability of suffering a personal victimization is directly related to the amount of time a person spends in public spaces particularly at night-time.
2. The probability of being in a public space at night varies as a function of lifestyle.
3. Social contacts and interactions occur disproportionately among individuals who share similar lifestyles.
4. An individual's chances of personal victimization are dependent upon the extent to which the individual shares demographic characteristics with offenders.
5. The proportion of time an individual spends with non-family members varies as a function of lifestyle.
6. The probability of personal victimization, particularly personal theft,

increases as a function of the proportion of time that an individual spends among non-family members.

7. Variations in lifestyle are associated with variations in the ability of individuals to isolate themselves from persons with offender characteristics.

8. Variations in lifestyle are associated with variations in the convenience, the desirability, and the vincibility of a person as a target for personal victimizations.

There are both strengths and weaknesses with these propositions. The strengths might be summarized in terms of the extent to which they help make sense of criminal victimization survey data and they do focus on the patterns of victimization, thus encouraging a move away from looking at victimization in terms of the individualized relationship between the victim and offender that was characteristic of von Hentig's early work. On the other hand, however, the idea that lifestyle can be measured is problematic (lifestyles tend to be rather more vague, fuzzy and changing), and the presumption that the structural variables that contribute to the patterning of victimization are age, sex, class and ethnicity, rather than ageism, sexism, classism and racism, is equally difficult. The latter observation offers a clue to what is absent in this approach – that is, an understanding of relationships of power.

So this approach to understanding the patterning of criminal victimization not only embraced positivism but also married with a functionalist view of society. This is evident in the use of the concept of social roles to which it is assumed that individuals adapt and consequently perform in accordance with social expectations. Such processes of adaptation offer little account of people's potential for strategies of resistance to social expectations or the potential for social conflict in relation to such expectations, or indeed an appreciation of the extent to which people may feel that they have no other choices. In downplaying these other possible explanations for the patterns or regularities of criminal victimization, Hindelang *et al.*'s propositions, and their subsequent embrace within the criminal victimization survey industry, implicitly offered a rather consensual, equal and democratic view of society in which it was only in the public domain that crime was a problem – thus ensuring the confinement of the study of victimization to that arena to the exclusion of the private home or the world of business. This framework had the effect of ensuring that the term 'victim' was understood as a rather structurally neutral concept and one in which one's status as a victim was given by the law.

Despite these inherent problems, the concept of lifestyle was embraced within the criminal victimization survey and was a research instrument that was harnessed by academic work on both the right and the left of the criminological political spectrum. Political conservatives have used the findings from these surveys both to downplay the risk of crime (see Hough and Mayhew 1983) and to emphasize the risk of crime (see President's Task Force on Victims of Crime 1982). The same research instrument has also been used in the UK and elsewhere to generate a more left-wing policy agenda in relation to understanding the focused nature and impact of criminal victimization on poorer and less powerful groups in society (see, for example, Kinsey *et al.* 1986; Crawford *et al.* 1990) and in this respect resulted in a reflexive refinement and development of the instrument itself as a result it is now used by government departments in such a way as to take account of a wider range of victimization experiences, especially of the less powerful in society, with some significant developments having taken place within this refinement process to access more sensitive issues such as sexual violence (see Walby and Myhill 2001; Piispa 2003). There are some additional qualifications about the international criminal victimization survey, though, and these are addressed in the next chapter.

So, arguably, the patterns and regularities revealed by positivist victimology have been used both expediently and to some effect in the political and policy arena. However, the connections between this kind of victimology and a more general political conservatism commented on above run somewhat deeper than observing mere political manipulation and utilization of survey findings. These connections emanate from the image of the victim and the presumptions about the nature of society which positivist victimology makes, partly discussed in reference to the work of Hindelang *et al.*, and they are worth further iteration at this point.

The three characteristics of a positivist victimology offered by Miers (1989) with which this discussion began are underpinned by a presumption that the term 'victim' itself is non-problematic. In the various forms of victimological work conducted under this scientific banner, the victim is taken to be either given by the criminal law or given by the self-evident nature of their suffering. This starting point enables the generation of data concerned with patterns and regularities since it presumes that what there is to be measured can in fact be measured and in itself is a static entity. As has been argued elsewhere (Walklate 1989), this initial presumption conceals an inherently static and functionalist view of society in which the themes of consensus, equilibrium and incremental change are predominant. There is little sense in this image of society or the individual in which the law or the state contributes to the social construction of the victim, the processes of criminal victimization, or processes of social change which may be unforeseen and/or dramatic as opposed to managed and incremental. So positivist victimology, and the survey work emanating from it, can provide snapshots of the regularities of criminal victimization but cannot provide an understanding of the social and historical production and reproduction of those regularities through time and space, and, as a consequence, cannot facilitate an understanding of the irregularities of criminal victimization. Such a concern demands minimally a different understanding of the term 'victim', and maximally a different theoretical starting point. As Dignan (2005: 33) states in relation to positivist victimology:

> Moreover, it fails to appreciate the fact that both the state itself, through its agencies, and also the legal and penal processes that it sanctions may themselves create new victims and also further victimize those who have already been victimized by an offender.

However, this non-problematic treatment of the notion of the victim offers only one way of thinking through those other connections with political conservatism.

Karmen (1990: 11) expresses some of these connections in this way:

> Conservatives within victimology and the victims' rights movement see the criminal justice system as the guarantor of retributive justice – satisfying victims with the knowledge that offenders are being punished for their crimes.

It is to this end that the 'powerful motif' of the victim, commented on by Bottoms (1983), was put to most effective use in the UK during the 1980s and 1990s and still has a good deal of contemporary resonance (as was discussed in Chapter 1). As Phipps (1988) has argued, this politicization of the victim led to a separation of the notion of criminal victimization from its *social* origins, seeing it as something that interferes with the 'normality' of an ordered society. He goes on to say:

> Further, the interventionist State must share the blame, for it has weakened authority of all kinds as well as tying the hands of the police and the courts by placing the rights of offenders above the rights of potential and actual victims to be free from harm and fear. (1988: 180).

The argument developed by Phipps (1988) suggests that what conservatism does is to transform the harm caused to individuals as a result of criminal victimization into a harming of the social order, of the rule of law, and of 'community'. Yet rather than this resulting in a social policy response to harm (Hillyard *et al.* 2005), it has increasingly been translated into a general commitment to repressive justice (see Garland 2001) that excavates people's feelings about being so harmed and that can take a number of different forms. Moreover, as Young (1996) argued, the use of the term 'victim' in the political domain serves more purposes than just a need to generate support for a particular policy initiative or direction. Those other purposes serve to signify the ideological mechanisms whereby the term 'victim' acts as both a strategy for including 'all of us' yet simultaneously excluding the criminal. Signifying the victim in this way, and the cultural and political processes that it reflects, is equally problematic for that victimology which sees itself as being of a more radical persuasion.

Radical victimology

Wright and Hall (2004) would argue that the kind of victimology drawn together under the heading 'radical' would be more accurately described as an 'interpretivist' approach to understanding society and the way in which knowledge about society is produced. Whilst this might constitute a more accurate label in relation to the knowledge production process, in the context of victimology it rather loses sight of the policy activism link that is so deeply embedded in this area of work. As a consequence the label 'radical' is retained here to capture the feelings engendered by those links. Arguably radical victimology has its origins in the work of Mendelsohn who, despite the more conservative implications of other aspects of his ideas, argued for a victimology concerned with all aspects of victimization, not just those which could be defined as criminal (i.e. law breaking). This concern can be traced through the work of both radical criminology (Quinney 1972) and radical victimology (Elias 1986, 1993).

The common threads that bind these different strands of work together can be identified as a concern with the role of the state alongside the law in producing victimization. These threads connect this version of victimology to a concern with the question of human rights. As Elias (1985: 17) states: 'A victimology which encompasses human rights would not divert attention from crime victims and their rights, but would rather explore their inextricable relationship to more universal human rights concerns.' Such concerns readily connect this version of victimology with the victims' movement through organizations such as Amnesty International. However, in the more localized political domain of party politics in the UK during the 1980s it was arguably the ideas of a radical victimology that underpinned some of the concerns of the left realists of criminology.

Radical left realism of the 1980s placed the requirement for an accurate victimology at the centre of the agenda as a way of highlighting the importance of recognizing in both political and policy terms that, as Dignan (2005: 33) states, 'the most predatory crime was directed not against the wealthy bourgeoisie but against the poorest members of society who tend to live among those responsible for such crime' (see also Dixon *et al.* 2006). Their own use of the criminal victimization survey enabled them to assert this claim and the importance of situating criminal victimization within the power structure of society on the basis of survey evidence – a claim that was rather different from the more normative claims made by Elias, cited above. However, as has been commented on elsewhere (Smart 1990; Mawby and Walklate 1994), radical left realism in particular, and radical victimology in general, failed to escape the chains of a positivist conception of science. Thus whilst the underpinning focus of radical victimology on questions of human rights might be considered laudable, their translation into standards which can be measured objectively, as articulated in the work of Elias for example, remained, and remains, problematic.

Nevertheless it is important to note that radical left realism argued for what has been called an 'engaged' criminology. In England this was reflected in an association between 'left realist' criminologists and some Labour-controlled local authorities, primarily in London, in an effort to reclaim the debate on law and order for the Labour Party. In very general terms these efforts presented a different conceptualization of victimization. As Phipps (1988: 181) points out, 'criminal victimization is but one aspect of *social* victimization arising from poverty and disadvantage – in which people are harmed by *normal* social and economic relations, a process which in turn results in their harming each other'.

Part of the consequence of endeavouring to reclaim the law and order debate in this way was that radical left realism elided the concern with crime with a concern with criminal victimization. Whilst Phipps was, and still is, right to assert the connections between criminal victimization and other aspects of social harm, this connection was not, and still is not, fully articulated in the realm of politics, though efforts to reconnect these concerns to issues of social justice persist (Dixon *et al.* 2006). What the concern with criminal victimization in this engaged sense did, without intention, was to facilitate the political gains to be made from focusing on crime as one of the issues that worried people both locally and nationally. It was a means for giving all of us a voice, albeit as victims of crime. As A. Young (1996) argued, this elision equated victimization with citizenship. One of the implications of this use was the idea of crime is a 'leveller'; something that we could all share in the experience of. Young (1996: 55) expressed this as follows: 'It [crime] provides a sense of community. . . . But our belonging comes not from the fact that we are all criminals but from the shared fact of victimization.' This sense of common victimization offered a basis to belonging that may be differently distributed by space, age, race or gender, but it is nevertheless the means through which 'all of us' as potential victims can be harnessed to participate in the democratic process. This is a process that has continued (see, for example, Home Office 2002). Thus our potential victimization acts as a mechanism whereby our activities as citizens can also be harnessed (this has again been referred to in Chapter 1). Signifying the victim in this way arguably resulted in the minimization of the political differences between left and right. As Karmen (1990) has suggested, the 1980s were characterized by a move from crime prevention to victimization prevention. This decade witnessed the collusion of those from both a left-wing and a right-wing political persuasion in the construction of a notion of social responsibility in relation to crime control. This became a responsibility for victimization reduction or what Garland (2001) has called 'responsibilization'.

However, the idea of a radical agenda for victimology has not been totally lost. Recently Kauzlarich *et al.* (2001) reopened the argument for such a victimology in proposing a 'victimology of state crime'. This framework defines crime victims as: 'Individuals or groups of individuals who have experienced economic, cultural, or physical harm, pain, exclusion, or exploitation, because of tacit or explicit state actions or policies which violate law or generally defined human rights' (2001: 176). They go on to suggest that ratified international law, domestic law and human rights standards can be used to look to the criminal activities of the state, and go on to produce a fourfold typology that might be used to iterate the nature of victimization by the state. From this they generate six propositions (2001: 183–9). They are worth reiterating here since they contrast quite nicely with the propositions of Hindelang *et al.* discussed above:

1. Victims of state crime tend to be among the least socially powerful actors.
2. Victimizers generally fail to recognize and understand the nature, extent, and harmfulness of institutional policies. If suffering and harm are acknowledged, it is often neutralized with the context of a sense of 'entitlement'.
3. Victims of state crime are often blamed for their suffering.
4. Victims of state crime must generally rely on the victimizer, an associated institution or civil social movements for redress.
5. Victims of state crime are easy targets for repeated victimization.
6. Illegal state policies and practices, while committed by individuals and groups of individuals, are manifestations of the attempt to achieve organizational, bureaucratic or institutional goals.

As the authors acknowledge, taking this kind of victimization into account is not without its problems. As Box (1983: 17) observed, 'the majority of those suffering from corporate crime remain unaware of their victimisation – either not knowing it has happened to them or viewing their "misfortune" as an accident or "no one's fault" ' – a phenomenon Geis (1973) referred to as 'victim responsiveness'. Yet the case for an understanding of the involvement of the state in criminal victimization remains a solid one, and it can be seen that in comparison with the agenda proposed by Hindelang *et al.* the propositions offered here clearly recognize the power dimensions to criminal victimization, the relative invisibility of some forms of criminal victimization (those associated with the workplace and those committed in the interest of the state in particular), and by implication the highly problematic issues associated with measuring the nature and extent of such victimization. In addition, this version of radical victimology presupposes that an important causal mechanism underlying patterns of criminal victimization is the capitalist state and how its interests are maintained. This presupposition posits a different political relationship between the individual and the state that places greater responsibility on the state for the processes of criminal victimization.

Thus it can be seen that, whilst radical victimology tries to construct and work with a much more general notion of the nature and extent of criminal victimization and with a relatively subtle and nuanced understanding of the sources of such victimization, in many of its guises (with the possible exception of the propositions discussed above) it still fails to break free of positivism. It has either relied on the criminal victimization survey in a very similar way to the reliance on such surveys found in positivist victimology, or looked for other forms of 'universal' standards either in the form of human rights or in other kinds of ratified legal frameworks. Moreover, whilst all of these avenues offer different and useful foci for policy, from Amnesty International to the European Community and the United Nations, at a fundamental level much of this kind of work results in a political and policy agenda not so dissimilar in its presumptions from that of a more conservative political persuasion as far as the victim of crime is concerned (again with the possible exception of the propositions discussed above). However, efforts have been made to break free of the conservative conundrum through what has been called 'critical victimology'. Before we go on to consider what might constitute such a theoretical perspective, it will be of value to reflect upon the theoretical and policy impact that work from another 'radical' perspective has had, if at all, on victimology. That work emanates from the feminist movement.

Feminism and victimology

As Chapter 1 has illustrated, research work emanating from the feminist movement has had some considerable influence in shifting and informing the policy agenda in relation to understanding the nature and extent of criminal victimization. For some commentators the success of this influence is demonstrated by the legislative changes put in place in England and Wales by the Sexual Offences Act 2003 and the Domestic Violence, Crime and

Victims Act 2004. Taken together, these two pieces of legislation stand as testimony to the achievements of the feminist movement in England and Wales since the late 1970s. (For a fuller discussion of these and related issues, see Chapter 6.) However, it is possible to argue that what these achievements illustrate is the important relationship between feminism and politics within the policy arena rather than the achievements of feminist theory. It is in this latter respect that feminist ideas and some victimological ideas, especially those emanating from positivism, have a rather unhappy relationship with one another.

The tensions between feminism and victimology, in their respective preference for viewing women as survivors and women as victims, have been commented on both earlier in this chapter and in Chapter 1, so it is not necessary to repeat them here. It is nevertheless important to reiterate the significant contribution of feminism to recognizing the private domain of the home as an important arena of criminal victimization. As Spalek (2006: 43) states:

> Although some women are killed by men, and some feel that certain aspects of their lives have been completely ruined by violence, many women nonetheless manage to reconstruct their lives, emotionally, psychologically, and physically, and this kind of reconstruction should be acknowledged through the use of the word 'survivor' rather than 'victim'; the same might also be said about all kinds of less powerful groups in society.

It is the recognition of the importance of power relationships and their impact on people's lives that not only renders feminism radical but also highlights the fact that the tension between feminism and victimology runs somewhat deeper than their different use of terminology. That tension returns us to the question of not only how we can know things about the world but also who can have knowledge about the world and what that knowledge might look like. It returns us to the question of the relationship between method and methodology.

Some time ago Stanley and Wise (1987: 110–11) made the following observation:

> If we wanted to 'prove' how terribly violent women's lives were, we'd go to women who live in violent places – run-down inner-city areas of large conurbations – who have actually experienced male violence and ask them about it. . . . However if we called this research a 'survey', then with exemplary motives and using 'scientific' means 'the problem for those women there' could be generalized into 'the problem for all women everywhere'. The consequence would be that we

would have over-estimated the amount of overt violence and actual powerlessness in the average woman's life.

We could, of course, insert any structural variable into this quote and the issue would remain the same; what are we actually finding out about, and why are we doing it in the way that we are? In the context of this chapter, given the earlier focus on the concept of lifestyle it will be of use to explore this in a little more detail by offering a different way of thinking about this concept. Genn (1988: 92–3) offers one:

> Becoming interested in what appeared to be examples of 'victim-proneness' in one geographical area, I visited one particular block on a council estate over a number of months, tape-recorded interviews with several families, their neighbours and friends, and eventually moved in for a short period with the woman who had suffered the greatest number of victimisations in our survey. The views which I formed after this period of intensive observation have a substantial bearing not simply on the experiences of multiple victims but on the limitations of victim surveys as they are currently designed . . . What also became apparent was the fact that events reported to us in the survey were not regarded as particularly remarkable. They were just part of life.

The quote above particularly relates to one woman's experience of criminal victimization, some of which she probably identified as criminal victimization and others she did not. However, for the purposes of the argument to be developed here the key phrase is 'They were just part of life'. This encourages us to think about lifestyle not as a series of discrete, measurable incidents, but as a process. Lifestyle as a process cannot be captured by survey methodology, as the quote from Genn clearly implies. It demands a different way of thinking about and exploring what 'just part of life' means for people. It is the case, of course, that much feminist-inspired work has always been committed to different ways of thinking about the routine nature of women's lives and has always been committed to challenging accepted knowledge(s). However, the impact of the feminist challenge not only is pertinent to the exploration of women's lives (and the lives of other powerless groups), but also encourages ways of thinking critically about how things get done, including criminal victimization research, in arenas that are valuable for understanding the knowledge production process in general. These are the questions that the phrase 'just part of life' connects us to. Inevitably this leads us to think about methodology rather than method, to think about the knowledge production process.

The differences between the different feminisms notwithstanding, the feminist work that is built upon in the arguments to be presented here is influenced by the work of Harding (1991). This work explicitly adopted a Hegelian stance to the knowledge production process, arguing that women, rather like the proletariat, had access to and information about the world from the perspective both of being powerless and of knowing who the powerful are in their lives. This access to knowledge, from both sides of this dichotomous relationship, made the kind of knowledge that women (and the proletariat for Hegel) have more complete. In this sense the knowledge that women possess is more objective. Thus the feminist concern with women as occupiers of both the public and private domain means that women's knowledge can render visible and name processes that were once invisible and unnamed. In this way the objectivity of the knowledge production process is enhanced, not by detachment – or as Fattah (1991) would say, by the separation of the humanist from the scientist, discussed earlier – but by re-cognizing that the researcher and the researched operate in the same critical plane. Hence the feminist claim for work by women, with women, for women. The implication of this argument is that the knowledge produced by the powerful is therefore less complete. In this context this points not only to the serious limitations of sole reliance on criminal victimization survey data, at a methodological level, in producing valid knowledge about the nature and extent of people's experiences of criminal victimization, but also to the theoretical paucity of such work. Spalek (2006: 43) goes further: 'It appears that a "white perspective" has underpinned research, so that what appears to be "normal", "neutral" or "common-sense", is in fact a particular lens through which the world has been viewed.' So feminist-informed work throws into clear relief the world-view of (positivist) victimology in particular as one that takes for granted the white, male heterosexual as the norm against which all other forms of knowledge are measured as well as all other forms of victimization. In this sense the possibilities for feminism and (positivist) victimology to talk to each other look very slim indeed.

So it is at this deeper level, at the level of what it is that can be known and who it is who can know things, that work emanating from the feminist movement poses a radical challenge to mainstream victimological work. This does not mean that feminist work has not influenced the academic and policy agenda. As Chapter 1 has demonstrated, this is clearly not the case. That work has clearly contributed to a contemporary agenda that not only has made it possible for a wider range of criminally victimizing concerns to be recognized (such as violence behind closed doors) but arguably has also contributed to a more subtly nuanced understanding of the 'just part of life' experience of other relatively powerless groups. This is not to say that that understanding could not be better, as Spalek (2006) clearly claims, and moreover the nature of the influence of feminism in the policy arena also needs to be thought about very carefully, with some suggestion of co-option clearly a possibility (see below and Chapter 6). Some of the issues that feminism and other versions of victim-centred work have traditionally glossed over will be returned to at the end of this chapter. However, it is against the backcloth of the kinds of concerns that feminism generated that some efforts have been made to call for a critical victimology, and it is that to which we shall now turn.

Critical victimology

The term 'critical' has been used in a number of different ways to articulate an agenda for victimology. Miers (1990: 224) offers one version of this usage when he states:

> Many groups and individuals may claim the label, but the key questions for a critical victimology are, who has the power to apply the label and what considerations are significant in that determination?

Here Miers is drawing both implicitly and explicitly on the theoretical perspective of symbolic interactionism to inform his use of the term 'critical'. In a similar vein, Holstein and Miller (1990: 4) state that:

> Conventional victimology, it appears, presupposes that some persons or groups are objectively 'victims' without explicitly considering the interpretive [and] definitional processes implicated in the assignment of victim status.

Understanding the processes associated with acquiring the label 'victim' is certainly a legitimate area of concern for victimology. Such an understanding highlights those assumptions that underpin what Christie (1986) has called the 'ideal victim'. Such questions have been developed latterly by Rock (2002) and have remained largely unanswered. Moreover, acquiring the label and/or status of victim, especially that of a 'deserving' victim, is crucial in some circumstances if the victim is to receive appropriate agency response and support. So, how and under what circumstances people acquire the label and then possible access to resources is of great importance. As Rock (2002) has argued, understanding these processes interactionally, in relation to how an individual comes to see themselves as well as how others see them, carries all kinds of implications for questions of personal identity. However, the question remains concerning the extent to which such an emphasis on this labelling process *per se* constitutes a *critical* victimology.

Sumner (1990: 23) has summarized the major shortcomings associated with the symbolic interactionist stance. He states that:

> it is equally problematic that 'labelling theory' (1) never specified in detail the ideological constitution of the moral and criminal categories, (2) never fully explored the links between these categories and the social structure, and (3) only dealt with the relationship between moral/legal condemnation and interest in an instrumental way.

So the label 'victim' is not negotiated in the vacuum of the interactive process; it is a label through which human beings display their competence as users of the socially constructed cultural values associated with notions of the 'ideal victim' commented on above. This is why such labels have such a powerful impact, especially on those to whom they are applied.

A second delineation of a critical victimology is found in the work of Fattah (1991). This too is defined as an interactionist stance but not in the same way as that discussed above. Fattah (1991: 347) argues that many of the problems of the discipline of victimology 'have to do with conceptual and measurement issues'. To overcome these problems he calls for an understanding of the dynamic relationship that exists between victims and victimizers (echoing earlier victimological concerns articulated by von Hentig), and for closer links to be made between victimological and criminological concerns, hence his use of the term 'interactive'. He goes on to generate a highly sophisticated conceptual framework in which he attempts to integrate criminological and victimological work (see Fattah 1991: Chapter 12).

Unfortunately, this interactive framework produces many tensions in the way in which it is developed, most aptly illustrated in the explication of gender issues. For example, Fattah (1991: 120) states that 'Males commit more crimes and are criminally victimised more frequently than females.' This statement is problematic in a number of respects, but primarily because of the empirical evidence concerning the criminal victimization of women by men which it denies, and consequently the deeply embedded conventional view of crime, and the crime problem which it lends credence to. In other words, not only is it difficult to establish what is actually critical about this version of the victimological agenda once it has been fully explicated, but it is also a version that fails to offer a substantially alternative methodological agenda for victimology.

To summarize: two different uses of the term 'critical' as applied to victimology have been explored so far, neither of which has genuinely reconsidered the domain assumptions of the discipline. Each in its own terms may be a more or less worthy candidate for making sense of victimological concerns, but is still rooted in fairly traditional and conventional conceptualizations of what would count as both good and legitimate victimological knowledge. At best, they are liberal in their intentions; at worst, they constitute a mere token effort to address some key problems within the victimological domain. There is, however, a third version of the use of the term 'critical' to delineate a particular way of thinking through questions of victimological concern. This version has been used by Walklate (1989, 1990) and developed by Mawby and Walklate (1994).

This version of critical victimology endeavours to address the problematic aspects of both positivist and radical victimology by applying a critical understanding of the achievements of radical left realism, a Bhaskarian understanding of scientific realism, and the way in which Cain (1990) has developed and applied some of these ideas from a feminist critique of criminology to victimology. This view of victimology takes seriously the need for a development of an empirically based, rational and objective science, but a science that demands that we go beyond the 'mere appearance' of things towards understanding the mechanisms that underpin and generate their appearance. Given the emphasis within this view of the knowledge production process on realism, one of the key issues in constructing a critical victimology informed by these ideas is to develop an understanding of what constitutes the real.

Leaning on Giddens's (1984) theory of structuration, the view adopted by Mawby and Walklate (1994) presumed that endeavours to research the real must take into account a number of processes which contribute to the construction of everyday reality: people's conscious activity; their unconscious activity (that is, the routine activity which people engage in, which can serve both to sustain and change the conditions under which that routine activity is constructed); the unobserved and unobservable generative mechanisms which underpin daily life; and the intended and unintended consequences of people's actions which inform both future action and knowledge. One of the basic premises on which these theoretical propositions are constructed is a notion of duality. As such it provides one way of understanding the dynamism between the structural location of people and their day-to-day negotiation of this structural location. Consequently, it is a theoretical vehicle whereby the concerns raised by standpoint feminism might be accommodated. For example, duality permits an exploration of the structural location of women (one way of understanding women's powerlessness, a defining characteristic of being a victim), and women's negotiation of their structural location (one way of understanding the term 'survivor'). It is this kind of theoretical starting point, which neither treats gender as a variable nor locates it purely as a definitional category, that permits the inclusion of the critical edge of feminist work into victimology and by implication issues relating to age, class and ethnicity. Such a theoretical starting point consequently leads to the construction of a differently informed empirical agenda.

Spalek (2006: 45) raises some interesting questions about this kind of starting point for a critical victimology that are useful to reflect upon. She asks:

> Is it possible to document individuals' own perspectives and yet at the same time to claim positions for them that they do not claim for themselves and is this ethically defensible? Can a researcher claim a source of knowledge beyond that held by the participants in the study? In so doing is this perpetuating a form of elitism?

Arguably these questions confuse method with methodology and are perhaps best addressed by returning to Bhaskar, who is quoted by Outhwaite (1987: 51) as saying:

> The conception I am proposing is that people, in their conscious activity, for the most part unconsciously reproduce (and occasionally transform) the structures governing their substantive activities of production. Thus people do not marry to reproduce the nuclear family or work to sustain the capitalist economy. Yet it is nevertheless the unintended consequence (and inexorable result) of, as it is also a necessary condition for, their activity.

The work of Sayer (2000) and Flynn (2006) suggests that this kind of critical realism allows for the possibility of envisaging alternative scenarios and outcomes and thus offers the opportunity of an emancipatory politics. What can be taken from this approach for an understanding of criminal victimization?

Put rather simply in the first instance it posits a meaningful, if not straightforward, relationship between individual action and the social conditions of and for action. This is a relationship that is not far from that posited by Giddens (1984). In the context of criminal victimization this means recognizing that there are real risks of such, independent of people's knowledge of them, there are actual risks of such (what happens when people encounter potentially victimizing situations) and there are the victimizations that people experience for themselves. If we take the example of the potential of being victimized by a terrorist event, in the current climate, those in positions of power have long known about the real risks of terrorist attack in London which are distinct from the actual risks for those people who encountered those attacks and how those who survived the 7 July attack dealt with that. Then, in addition, there is the empirical reality of what people may choose or choose not to do in the aftermath. The latter two types of decision making have little, if any, relationship with the real risks of further terrorist attack. So, to answer the questions raised by Spalek (2006), this way of thinking about the nature of social reality is not about researchers making claims that people do not make for themselves, it is about situating and understanding those claims within particular socio-structural conditions. Doing so, critical realists would argue, makes possible a better understanding not only of those social conditions but also how best to enter into them *politically*. How this might be subjected to empirical investigation (a question also raised by Spalek 2006) is also neither simple nor straightforward.

If we take the considerations of critical realism, structuration theory, and the concern to understand the complexity of human interaction through time and space, this also demands a research agenda that can take account of and document these processes. Pawson (1989) and Cain (1990) have attempted to delineate what such a research agenda, informed by realism, might look like. At a minimum their recommendations point to three defining characteristics that such research should possess: a breaking down of the barriers between quantitative and qualitative research, comparative studies, and longitudinal studies. How might such a theoretical and empirical starting point better inform the victimological agenda? In other words, what makes this a *critical* victimology?

Put rather simplistically, this kind of framework postulates the importance of understanding the processes that 'go on behind our backs' which contribute to the victims (and the crimes) we 'see' as opposed to those we do not 'see'. In other words, it ensures that we get beyond the 'mere appearance' of things. Identifying the processes that go on 'behind people's backs' can really take us beyond those issues that people take seriously to fully understanding their 'lived realities' (Genn 1988; Crawford *et al.* 1990). To use the work of feminists again as an example, feminist work forces the recognition of women as occupiers of both the public and the private domain, rendering visible and naming processes and experiences that were once unspoken and hidden. Moreover, feminist work has been keen to document women's strategies of survival and resistance. Such concerns demand an understanding of human subjectivity ('conscious' and 'unconscious' action) to be taken seriously. In addition, this kind of theoretical framework renders problematic both the law and the role of the state in their contribution to the processes of victimization, both of which are not always or consistently at the forefront of victimological work, and thereby might well incorporate the agenda of Kauzlarich *et al.* (2001) discussed above. In other words, it is possible to set an inclusionary rather than an exclusionary theoretical and empirical agenda. In the context of criminal victimization, Mawby and Walklate (1994) have argued that the kind of theoretical starting point outlined above not only generates a challenge to the domain assumptions of victimology as a discipline but also presumes that the state is neither necessarily neutral nor benign in its activities. Such a view stems from the work of Offe (1984).

Appreciating the ways in which the state operates sometimes in the interests of its citizens, but always in the interests of self-maintenance, is central to understanding the underlying (generative) mechanisms that contribute towards the kinds of victimizations which we 'see' as compared to those which we do not 'see' – in part, the way in which the 'victim' has been used symbolically in the political arena commented on in Chapter 1. Moreover, as MacKinnon (1989) has cogently argued, this state is a gendered state that also has notions of class, gender, race and ethnicity embedded within it, all of which permeate its activities whether or not we see this to be the case – recognition of, for example, 'institutional racism' notwithstanding (see Chapter 6). In relation to a rather different debate, McRobbie (2006: 82) expresses this issue in this way:

> The shoot to kill policy introduced suddenly in the aftermath of 7th July and without due discussion across the departments of government, only seemingly to be re invoked following the killing of an innocent young Brazilian man on his way to work, reflects this cavalier relation to existing law. Law is downgraded and is even seen to be an impediment to the success of the fight against terrorism.

The value of what she is drawing attention to here is how power can work to render some people potential victims (in this case of the state) and at the same time protect those same perpetrators. Such an analysis does not mean that the state cannot be challenged. What it does imply, however, is that any challenge posed to the state and its activities of self-maintenance may not always have the 'progressive' outcome intended. Matthews (1994), for example, comments on the way in which the adoption of feminist-informed rape crisis programmes has in some circumstances resulted in their co-option by the state. Smart (1989) raises a similar dilemma for feminists who look to changing the law as a way of enhancing women's rights before the law. Such an outcome is not always or necessarily guaranteed. It remains to be seen, for example, how the changes introduced by the Sexual Offences Act 2003 impact or fail to impact upon declining rates of conviction for rape. Indeed, the embrace of 'institutional racism' has yet to be fully documented as a 'progressive' moment. All of these examples fit quite nicely with Jessop's (2002) suggestion of the importance of appreciating the move from the determined state of the 1950s to the hegemonic state of contemporary times that requires keeping 'imagined political communities' on side.

For this version of critical victimology, then, the state is not an objective, neutral arbiter of the 'facts', but a self-interested and self-motivated mechanism in which its interests, at different historical moments, may be more or less paramount, dependent upon economic circumstances. This does not mean that the state always remains impervious to questions of gender, race or class; but it does mean that the ways in which those questions may or may not be articulated in policy terms are connected with the underlying activities of the state itself. These issues, then, set the scene in which some aspects of criminal victimization become visible and other remain invisible.

To summarize, a key concern of critical victimology is to challenge the use of the term 'victim' and the circumstances under which such a term may be applicable. In so doing, it constitutes a fundamental challenge to the domain assumptions of victimology as a discipline. It does this by positing quite a different methodological starting point for addressing concerns about criminal victimization. Rather than being occupied with measuring the patterns and regularities of criminal victimization, the 'mere appearance' of things, as in positivist victimology, it is concerned to capture what the underlying generative mechanisms of those appearances might be. In this sense it endeavours to build on the considerations of radical victimology and its variants and takes seriously the white, male, heterosexist view of criminal victimization and consequently eschews sole reliance on the criminal victimization survey. This does not necessarily mean that the regularities associated with the patterning of criminal victimization are denied. They are, however, set in a somewhat different explanatory framework in which what constitutes the real is always necessarily more than that which people (individuals) are perceptually aware of as real. This does not of necessity result in elitism, but potentially opens up debate to those who are prepared to listen. This challenge to positivist victimology, whilst still underdeveloped in some key respects (see below), is a deeply critical one, and a more detailed appreciation of that challenge will facilitate a deeper understanding of both the theoretical and the potential policy agenda of this version of victimology.

The challenge of critical victimology

As was stated earlier, the work of Mendelsohn (1974) and von Hentig (1948) is frequently taken as the starting point for victimological concerns. Whilst neither of these writers intended to suggest that there was such a being as the 'born victim', they were nevertheless searching for ways of *differentiating* the potential victim from the non-victim which could be applied in all victimizing situations. This concern with differentiation is clearly consonant with the work of the early criminologists, and implicitly took the view that the risk associated with such victimization was at best unfortunate or at least shared between the victim and the perpetrator. Later versions of this kind of work are much more sophisticated than those of von Hentig and Mendelsohn, but they nevertheless share in the early criminological worldview that if criminals could be identified in some way then so could victims. Not only could victims be identified, but more often than not they could be identified by some personal characteristic which marked them as being different from the norm. This was what put them at risk. What constituted that norm was differently interpreted for different writers, but what they shared in common was an underlying presumption that normality was characterized by the white, heterosexual male, deemed less at risk (see Walklate 2004: Chapter 2; Spalek 2006). In this way victimology, unsurprisingly, shared in those fundamental tenets of early criminology – determinism, differentiation and pathology. These concerns are reflected in the work of the early victimologists whose typologies focused on either the personal characteristics of the victim (whether they were female, old, mentally defective, etc., for von Hentig) or the contribution that their behaviour made to the commission of a crime (from being totally innocent to the criminal who became the victim, for Mendelsohn). They are also reflected in the subsequent development of the discipline and its focus on the concepts of victim precipitation and lifestyle.

These two concepts, victim precipitation and lifestyle, constitute the core of much victimological thinking, despite the other theoretical interventions that have been discussed in this chapter. As concepts they have generated a significant amount of empirical work and consequently have contributed to the development of the victimological agenda. As concepts they also both implicitly and explicitly focus our attention on the behaviour of individual victims and the extent to which their behaviour puts them at a greater or lesser risk of victimization. Indeed Fattah (1991), in reviewing the available data and explanations for differential patterns of victimization, attempts to integrate a range of victimological work generated in this way into a general schema. In doing so he groups 40 propositions about criminal victimization under ten key headings: available opportunities; risk factors; the presence of motivated offenders; exposure; associations; dangerous times/dangerous places; dangerous behaviours; high-risk activities; defensive/avoidance behaviours; and structural cultural proneness. This listing, whilst evidently more sophisticated than the simplistic assertion of a notion of lifestyle or victim precipitation, still reflects the central influence that these concepts have had on victimology, and clearly articulates a calculable and situational understanding of risk that largely resonates with that to be found in mainstream criminology. But more importantly, they all, with one exception, direct attention to trying to differentiate the (potential) victim's behaviour from that of the non-victim. This concern to differentiate the victim from others, whether in terms of their personal or their behavioural characteristics, has constituted a key assumption of much victimological work. It is the individual who is more or less risky. A critical victimology, as outlined above, clearly challenges the presumption that victims can be differentiated in this way. Critical victimology articulates the view that it is within the routine practices of everyday life that the processes of 'victimization' are produced and reproduced, thus rendering the term 'victimization' itself as problematic.

There is, however, another theme implicit in this discussion. What has also been very powerful in the policy domain is the idea of the victim as being structurally neutral. We have addressed this here by reference to the elision between victimization and citizenship in this chapter and additionally, in Chapter 1, in the discussion of the movement of the victim of crime from the periphery to the centre of policy concerns since the 1950s. This neutral image and the associated cultural processes that encourage the view that 'we are all victims now' have proceeded apace in policy terms and are self-evident in the contemporary policy agenda addressing the victim of crime under New Labour. As Richard Young (2002) comments, in the relatively new arena of restorative justice policy initiatives, more often than not these initiatives work with an undifferentiated view of the victim. There has been a lack of a critical stance within the victimological gaze on these processes that has had the resultant effect of rendering a number of issues in relation to criminal victimization relatively invisible. It is to a discussion of these invisible issues that we shall now turn. One way of rendering them visible is to reflect upon what constitutes the Victimological Other.

The Victimological Other

As the previous discussion has intimated, the idea of the structurally neutral victim of crime, whether that idea be embedded within mainstream academic victimology or victim activism, has been very powerful both in harnessing the symbolic power of the victim motif and in the kinds of policy 'successes' that have resulted from this power. However, the success of this neutral image notwithstanding, there are various images of the victim of crime hidden from view here. For example, one of the dangers of some feminist work in the arena of sexual violence is that it is clearly suggestive of the equation victim = female, perpetrator = male. This equation, perhaps rather perversely, is also endorsed in mainstream victimological work in which the white, heterosexual, reasonable male constitutes the measuring stick that has been used implicitly to differentiate the non-victim from the victim. Women are risk-prone. Men are risk-free. Such a view, not only resonating with Lombrosian criminology, leaves men, and their experiences of victimization, out of the picture. Their victimization and their experience of victimization are hidden. In this view they constitute the Victimological Other. Over the last decade the invisibility of men's experiences of victimization has been significantly challenged (see, for example, Newburn and Stanko 1994; Goodey 1997; and Allen 2002; see also Chapter 3 below). However, despite the increasing recognition that men can be victims too, and the political and ideological efforts to elide victimization and citizenship, the claim to victim status is still a reserved one. In many ways the notion of a Victimological Other remains strong since it is rooted within the historical image of the 'innocent victim of crime' found within the first formation of the Criminal Injuries Compensation Board, and it is worth reflecting on the continued power of this imagery.

The idea of the 'innocent victim of crime', as first formally formulated, tapped into earlier conceptions of the 'deserving' and 'undeserving', a distinction that was more often than not used in relation to the poor and the appropriate support that might be offered to them in the light of that distinction. In relation to practice, it is a distinction that has also been found to be meaningful in responses to victims from domestic violence (Stanko 1985; Allen 2002), to victim participation in the criminal justice system (Sanders 2002) and to constructions of victimhood in relation to offending behaviour. In this latter respect see, for example, the provocative discussion offered by Winter (2002) on the construction of Rosemary West as victim and Walklate's (2006a) discussion of the young offender as the victim of restorative justice policies. But of course, the innocent victim cannot be blamed and is risk-free in that process. Risky subjects – or, as Miers (2007) calls them, 'delinquent victims' – are highly problematic subjects for the state to be seen to respond to, it would seem, since such a response blurs the distinction between being a victim or being an offender. As O'Malley (2004: 325) states: 'Risk-avoidance negativity has been taken as the hallmark of risk in criminal justice, just as it has in critical and liberal analysis of government more generally.'

Arguably, consideration of the Victimological Other, those who fall outside the normative imagery of theory and practice, returns us to the fundamental tension that exists between academic victimology and activist or policy victimology: those who are identified by mainstream academic work as (legitimate) victims and those whose presence is often only known and felt by those working in the field, the activist working with the (less than legitimate) victim. Although drawn rather starkly here, this is a tension that we have alluded to throughout this chapter utilizing Fattah's distinction between the scientist and the humanist in the victimological domain, and it is a tension that has been usefully summarized by Goodey (2005: 92–6). She suggests that despite the various efforts that have been made to analyse the complex interrelationship between academic victimology, victim policy and victim advocacy (see, for example, Karmen 1990; Mawby and Walklate 1994), these analyses have for the most part neglected the policy element in this relationship. This is not the place to engage in a critical evaluation of Goodey's (2005) agenda on this, though suffice it to say at this juncture that Goodey believes that it is through the avenue of developing 'good' practice that the work of academics, activists and policy makers is brought together. This view is interesting and very practical; however, it does not necessarily resolve the questions raised by the Victimological Other. Those questions imply the bigger question of justice and what the function of the criminal justice system has in relation to the state.

Briefly, as we shall revisit this issue in Chapter 5, some time ago McBarnett (1988: 300) made the following observation:

> The civil trial takes the form of victim v offender, but the criminal trial takes the form of state v offender. The offence is not just against the victimised person, the offence is against the state. The state is not just the arbiter in the trial between victim and offender; the state is the victim ... If the victim feels that nobody cares about their suffering, it is in part because *institutionally* nobody does. (Emphasis added)

In an adversarial system of justice, this structural relationship is crucial to any understanding of the (potential) ultimate response of the state towards the victim of crime, no matter whether or not that response is informed by activism, academia or policy. Arguably it is the state's role in this respect in the adversarial system that is a key contributing factor to who is and is not seen as the Victimological Other, including, of course, the state itself as a perpetrator of criminal victimization, and this role frames what can and cannot be understood as just and/or fair practice. The state does not take this role in other systems of justice, such as the inquisitorial system that operates in some European jurisdictions. This is an important distinction to appreciate not only in terms of understanding the possibilities of the various forms of victimology that have been discussed in this chapter and their associated political implications, but also for understanding the problems and possibilities of policy transfer and good practice within the realm of victim policy. As Goodey (2005) suggests, issues of transferability need to be 'matched' in terms of similarity of legal frameworks, levels of development with respect to victim-oriented policies, and levels and experience of different types of crime. A consideration of all of these issues, of course, ultimately lead us to the question of what might be considered to be fair and just for the victim of crime within different structural frameworks. This is a question that we shall return to later in this book. However, the question that remains to be discussed is what is it that has been overlooked by those who call themselves victimologists.

Conclusion: the deeper world of victimology

As Goodey (2005: 53) has observed, most people's experience of crime is 'home grown'. However, how this is understood can vary quite considerably. A positivist victimology, in identifying the patterning of criminal victimization, would observe that the 'home grown' nature of such criminal victimization would comprise experiences that are geographically, economically, racially and age focused, that are disruptive to people's everyday public lives.

A radical victimologist would want to include in this equation those victimizing experiences that go on 'behind our backs' but are nevertheless still home grown in the form of the activities of the state and/or those that go in within the 'safe haven' of our own homes. A critical victimologist, in the form adopted in this chapter, would want to posit the importance of both the public patterning of criminal victimization along with the private experience of it, but within a framework that offers a challenge to the presumption that victimhood is either a differentiating or a gendered (or by implication an aged, ethnicized, classed or sexualized) condition. Each perspective offers, at a theoretical level, a wider embrace of who can be criminally victimized by what. Yet even within these theoretical developments there are voices who have yet to be heard. Goodey (2005) points to how little is known about those victims who do not engage in the criminal justice system and the services that it offers. Do they share anything in common? Is there anything to be learned from how they manage and respond to their experiences? As Spalek (2006) rightly indicates, victimological work has rarely posited a framework that can account for the interchangeable nature of being a victim or being an offender and has tended to presume that these two categories are not only dichotomous in criminal justice terms but also experientially. This is despite the increasing evidence emanating from criminological research that such thinking is empirically not sustainable (see, for example, in the context of women's experiences, Chesney-Lind and Pasko 2004; Rumgay 2005). Arguably this observation can be linked to the similar failure of theoretical victimology to adequately account for how and under what circumstances individuals embrace a victim identity (Rock 2002). Spalek (2006: 157) is also very critical of victimology's endeavours to fully embrace an understanding of ethnic minorities and members of other marginal groups experiences in relation to victimization. As she states;

> it seems that differences between victims have rarely been acknowledged or fed into research plans, so that generalised accounts of victimisation have resulted. ... However, social scientists here have rarely questioned the applicability of generalist frameworks of understanding to individual victims who may differ according to their class, race, religion, gender (etc.) subject positions. As a result, diversity issues have been somewhat neglected, amidst the use of rather essentialist categories that overlook significant differences between individual victims.

It is at this juncture that the deeper world of victimology emerges.

The ever-increasing demand of different groups to be recognized in terms of their different and/or differential experiences is clearly located within the cultural changes observed by Furedi (2002) with which this chapter began. In what is now frequently referred to as a late modern or post-modern world in which many traditional bonds between individuals have been subjected to change and realignment, individuals look for other senses of belonging (Bauman 2000). The ability or otherwise of the different strands of victimological thought discussed in this chapter to account for those experiences is clearly questionable. However, in asking the question it is important not to blur risks from and responses to victimization with understanding the harm done by criminal victimization. Arguably, harm done is as variable as the individual and the impact that it has is as variable as the individual's coping mechanism for dealing with what has happened to them. Risks from, and policy responses to, victimization are structured and patterned and therefore inevitably gloss individual, and even individual group, differences. Arguably, this blurring is a direct consequence of the failure to appreciate the victimological embrace of modernism.

Victimology, like criminology, is tied to the modernist project. This project embeds both areas of concern into policy. Policies in their very form are not *per se* concerned to address the particular demands of every individual, though practitioners within the framework of policy might endeavour to do this. Policies are formulated in the interests of us all – in other words, in such a way that if anyone were to present themselves as a victim of crime, the criminal justice system would respond in much the same way to all of us. Recognizing that victimology is tied to modernism in this sense also means recognizing this inherent limitation. As a set of domain assumptions victimology cannot see the post-modern world, in much the same way as criminology is also limited in its vision.

So victimology and its associated ways of thinking cannot readily see the individual. Of course, there will be people within psychology and psychiatry who may well be preoccupied with understanding how particular individuals cope with, fail to cope with, embrace or resist the victimizing events that happen to them in their lives, and such people may well associate themselves with victim organizations. In order to embrace 'subject positions' it would be necessary to divorce victimology from its policy imperative, and whilst, as Sebba (2001) has lucidly argued, the existing relationship between victim research and victim policy could be much improved, to separate them further would, from his point of view, result in the further (worsening?) politicization of the victim. Victimology also struggles to see the victimization that goes on 'behind our backs' and that struggle too is evident in the chapters that follow. In the next chapter we shall consider some of the evidence of the nature, extent and impact of criminal victimization and as a result will have a more complete picture of both the strengths and limitations inherent within the domain assumptions of victimology.

3   Exploring criminal victimization and its impact

Introduction

It is self-evident that crime does not impact on all members of society in the same way. Indeed, for some critical criminologists, the recognition of the harm done by criminal victimization renders the legal definitional framework invoked by the work of criminologists and victimologists alike highly problematic (see, for example, Hillyard *et al.* 2005). However, leaving such debates aside for a moment, it is important to note that the experience of criminal victimization, like many other aspects of social life, is a highly structured one. In this chapter we shall explore some of the key features of this structuring in three different ways. First of all, this chapter will offer a critical assessment of the main sources of data on criminal victimization by focusing in particular on the criminal victimization survey industry. Secondly, drawing on data that this industry has produced, this chapter will offer an overview of the nature and distribution of criminal victimization. Thirdly, it will consider the differential impact that crime may have on individuals. Such impact can take a number of forms but can be considered to be particularly problematic in those circumstances in which victimization is a recurring feature of people's everyday lives, frequently referred to as repeat victimization. Much of the discussion in the first part of this chapter will reflect a fairly conventional understanding of what constitutes crime and criminal victimization, thus developing our appreciation of the role and influence of positivist victimology discussed in Chapter 2. In the latter part of this chapter we shall consider some aspects of those kinds of criminal victimizations that go on 'behind our backs' and that are linked with a much more radical interpretation of what counts as victimology. Here our discussion will focus on the nature of 'the crimes of the powerful' and the impact they may have upon individuals' everyday lives. However, it must be noted that, given the wealth of data now available on the nature and extent of criminal victimization, this chapter does not claim to offer a comprehensive coverage of those data but merely to give a flavour to how different constructions and understandings of victimization and victimology, discussed in Chapter 2, produce different accounts of the nature and extent of that victimization. Wherever possible, data will be drawn from legal jurisdictions other than

England and Wales. But first a few comments on the nature of the criminal victimization survey industry.

Measuring victimization: national surveys

The criminal victimization survey was first deployed in the USA in the late 1960s in part as a response to the then increasing awareness of the limitations of police statistics as a measure of the nature and extent of crime (often referred to at that time as the 'dark' figure of crime), and in part also as a result of increasing awareness of the kinds of social problems that concerned people, which clearly included crime. In England and Wales the first survey of this kind was conducted in 1982, and they are now conducted annually. Similar data sources exist for Canada and Australia. On the other hand, apart from their involvement in the International Criminal Victimization Survey first conducted in 1989, many European countries have resisted the move towards developing national databases of this kind. As a consequence, such data are not available in the same shape or form across all jurisdictions, making some cross-cultural comparisons problematic. Such difficulties not-withstanding, as a source of data, criminal victimization surveys are them-selves inherently limited in what they can tell us.

The criminal victimization survey, in asking people about their own ex-periences of crime, endeavours to overcome some of the limitations inherent in officially recorded crime statistics – limitations that have been summarized by Walklate (2005b) as recognizing an event as criminal, reporting that event, and the event subsequently being recorded as criminal. Some of the main limitations of the criminal victimization survey can be summarized in two words: the respondent. Asking people questions about their own experiences assumes that they can remember accurately what has happened, that they define what has happened in the same way as the survey (a particularly acute problem in relation to crimes of violence), and that they define what has happened as criminal (again particularly acute for people whose everyday experiences comprise behaviours that are defined as illegal but which they may not recognize as such). It should also be remembered that these surveys address the concerns of people aged 16 and over, thus excluding younger people for whom other studies have shown that criminal victimization in the form of 'bullying' can constitute a routine feature of their everyday lives (see, for example, Anderson et al. 1994; Armstrong et al. 2005). (However it should be noted that the advent of the crime and criminal justice surveys has, in England and Wales, afforded the opportunity to ask younger people about their experiences of victimization. For example, Wood (2005) reports that 35% of 10–15-year-olds were victims of crime in 2003, with 19% of them experiencing five or more incidents. It remains to be seen what patterns of evidence this source of data produces over time.) In addition, the focus of national criminal victimization surveys is limited to those kinds of crimes largely considered to be the conventional crimes that emanate from the lifestyle model of victimization on which they are built (see Chapter 2). As a consequence, all sorts of criminal activity are frequently excluded from their frame of reference, such as fraud, health and safety offences and possession of drugs. As Spalek (2006: 53) observes, surveys could be used for these purposes, but

> there is little political incentive to include white collar offences in a national crime survey, as their inclusion would mean an increase in the overall level of victimisation recorded, and thus politicians would have to tackle this large area of social injustice.

It is a moot point whether or not such political activity would be the end product of the inclusion of such crimes within this kind of survey. However, Spalek (2006) does raise the important question of the political context both in which such surveys emerged and the way in which the data generated by them have been used. In England and Wales this political context was at its most self-evident in the 1980s, and the debate that this survey data technique generated, concerning the fear of crime in particular, is discussed in Chapter 4. However, arguably the political dimension underpinning this data gathering process still remains, but is perhaps more subtle in its effects contemporarily than in the 1980s. In this respect Spalek (2006: 51–2) discusses the implicit association that such surveys made between identifying people at risk from criminal victimization and the concomitant policy move towards increasing individual responsibility for that criminal victimization – a process also commented on by Mawby and Walklate (1994). This link has clearly been sustained in the UK as policies have increasingly reflected the individualized punitive stance of Garland's (2001) 'culture of control' rather than a social welfare approach that one might still find in France (Roché 2002) or Germany (Zedner and Lacey 2000) or that might be preferred by those arguing for a 'harm done' frame of reference mentioned earlier (Hillyard *et al.* 2005; see also Dixon *et al.* 2006).

Despite this criticism and the obvious limitations that the early surveys of this kind reflected, especially with respect to their ability to tap into crimes of sexual violence and or racial harassment, the way in which they are conducted has evolved significantly. Later surveys have dealt much more sensitively with the issues of sexual violence and racial harassment, resulting in a higher rate of reporting of incidents of these kind (see Spalek 2006: 55). In addition, it should be remembered that this same survey method was central to the development of local crime surveys that became the hallmark of left realism (discussed in Chapter 2). One of the effects of this work was to ensure a fuller appreciation of the structural dimensions to criminal victimization. Left realism embarked upon a series of geographically focused surveys that took the variables of class, sex, age and ethnicity as being central to the sample design and as a result offered a differently informed picture on the impact of crime. Moreover, contemporarily, the criminal victimization survey has become the accepted way of gathering data to inform such local policy priorities. The 1998 Crime and Disorder Act required local authorities in England and Wales to engage in consultation processes with local people in order to set crime reduction priorities for their area, and the criminal victimization survey became part of the accepted way of gaining information about local problems throughout urban and rural areas in England and Wales. All of this arguably constituted a strengthening of the link between the criminal victimization survey industry and not only national policy agendas but also local ones. Contemporarily many of those local policy agendas have a remit that focuses on criminal victimization including some of the features that were once hidden from view in the first British Crime Survey of 1982, such as domestic violence and racial harassment. Though it has to be said that this resultant focus is as much a result of the kinds of targets set for local authorities by the Deputy Prime Minister's Office as it is a result of the findings of local data (see also Squires 2006).

So despite the conservative overtones inherent in the first use of this method of gathering information about victimization, especially in the kinds of questions it asked about what kind of crime, it is a method that has been responsive to both political and methodological critique. The nature and influence of that response will be documented more fully later in this chapter and in Chapter 6, but it is important to appreciate the intermeshing of this method with the wider political policy context. Interestingly, politics of a different kind underpin the International Criminal Victimization Survey, and given that data from that survey, alongside the findings of national victimization surveys, will be referred to here, it will be of value to consider some aspects of those politics in a little more detail.

Measuring victimization: international surveys

International criminal victimization surveys obviously share the same problems as national surveys, but with the additional problems of comparison. Nelken (2002) has offered a thorough analysis of the problem of comparison for criminology, and by implication victimology, but in this context, put quite simply, the key issue is whether asking the same questions in different socio-cultural and legal settings elicits sufficiently similar answers to make sense of the data. How well does the International Criminal Victimization Survey (ICVS) manage this problem?

The ICVS is organized by an International Working Group of criminologists with interest and expertise in survey methodology. This group began its life in 1987 and, whilst its membership has changed in the intervening years, its work is still sponsored by the Dutch Ministry of Justice. Following in the footsteps of national surveys, the first ICVS was conducted in 1989 and there have been another three since then, in 1992, 1996 and 2000. During that time there have also been 'supplementary surveys', conducted in non-industrialized societies using the ICVS methodology under the auspices of the United Nations Interregional Crime and Justice Research Institute (UNICRI) based in Rome. These have been city-level surveys largely with the purpose of trying to inform regional governments of problems in their urban areas. There have been two survey sweeps of this kind. Not every survey has involved the same country on every occasion, but as the authors of the 2002 report state: 'All told there have been about 140 singular surveys of the ICVS around the world. These have involved interviews with over 200,000 respondents, of which 110,000 were interviewed in industrialised countries' (van Kesteren et al. 2002: 14). The ICVS planned for 2004 intended to look for better ways of including more 'developing' countries, though much of this work remains to be reported on at the time of writing.

In this brief pen portrait it is simply not possible to do justice to the wealth of data that all this activity has produced. Indeed, in many respects one of the features of the work conducted by the ICVS and the UNICRI is the apparent transparency that is associated with the work done under the umbrella of these organizations. Reports on the findings are carefully worded and every effort is made both to make clear how data have been collected and analysed and what can and cannot be read into them. The historical legacy of the ICVS, emanating as it does from the national survey methodology, which, as was observed above, has been embraced most effectively and consistently by the Anglo-American axis, gives us some clues as to its political framing and the (potential) problems inherent in the occidentalism (Cain 2000) that such a framing implies. For the purposes of this discussion the issue of occidentalism raises two main questions: that of method and that of methodology.

The question of method refers to what might be called the 'technical' problems that are associated with trying to engage in comparative research work of this kind. Such technical problems range from how to take account of the different legal frameworks within which the survey might be being conducted, the data collection process, to the problems of language translation each of which may differently have an impact on the findings produced. All such problems are problems of data reliability: whether the research instrument can be used repeatedly. For example, Mawby et al. (1999), in a comparative study of burglary victims, opted for a definition of burglary as being 'a situation in which someone entered the home without legal permission and either stole or tried to steal something'. This did not match the legal definition of burglary for either Poland or Hungary (two other partners in the research) but was the definition that was the most easily translatable for the purposes of interviewing burglary victims. Given the purpose of the research, it was more important in that instance to get people to talk about their experiences than it was to be able to accurately match with official statistics. The ICVS, however, has different concerns.

During the time since the first ICVS much work has gone into refining and 'standardizing' the survey questions. In so doing, the researchers report efforts to take account of different legal frameworks, different language translation issues and changing crime agendas. Indeed, the kinds of things that people are asked questions about have changed relatively little. So, for example, the 2000 ICVS asked respondents questions about 11 forms of victimization, from household crime to personal crime, consumer fraud and street-level corruption (del Frate and van Kesteren 2004). In addition, respondents were asked questions about their reporting behaviour, and their experiences of the criminal justice system. (The English versions of all four sweeps of the ICVS questionnaires can be found on the Internet at http:// www.unicri.it.)

Just as an example, we shall consider some of the implications of the 2000 ICVS for the purposes of this discussion. The main method of data collection for the 2000 sweep of the ICVS was a random sample of computer-assisted telephone interviews, though face-to-face interviewing was used in some countries. Face-to-face interviewing has certainly been the main method of data collection for the non-industrialized societies surveys conducted by the UNICRI. The use of the telephone obviously raises questions of telephone availability that the ICVS seems well aware of, with face-to-face interviewing raising a range of quite different questions, some of which will have a greater or a lesser impact on what the respondent will tell you, dependent upon the topic under discussion. Much has been made of the importance of these dynamics in relation to crimes of a sexual nature, and it is well known that this may be as relevant for males as for females. It should not, however, be assumed that these are the only circumstances in which such dynamics might impact upon the data gathering process. Any crime in which the 'offender' is known to the 'victim' (the use of the inverted commas is deliberately intended to convey the problematic nature of these terms), either as a relative or as a member of the local community, may result in the presence of interviewing 'dynamics' that cannot necessarily be controlled for. Issues such as these may all differently impact upon the response rate of the survey. The 2000 ICVS reports an overall response rate of 64% which, given the chosen method of data collection, is quite impressive, though as the ICVS itself comments, not much can be said about non-respondents and as a result different data weighting techniques are employed to ensure the representative nature of the sample subsequently obtained. It is at this point that technical questions of method (the issue of standardization that the ICVS is so focused on) begin to merge with more philosophical questions of methodology.

To clarify, it is useful to return to the quote taken from the work of Stanley and Wise (1987: 110–11) and used in Chapter 2.

> If we wanted to 'prove' how terribly violent women's lives were, we'd go to women who live in violent places – run-down inner-city areas of large conurbations – who have actually experienced male violence and ask them about it. ... However if we called this research a 'survey', then with exemplary motives and using 'scientific' means 'the problem for those women there' could be generalized into 'the problem for all women everywhere'. The consequence would be that we would have over-estimated the amount of overt violence and actual powerlessness in the average woman's life.

We could, of course, insert any structural variable into this quote and the issue would remain the same: what are we actually finding out about, and why are we doing it in the way that we are? Indeed, this same issue is self-evident in the use of both national and local victimization surveys, though in these two cases there is also evidence of some responsiveness to the questions that this issue raises, as has been suggested above. It is at this juncture that it is important to reconsider the relevance and impact of positivism and gender on the subdiscipline of victimology that were discussed in Chapter 2 and their relationship with the development of the ICVS. These are questions of methodology.

I have mapped the impact of positivism and gender on both criminology and victimology elsewhere (see Walklate 2004) and this is not the place to re-present it in great detail. However, briefly, what these traditions built upon were already well-established conceptions of science, in terms of not only what counted as knowledge, but also who could know things. As Smith (1987: 74) remarked, 'the knower turns out after all not to be an "abstract knower" perching on an Archimedean point but a member of a definite social category occupying definite positions in society'. Thus positivism, in victimology identified as a 'search for factors that contribute to a non-random pattern of victimization' (Miers 1989: 3, see also Chapter 2 above) reflects a search for male knowledge. But more than this, in the context of this discussion, this knowledge also became equated with what kinds of questions can be asked and how it might be possible to ask them. These factors, taken together, have contributed to the powerful influence of the criminal victimization survey and its extension to the ICVS. Thus the deep-rooted assumptions of positivism implied in the use of the criminal victimization survey methodology, the assumptions of a white, male, middle-class, western industry, became the domain assumptions bounding what can be asked, how it can be asked, and what sense might be made of the data in relation to the experience of crime. Taken together, these assumptions comprise part of the occidentalism inherent in the ICVS and frame the resultant political and policy agendas that may flow from this database and its associated 'standardized' approach, from the above discussion now recognizably problematic.

Assumptions such as these do not necessarily make the findings of the ICVS and associated surveys worthless. The ICVS does provide quite detailed information on reported trends in victimization, and people's levels of satisfaction with the various criminal justice agencies with whom they have contact. They can and do offer an understanding of the patterning of criminal victimization, albeit a patterning that is subject to 'standardization', to use an ICVS term. The question is what this standardization makes visible and renders invisible and how it connects to the deep-rooted assumptions of what it is that can be asked, referred to above. One example will be used by way of illustrating this wider problem.

The investigation of São Paulo by Caldeira (2000) is not a criminal victimization study but an anthropological study. She calls it with 'anthropology with an accent', as she moved between North and South America over a ten-year period concerning herself with crime, the fear of crime and the urban response to it. Whatever methodological label is applied to this study, it is a thought-provoking analysis of violent crime, its place in democracy, and the policing and public response to it. In this work Caldeira presents a convincing argument for understanding the extent to which 'Violence is constitutive of the social order' (2000: 142) in São Paulo in which 'routine abuse [including torture] is the modus operandi of the police' (2000: 145). In this social order the rich can buy torture from the police for their suspected offenders much in the same way that they can buy private security. Indeed, it is this social acceptance of torture that Caldeira (2000) connects to the cultural belief that with pain comes knowledge and thereby truth – a belief she connects with other social beliefs to do with carnival and the unbounded body that she associates with Brazilian culture. She argues that the propensity of Brazilians to engage in invasive surgery, from Caesarean sections to cosmetic surgery, is linked to the social acceptance of torture, and both are a manifestation of different attitudes to the body. It is these cultural values, she argues, that need to be understood before one might begin to intervene on questions of human rights, civil rights and, more specifically, crime. This analysis compares interestingly with the UNICRI survey findings on corruption reported by del Frate (1998: 46). She states:

> In the third sweep of the ICVS, the highest levels of bribery are exhibited in Latin America, Asia, Africa, and countries in transition, all of which are far beyond the 10% threshold. ... While possible

explanations cover a range of factors, including specific cultural ones, these findings do indicate that it is most likely that street level corruption by public officials has to do with standards of public administration on the one hand and with the overall position of citizens on the other.

In comparing these two differently constituted images of Brazil on the one hand and South America on the other it is possible to see that Caldeira's study offers an in-depth, socio-structural explanatory framework for the surface manifestation of the general findings from the ICVS data. In the one (the ICVS derived report) the talk is of levels of bribery. In the other the cultural belief that with pain comes truth is the context in which the police are paid to secure offenders. These contrasting interpretations and understandings make a very strong statement for understanding the local context that produces the surface pattern of criminal victimization statistics. Moreover, these contrasting interpretations also make a very strong statement, by implication, about the ICVS search for standardization. The drive to produce questions and thereby data that are standardized is at the cost of understanding the specificity of the local socio-cultural context. It is in this drive for standardization that it is possible to trace the political influence of occidentalism: of using the Anglo-American axis of standards as the measuring rod against which other countries' responses to crime and the criminal justice system are compared and, by implication, measured and judged. Caldeira's study not only puts to the fore the importance of locale (that is, the developments in São Paulo itself) but also the wider cultural context of attitudes and values in Brazil, in particular the importance of being rich in securing a convictable defendant for your crime. Of course, Caldeira's study goes beyond the boundaries of criminology and victimology in order to make sense of its findings, in this case reaching out to the sociology of the body for its theoretical framework. Nevertheless the point is well made in the context of the usefulness and relevance of the ICVS and the problem of occidentalism as well as the problem of comparison.

As has been said before, this does not mean that ICVS findings are meaningless, just rather limited in terms of providing understanding or explanatory potential. Indeed, their value, apart from endeavouring to map cross-cultural patterns in relation to criminal victimization, also lies in the way in which they are used to inform policies and directives on criminal victimization at both European Council and United Nations levels, some of which do benefit crime victims. However, the embedded link to positivist victimology that this work articulates, alongside its occidental tendencies, needs to be borne in mind when considering the findings that it offers. Moreover, as we shall see in the findings to be discussed in this chapter and the next chapter on the fear of crime, the importance of socio-cultural context should not be dismissed, nor should the importance of other structural variables that are made more or less hidden by this kind of data (see also Walklate 2003b).

Obviously criminal victimization survey data are not the only source of information about victims of crime. Other sources of data, from the reports of the various voluntary groups involved in victim support organizations and academic sources, use a range of different methods to access information about people's experiences of crime. One of the key differences between these different sources of data is whether or not the study is concerned with measuring the incidence of victimizations (that is, how many times something happens within a particular time frame which is the prime concern of the criminal victimization survey industry) or whether or not they are concerned to measure the prevalence of victimization (how many times an event occurs in an individual's lifetime, as with feminist-informed studies of sexual violence, for example). These differences, alongside the other issues addressed in this chapter so far, are crucial to understanding what is being measured, and can add another dimension to making sense of the nature and extent of criminal victimization. For the purposes of this chapter attention will be focused primarily on incidence measures in building a picture of the patterning of criminal victimization, and as and when other measures are being referred to this will be made clear in the text.

Patterning criminal victimization: on the streets and behind closed doors

Put simply, the patterning of criminal victimization – who is most likely to become a victim of crime – is dictated by four key variables: social class, age, ethnicity and gender. The importance of these variables is evident in different socio-legal contexts, and it will be useful for us to consider the salience of each of them in a little more detail. But first of all, what follows is a short review of some of the currently available data that supports the assertion of the relevance of these variables.

The 2000 ICVS conducted in 17 countries reports that those living in conurbations of populations over 100,000 were most at risk from crime. Households with higher incomes were more at risk than poorer ones, though this distribution was subject to variation according to whether it was the individual or the neighbourhood that was taken as the unit of analysis. People under 55 were at twice the risk from crime compared to older people. Those who went out more often were more at risk, as were those who were unmarried. In relation to robbery, assaults and threat, men were 20% more at risk than women (van Kesteren *et al.* 2002). From this data source it would appear that car-related crime constitutes one of the main problems for victims, accounting for over 40% of incidents reported to the survey, with personal (contact) crimes comprising 25% and household crimes (including bicycle and motorcycle theft) 10% (Goodey 2005: 56). However, within the spread of countries covered in a survey of this kind there are important national variations, and whilst England and Wales has moved down the international table of crime risks that reports such as these generate, the 2000 survey findings still placed England and Wales in pole position when crime seriousness was taken into account (van Kesteren *et al.* 2002: 48). A further report, which supplements the general findings of the 2000 ICVS, explores criminal victimization findings in relation to the experiences of people in 16 cities in central-eastern Europe and nine urban areas in western Europe. This analysis suggests that whilst overall levels of victimization appear to be lower in non-EU countries, there were higher levels of feelings of unsafety and concerns about police performance in these countries than in EU countries, suggesting some areas for further investigation (del Frate and van Kesteren 2004).

The Home Office report on crime for England and Wales 2004/2005 (Nicholas *et al.* 2005) offers an analysis of the nature and extent of criminal victimization that combines criminal victimization survey data with the data recorded by the police. It reports that whilst the extent of criminal victimization is overall in decline, the risk of becoming a burglary victim varies considerably between households. At particular risk were households in which the primary occupier was aged 16–24, single-parent households, households with an overall income of less that £5000, households left unoccupied for more than 5 hours a day and households with no security measures. In addition, it reports some regional variations in these risks, including urban and rural differences. The chances of your car being subjected to criminal damage varied along similar lines, with increased risks for those living in areas 'hard pressed' or of 'moderate means' (according to the ACORN classification of housing areas), single-parent families and households in which the main occupier was under 60. In the context of violent crime, the strongest predictor of all violent victimizations was being aged 16–24, being divorced, single, separated or cohabiting, and being male.

Similarly, the Bureau of Justice of the United States reports that criminal victimization patterns for 2004 (based on the national criminal victimization survey), whilst again in overall decline, were more concentrated for some sections of society than others (Catalona 2005). For example, households in urban areas with an annual income below $7500 were much more likely to be burgled and people living in those households were also much more likely to be victims of robbery and assault. Individuals aged 12–19 were much more likely to be victims of violence than other age groups, and males were much more likely to be so victimized that females. In addition, people who had been so victimized in the past were much more likely to continue to be so victimized.

Reporting on data from Australia generated as part of the 2004 ICVS, Johnson (2005) states that whilst the likelihood of being a victim of crime appeared to be on the decline, the risk of being a victim of personal crime was increased for individuals who were unmarried, had a relatively higher income, had been at their address for less than a year, were unemployed or had an active social life outside the home. The risk of household crime was increased when the household had a higher income and the occupier had been there less than a year. Interestingly (Johnson, 2005: xi) states that 'This [report] lends support to research that has found that the best single predictor of personal victimisation is previous victimisation'. This is an issue that we shall return to.

These more recent findings cited above add to the wealth of already existing data that supports the claim that social class and age are key variables within the criminal victimization experience. Whilst there are some inconsistencies between countries in how these two variables manifest themselves (for example, the findings in relation to household crime in Australia), and despite the general observation that rates of criminal victimization appear to be on the decline at least in the English-speaking world, it remains the case that those living in the most deprived areas and with the least economic resources to manage their situation are also the most likely to be criminally victimized. As Dixon *et al.* (2006: 12) report, in England and Wales, people on an income of less that £10,000 are 1.6 times more likely to be mugged; 1.3 times more likely to be burgled; and 4.2 times more likely to feel insecure walking alone after dark in their neighbourhood than people on incomes of £30,000 and more. In addition, age features in all of these findings as a factor in the processes of criminal victimization. Contrary to popular opinion, children under the age of 1 are the most vulnerable to crimes of extreme violence, especially murder, and are most likely to be killed by their parents. Moreover, if this finding is placed in the context of understanding the nature and extent of child abuse in general then age, as a feature of criminal victimization, is actually crucial to understanding the nature and extent of personal crime (violence). For ethical reasons criminal victimization surveys generally do not tap into the experiences of those under 16 (though other research has – see, for example, Anderson *et al.* 1994, Armstrong *et al.* 2005; Wood 2005), nevertheless the findings cited above do point to the unequal distribution of the crime experience by age. So younger people rather than older people seem to be most at risk from crime of all kinds, but at risk from personal crime in particular. Again this holds so long as the focus of the victimization is that which can be measured by the criminal victimization survey. If the context of personal crime (violence) or other forms of criminal victimization is reconfigured to include issues of elder abuse, then the relationship between age and criminal victimization might shift a little – again a shift in focus that some would argue is crucial in understanding the nature and extent of the criminal victimization experience (see, for example, Brogden and Nijhar 2000).

Of course, as the previous observations imply, offering a more complete picture of the relationship between age and criminal victimization moves the victimological agenda away from that which can be measured by the criminal victimization survey methodology and its associated frame of reference. Put rather simply, this can be categorized as a concern with 'crime of the streets' or conventional crime (Walklate 1989). Crime 'behind closed doors', child abuse, woman abuse and elder abuse, for example, are all arenas that have only limited exploratory potential via the criminal victimization survey and as a consequence have remained relatively invisible to the mainstream victimological agenda (though for an appreciation of the more recent impact that awareness of some of these issues has had on the policy agenda, see Chapter 6 in particular). The similar observation of relative invisibility can also be made in respect of one of the other consistent findings in the data cited above – the extent to which it is young males aged 16–24 that run the most risk of being a victim of violent crime (see also Simmons and Dodd 2003). So in terms of what is actually being measured by the criminal victimization survey, this general finding is worthy of some further explication.

The Home Office report referred to above clearly states that the strongest predictors of victimization violence were being young, male and single (in all of its various forms); however, these risks are mediated by whether or not the person knew the offender. So, for example, that same report states that domestic violence was the only category of violence for which the risks for women were substantially higher that those for men. Similarly, the Bureau of Justice of the United States says that in 2004 'males were about as vulnerable to violence by strangers as by nonstrangers while females were most often victimised by nonstrangers' (Catalona 2005), with the female experience of violence most likely to be rape or sexual assault – thus supporting the assertion that the patterning of criminal victimization in general, but also in relation to violence in particular, is gendered. In a more detailed analysis of British Crime Survey data, Walby and Allen (2004: v) report that:

> Inter-personal violence is both widely dispersed and it is concentrated. It is widely dispersed in that some experience of domestic violence (abuse, threats or force), sexual victimisation or stalking is reported by over one third (36%) of people. It is concentrated in that a minority, largely women, suffer multiple attacks, severe injuries, experience more than one form of inter-personal violence and serious disruption to their lives.

They go on to report that whilst the British Crime Survey estimates that 13% of women and 9% of men had been subject to domestic violence, sexual intimidation or stalking in the 12 months prior to interview,

> Women are the overwhelming majority of the most heavily abused group. Among people subject to four or more incidents of domestic violence from the perpetrator of the worst incident (since age 16), 89 per cent were women. Thirty-two per cent of women had experienced domestic violence from this person four or more times compared with only 11 per cent of men. (2004: vii)

These findings concur with earlier British Crime Survey findings (see Mirrlees-Black 1999; Simmons and Dodd 2003) and seem to reflect a pattern that is repeated in other countries. For example, according to Mouzos and Makkai (2004), reporting on the Australian component of the International Violence Against Women Survey, conducted under the auspices of the Helsinki European Institute for Crime Prevention and Control (HEUNI), 10% of women surveyed reported at least one incident of physical or sexual abuse in the previous 12 months and over one-third reported such experiences over their lifetime, with Newman (1999) suggesting that this pattern has global dimensions.

All of the above variables are, more often than not, seriously compounded by ethnicity, although to what extent is frequently difficult to discern from much of the available data. However results from the 2003–4 British Crime Survey show that Asian people, along with those of mixed race origin, have a higher risk of criminal victimization than people of white or black origin. Earlier findings suggest that these differences disappear when age and type of area lived in are controlled for in all groups other than those of mixed race or ethnic origin (see Salisbury and Upson 2004). A similar finding is echoed in the US Bureau of Justice report on criminal victimization for 2004 (Catalona 2005). Johnson (2005) also reports that, with the exception of racially motivated crime, migrant communities in Australia suffer from levels of criminal victimization comparable to those experienced in the area in which they live. One of the key points of difference in Johnson's findings, however, lies in the experience of racially motivated incidents. This issue is discussed more fully in Chapter 6.

From this brief overview of a selection of the data that are available on criminal victimization it can be seen that the experience of criminal victimization is not evenly distributed across all population groups. Indeed, quite the reverse is the case: depending upon what kind of crime is being considered, your chance of criminal victimization is clearly enhanced (or diminished) by the factors highlighted above. This experience of criminal victimization, which has so far been focused on what might be conventionally understood as crime – that is, household crime and/or interpersonal violence – is often compounded by those kinds of crimes that go on 'behind our backs', many of which are just not touched upon by the data sources referred to here. A focus on the harm done by this kind of criminal victimization is largely associated with that kind of victimology and/or criminology that defines itself as radical in orientation (see Chapter 2). This kind of victimization may or may not be recognized and/or responded to as criminal by either the victim or the state, but this does not deny its importance as a dimension to either the harm it does or its structural dynamics. A consideration of the impact and patterning of this kind of criminal victimization also takes us outside of the realm of the criminal victimization survey, and since it lies outside of the domain of this survey methodology, it is an aspect of the victimization process that is also frequently rendered invisible by it. This does not mean, however that, as an experience, it does not have real consequences.

Patterning criminal victimization 'behind our backs'

Box (1983: 17) stated some time ago that 'the majority of those suffering from corporate crime remain unaware of their victimisation – either not knowing it has happened to them or viewing their "misfortune" as an accident or "no one's fault"'. This disaster scenario has been subjected to critical scrutiny by Walklate (1989) and Pearce and Tombs (1998), and it remains a key strategy in the management of events simply seen as a result of misfortune or, as Geis (1973) once said, 'victim responsiveness'. Interestingly, Carrabine *et al.* (2004: 200–1) list the numbers of events that might come under the heading of this kind of criminal victimization that occurred in England and Wales during the 1990s, illustrating just how persistent these kinds of experiences are. Such events are not, of course, limited to the UK Reiman (2001) and Elias (1993) have documented their prevalence elsewhere. In the context of this discussion it is important to remember that such victimizations also include offences against health and safety legislation. A visit to the Centre for Corporate Accountability website (http://www.corporateaccountability.org) offers some data of the number of deaths that occur worldwide as a result of just being employed – figures that are supported by the analysis offered by Tombs (2005) on a whole range of workplace 'harms' and the associated processes of (lack of) law enforcement in that setting. If we add the costs of the pensions scandal of the 1990s to this catalogue of criminal victimization, it is relatively easy to conclude that it is not victim responsiveness alone that permits such crimes to happen. This is also the space in which the (global) hegemonic capitalist state arguably makes more than a theoretical contribution (see Chapter 1).

Spalek (2006: 59) reports there have been very few surveys conducted with victims of white-collar crime and suggests that this kind of crime does not necessarily reflect the same patterning of criminal victimization that is evident for other kinds of crimes. However, one suspects that in terms of *impact*, that patterning might look somewhat similar – in other words, it is the poorer members of society who are likely to be the least well equipped to deal with loss of pension funds or long-term loss of work as a result of some accident or 'disaster', welfare state provision notwithstanding. Indeed, this is somewhat in contrast to what is known to be harmful and the continued use of harmful practices and/or substances in poorer countries – see Tombs and Whyte (2006) on the continued use of white asbestos in poorer economies despite its known carcinogenic effects, for example. Taking these factors together, Box (1983: 67) stated that:

> If employees, consumers, and other corporate victims had their awareness sharpened and supported by trade unionism, consumerism and environmentalism, and the state and legal institutions could be shamed into closing the gap between lofty principles and tawdry practices, then some of these old ideas could be put into effective operation.

Some would argue that 20 years on from this observation, things have much improved, given the growth in the kinds of movements that Box identifies as being important to the process of change (with perhaps the exception of trade unionism, in the UK especially). However, others, most notably Elias (1993), Pearce and Tombs (1998) and Slapper and Tombs (1999), would disagree. From their point of view the growth and development of movements that have been concerned with crime victims in general, and some pressure groups concerned victims of white-collar crime in particular, have, since the initial observations made by Box (1983), amounted to little more than political manipulation of the victim of crime. However, such debates notwithstanding, the recognition that there is a much broader remit to criminal victimization than that routinely captured by criminal victimization (and other) statistics, usefully reminds us of the wide ranging physical, economic, social and psychological damage that can result from such victimization, and it is to a consideration of the impact of criminal victimization that we now turn.

Understanding the impact of criminal victimization

Of course, it is fair to say that those who have been involved in the development of the increasingly varied and vociferous organizations that now exist and claim to speak for and support victims of crime have always been concerned with the impact that crime has on individuals, hence their concern to alleviate the worst aspects of that impact. Moreover, some would say that the now well-documented 'fear of crime' is one of the key areas in which crime, to a greater or lesser extent, has impacted upon us all over the last 25 years (see the next chapter). Spalek (2006) offers an excellent and very detailed account of the nature and extent of the impact that criminal victimization can have, and there is no intention to repeat that coverage here. The central purpose of this discussion is simply to offer an overview of the different ways in which criminologists and victimologists have conventionally thought about the impact of crime. For the most part they work with four important distinctions in understanding the impact that crime may have on individuals: primary victimization; secondary victimization; indirect victimization; and vulnerability. We shall discuss each of these in turn.

Primary victimization refers to the direct impact that a crime has on the victim. For example, Dixon *et al.* (2006: 21) state that in 2002/3, 850,000 people suffered loss of earnings as a result of being a victim of crime, 180,000 people moved home, and 32,000 changed jobs. Moreover, they go on to state that the global cost of crime, including the property taken, the health service costs, insurance and the physical and emotional costs amounts to £36.2 billion each year. Of course, at an individual level, the impact may vary with the nature of the crime, from physical injury to loss of earnings as a result of the required involvement in the criminal justice process. However, for some people this kind of impact is made worse by the stress, shock and sense of invasion of privacy that may go along with burglary, along with feelings of fear and difficulty in sleeping, to the post-traumatic stress disorder reported by some victims of rape. (For a good theoretical discussion of this in relation to burglary, for example, see Kearon and Leach 2000.) The *Handbook on Justice for Victims* (United Nations 1999: 4) offers a thorough documentation of the various ways in which crime may directly impact upon the victim, starting with the physical reactions to the event which

> may include an increase in adrenalin in the body, increased heart rate, hyperventilation, shaking, tears, numbness, a feeling of being frozen or experiencing events in slow motion, dryness of the mouth, enhancement of particular senses, such as smell, and a 'fight or flight' response.

Such reactions may occur regardless of any physical injury that results from the event. In addition, of course, there are a whole range of ways in which criminal victimization may impact upon an individual financially, from having to replace stolen goods to losing pay as a result of having to take time off work. It is difficult to predict the nature and extent of this kind of primary victimization but, as Maguire (1982) observed some time ago in his study on the impact of burglary, it is likely to take its greatest toll on individuals who are already experiencing or trying to cope with other events of significance in their lives (such as bereavement or divorce). For some individuals, of course, the nature and extent of what has happened to them may result in what is called post-traumatic stress disorder, and again it is difficult to predict how and under what circumstances criminal victimization may result in this kind of problem. For most people, however, after the initial event, they search for ways of making sense of what has happened and endeavour to put their lives back in order, though for some (especially men) this process of being rendered vulnerable in this way leaves them feeling very angry (see also the discussion on vulnerability and the fear of crime in the next chapter). All of this may also take its toll on the victim's immediate family relationships and may spill over into other aspects of their life (Hodgson 2005).

Moreover, if we expand our understanding of what might count as crime to include transgressions of human rights, the kind of agenda that would fit with the radical victimology proposed by Elias (1986), the impact of that kind of activity can take its toll on whole communities through tribal warfare or 'ethnic cleansing', for example, or on sections of a community as in the case of children used for the purposes of sex tourism. As United Nations (1999: 5) states:

> The effects of victimization strike particularly hard at the poor, the powerless, the disabled and the socially isolated. Research shows that those already affected by prior victimization are particularly susceptible to subsequent victimization by the same or other forms of crime. These repeat victims are often found in many countries to reside in communities with high crime levels and are also a common phenomenon during times of war.

Both of these observations will be reiterated in the discussion to follow.

These kinds of observations on the general way in which crime may impact upon individuals, of course, presume that the kind of crime that is being discussed, whilst not necessarily being an ordinary experience for the victim, is fairly ordinary and mundane for the criminal justice system; they can sometimes be made worse by the way in which the criminal justice system responds to such victims. This is what is referred to as secondary victimization. Research has indicated that individuals who are involved in the criminal justice process as either victims or witnesses frequently feel let down by that process through not being kept informed of what was happening in their case, being treated unsympathetically by the professionals working in the criminal justice process, or not being believed when they are giving their evidence (the latter experience is not solely confined to the rape victim, for example). These kinds of experiences all arguably add to the feelings of victimization. In other kinds of cases, such as those involving murder, the families of both the murderer and the murder victim can also feel victimized by their experiences in relation to feelings of bereavement, perhaps being under suspicion themselves for what has happened, or just not being able to make sense of what has happened (on the experience of the families of murder victims see Rock 1998; Howarth and Rock 2000). All of this is referred to as indirect victimization. However, the extent to which any individual may experience crime in any of these ways is frequently related to their personal or structural vulnerability. In other words, not all victims of crime will experience their victimization in the same way or with the same level of impact. As Spalek (2006) usefully reminds us, this diversity of experience has often resulted in some aspects of the impact of crime being overlooked. For example, she discusses the notion of 'spirit injury' that has been used to make sense of the experiences of ethnic minority women. As she says (2006: 88):

> Embedded within the notion of 'spirit injury' is an assertion of the interconnected self, so that common and recurrent experiences of racist and sexist abuse amount to a brutalisation of an individual's self-identity and their dignity.

She goes on to suggest that this concept allows an understanding of the impact of victimization not only on the individual but also on the wider audience who might be indirectly victimized as a result of their shared 'subject position'. This concept offers an interesting intervention into understanding not only the impact of crime but also how to support someone so victimized, and our attention will be drawn to it again in our discussion of repeat victimization below.

Overall those most affected by crime are very similar to those most likely to experience criminal victimization (Mawby and Walklate 1994). When risk from, experience of, and impact of crime are combined, the pattern of those most affected by crime has changed little in the last ten years and is shown in Table 1. From this table it can be seen that those for whom crime seems to have the most impact are those least at risk, elderly females. This relationship between risk and impact seems to hold for both UK data (on which it is based) and US data. Indeed, it seems reasonable to suggest that vulnerability works in this way in other societies too. However, it is important to remember that Table 1 is derived from criminal victimization survey data, and that if we were to incorporate some of the data referred to earlier in relation to the kinds of crimes that such data does not capture, then the impact of being criminally victimized by someone you know, an intimate, would need to be taken into account along with the experience and impact of corporate victimization. Whilst there may be some variations in the relationship posited by Table 1 as a result of these inclusions, it seems to be reasonable to suggest that those on low incomes, those from ethnic minorities, those living in rented accommodation, the elderly, the very young, single-person and one-parent households, and women are the people more likely to be in a structurally vulnerable

Table 1 Relationship between risk from crime and impact of crime according to victim survey data

	High risk	High impact
Class	Poor, living in private rented housing	
Gender	Males	Females
Age	Young	Elderly
Ethnicity	Ethnic minority groups	
Marital/family status	Those living in households with no other adults	

Source: Modified from Mawby and Walklate (1994: 55).

position and consequently more likely to feel the impact of crime, especially when these variables compound one another. As Mawby and Walklate (1997: 293) comment in the context of a comparative study of burglary: 'Crime does not take place in a vacuum, and reactions to crime are more readily understood in terms of the quality of life "enjoyed" by victims.' This conclusion – which supports the much earlier findings of Maguire (1982) – might also apply to the impact of other forms of criminal victimization. However, such a statement notwithstanding, it is evident that some victims receive more attention that others; the question is why.

Why do some victims get more attention than others?

Part of the answer to this question returns us to the issue of vulnerability. In one sense it is obviously quite reasonable, at the level of understanding the harm done to an individual, for a highly vulnerable elderly female who has suffered the trauma of being attacked in her own home by an intruder intent on burglary to receive all the attention necessary from victim support workers and the criminal justice process. This kind of response to this kind of individual clearly returns us the image of the 'ideal victim' (Christie 1986) discussed in Chapter 2. So in some respects the nearer an individual fits the 'ideal' stereotype the more attention they are likely to receive – indeed, the more sympathetic attention they are likely to receive. However, it is also clear that whilst there are differences in attention received at an individual level, there are also differences in attention received by victims of crime at a structural level. In our review of the structural dimensions to criminal victimization in this chapter the relative invisibility of criminal victimization in the workplace has been commented on. We might also add to this observation the relative invisibility of a wide range of others whose victimization is also criminal (victims of fraud, 'disasters', etc.) There are criminologists and victimologists who spend their time exploring these less visible crimes and victims despite the lesser attention that they receive. For the purposes of this chapter it is sufficient at this juncture to be aware that a criminologist/ victimologist would argue that there are both individual reasons and structural reasons as to why some victims of crime receive more attention than others. In relation to this question, it is also important to remember that recognizing the process of victimization, of who may become a victim of what kind of behaviour, is not a static one. New 'victimizations' can be recognized and responded to. So in exploring the differential impact of crime in just a little more detail we shall consider one issue of criminal victimization that has been the subject of much policy debate and intervention, namely, repeat victimization.

Exploring repeat victimization

Tseloni and Pease (2003: 196) state that 'Victimization is a good, arguably the best readily available, predictor of future victimization.' Citing Farrell and Pease (2001), they go on to state that 'This appears a robust finding across crime types and data sources.' Indeed, some of the data cited above adhere to this proposition – a proposition, which like some other aspects of victimological work discussed elsewhere in this book, appears to have gained a global audience. The question remains as to how to fully understand the phenomenon of repeat victimization. One of the first statements acknowledging its existence comes from the National Board for Crime Prevention (1994: 2):

> Research has shown that repeatedly victimised people and places account for a significant proportion of all crime. One study found that of the 1992 British Crime Survey respondents, half of those who were victimized were repeat victims and suffered 81% of all reported crimes. Of these 4% were chronically victimized. That is, they suffered four or more crimes in a year, and accounted for 44% of all the reported crime. Effectively preventing crime against these people and places should ultimately have an overall impact on crime levels.

The policy focus that this finding suggested was hardly a surprise, given that it was a logical outcome of what Karmen (1990) has identified as a move away from crime prevention towards an emphasis on victimization prevention. However, Farrell (1992) endeavoured to give this concept some greater theoretical respectability by tracing its genealogy.

As a concept it appears to have been first used by Johnson *et al.* (1973) in *The Recidivist Victim: A Descriptive Study*. However, as Farrell (1992) goes on to point out, Hindelang *et al.* (1978) also devoted some time to the phenomenon of multiple victimization in support of their lifestyle exposure model, as did

Sparks *et al.* (1977). The latter work afforded the opportunity for one of the researchers, Genn, to return to one of the London boroughs in which this first criminal victimization survey work had been conducted in order to engage in some supplementary participant observation work (Genn 1988). This offered some insights into the tensions between conventional victim survey work, informed by the lifestyle model from which this focus on repeat victimization has emanated, and how people actually routinely experience criminal victimization. Her work offered us another 'story' about repeat victimization that was quoted at length in Chapter 2.

As Farrell's (1992) review of the literature on multiple victimization documents, and Genn (1988) implies, much of the focus of the work in this area has been 'event'-oriented and individual-centred. Yet Genn's work quite clearly indicated that such repeat victimizations were part of ordinary life – that is, part of the routine daily *processes* that people engage in, processes that feminist work on domestic violence, for example, had long been aware of. If repeat victimization is understood as part of daily life as opposed to an event, then the potential for victim blaming that is implicit in much of the work that has been developed under this heading is undermined. Yet, despite Farrell's (1992) persistent recognition of the 'unfortunate' victim-blaming connotations underpinning multiple victimization work, that work has proceeded apace within the event orientation, Genn's (1988) caveats notwithstanding. For example, more recent work on this phenomenon has become embroiled in trying to untangle the cause of repeat victimization by addressing two causal possibilities. Is the repeat victimization dependent on the crime event that then increases the chances of further victimization, or is the repeat victimization related to heterogeneity in which the crime event simply signals a long-lasting risk of victimization (Tseloni and Pease 2003)? This increasingly focused concern is largely a consequence of the powerful influence of the lifestyle-exposure model and its implicit concern with differentiation (what makes victims different from non-victims) that underpins the victim survey work from which the data illustrating the nature and extent of multiple victimization are drawn. However, as Genn's (1988) analysis implied, there is at least one other way of thinking about multiple victimizations: 'They are just a part of life.' What might a view such as this imply theoretically?

Genn's (1988) analysis of living with a multiply victimized woman in 'Bleak House' could have been drawn from a whole range of studies which have been concerned to document the nature of many women's routine lives. These are largely located within feminist analyses which reject the refusal of the literature to adopt an individualized event-oriented approach to women experiences (including their experiences of criminal victimization), preferring instead to locate an understanding of such experiences within the reality of women's routine lives in relation to men that they know. Put more simply, this latter approach privileges processes over events. In some respects, then, feminist work, especially on 'domestic' violence for example, articulates an understanding, *par excellence*, of the processes surrounding multiple victimization.

Hope and Walklate (1995) argued that the repeat victimization approach represents only a partial conceptualization of the process of victimization since it focuses mainly on the 'first' victimization. In other words, in this formulation, the differentiation of the victim (following the positivist line) is achieved in the moments following the victimizing event. In contrast, Hope and Walklate (1995) suggested that various 'victimizing relationships' have structural properties that shape their duration over time and space in ways that cannot be entirely reduced merely to the subsequent reinforcement of a priori individual risk. One of the basic premises on which these theoretical propositions are constructed is the notion of duality – that is, an emphasis on the interrelationship between agency and structure. Crucially, this is a dynamic relationship over time-space. This provides one way of understanding the dynamism between, for example, the structural location of women (one way of understanding women's powerlessness, a defining characteristic of being a victim), and women's negotiation of their structural location (one way of understanding the term 'survivor'). It is this kind of theoretical starting point, which neither treats individual characteristics as given nor individual events as products of such givens, that permits the development of a critical victimological edge to the work on repeat victimization (see also Chapter 2 on critical victimology). As Hope and Walklate (1995) stated:

> Yet it may be that all victimization has a potential for repetition; the crucial point being why do many avoid it. Arguably, a focus on victim-precipitation and differentiation has obscured defining aspects of victimization, especially issues of power and dominance in personal and social relations, which a focus on the structuration of victimization, and its routinization, clarifies.

The consequence of these theoretical concerns may be that it is the *processes* underpinning 'domestic' violence (as in Genn's comment; they are just part of life), bullying, racial attacks (see, for example, Hesse *et al.* 1992; Bowling 1998) which are the 'normal' case of victimization, and it is the 'one-off' victimizing event which is much more difficult to explain. In other words, some sections of society feel the impact of criminal victimization not only repeatedly but also *routinely*, and understanding the impact that that has lies in understanding its routine nature and all that that implies – thus, perhaps, identifying a connection here with Spalek's (2006) introduction of the concept of 'spirit injury'. If this is the case, then, the targeting of repeat victims, predicated as it is on the notion that these are somehow different than other forms of victimization, is not only theoretically misplaced but also, in policy and resource effectiveness terms, only ever going to be at best partially successful.

Understanding the distinction between victimization as a one-off event and as part of routine daily life has important implications for not only how we understand the nature of repeat victimization in the context of 'domestic' violence or racial harassment but also how we understand the nature of criminal victimization more generally, since it raises the spectre of how to make sense of criminal victimization when the perpetrator is known to the victim, and what that knowing process actually looks like. This, of course, can be the case in many different kinds of crime, not just those routinely recognized as 'interpersonal'. It can be the case, for example, that a burglary event is the product of a relationship dispute that might be 'domestic' in nature or might be less intimate than the term 'domestic' implies. Nevertheless the perpetrator is 'known' in some form or another to the victim. Recognition of this possibility not only strengthens the importance of understanding the processes that lie behind 'events' but also poses some questions for our second example in which in recent years much has been made of the impact of criminal victimization: hate crime, discussed in more detail in Chapter 6.

Conclusion

The purpose of this chapter has been to document a number of features of the criminal victimization industry. That industry, dominated as it is by the national and international use of the criminal victimization survey, has been very productive in demonstrating the structural dimensions to the experience of criminal victimization. By implication, in exploring the impact of criminal victimization, this chapter has also offered an insight into the changing nature of not only our understanding of the impact of crime and the emergence of more subtle ways of appreciating that impact, but also the links between those more subtle understandings and the development of policy responses to them. A more detailed picture of the structural dimensions to criminal victimization, and the policy response to them, is offered in Chapters 5 and 6. In those chapters it becomes evident that in the world of criminal justice policy significant tensions exist between those policies that endeavour to work with a structurally neutral image of the crime victim (Chapter 5) and those that engage a structurally informed image of the crime victim (Chapter 6). In other words, despite the clear evidential base from the most conservative of methods (the criminal victimization survey) of the structural foundation to the experience of crime, a structural foundation that seems to hold in different socio-economic settings at least for conventional crime, policies can struggle to reflect a sense of that structure.

In addition, this chapter has offered a flavour of the influence of positivist victimology alongside the strengths and weaknesses of this influence. In particular, it has alluded to important ways in which the development of the international criminal victimization survey can serve to provide much more information about the nature and extent of victimization yet simultaneously hide the importance of understanding the local context in which such victimization occurs. This tension between the global and the local, the general patterning as compared with specific local experiences, is also evident in debates on the fear of crime to which we shall now turn.

4 Victimization, risk and fear

Fear of crime affects far more people in the United States than crime itself and there are sound reasons for treating crime and fear of crime as distinct social problems. (Warr 2000: 451)

Introduction

The previous chapter developed an appreciation of the patterning of criminal victimization and explored the impact that such victimization might have in the light of both personal and structural vulnerabilities. In this chapter we shall consider the impact of crime from a slightly different perspective. The purpose of this chapter is to unpick some of the issues that relate to the fear of criminal victimization, more usually referred to as the 'fear of crime' debate. That debate has taken on different contours since the 1970s and in some key respects, as Lee (2006) articulates, now has a life that is somewhat independent of the actual experience or risk from crime itself (see also Hale 1996; Warr 2000; Dixon et al. 2006). In others words, people feel the impact of crime and/or the potential for some harm to happen to them, whether or not they have been or are likely to become victims of such harm. Yet the criminological and victimological debate on how and why this is the case is rather confused and to some extent theoretically impoverished. The confusion stems, as Warr (2000) suggests, from an inability of work in this area to take on board the differences between what people perceive to be the case, from what they know about the social world, and how they feel about it. Fear is, after all, a feeling that produces a physical, and arguably a mental, reaction in the immediate presence of a threat or danger. Indeed, such feelings may well be present when an individual is faced with an intruder in their home, but to assume that such feelings are an ever-present condition in relation to crime is perhaps mistaken. However, an individual coming to this debate for the first time might be forgiven for understanding this to be the case given the state and the status of understandings of the fear of crime. It is nevertheless evident that the way in which crime and its relationship with fear has been investigated has muddled together how an individual might feel when placed in a situation of immediate threat, with how they might feel in anticipating something happening to them, along with how they might feel about something happening to someone close to them or indeed someone they merely know. Suffice it to say that, as will be illustrated in the pages that follow, little in the fear of crime debate offers a concerted effort to make sense of this kind of complexity, preferring instead to remain locked into the tried and tested questions of the criminal victimization survey that have been designed to explore this issue. In some respects, as a consequence, we have all become vulnerable to criminal victimization as a result of this rather uncritical exploration of fear.

From one point of view such vulnerability is being driven, contemporarily, as much by what might now be called the 'politicization of fear' (Furedi 2005), a politicization that is evident in governmental endeavours to harness people's fears in the interests of the global insecurities associated with terrorism (see, for example, Mythen and Walklate 2006a). This view lends some weight to the culture of fear thesis offered by Furedi (1997, 2002), discussed elsewhere in this book, and more weight to what Valier (2004) has called the 'power of horror' and the role of teletechnologies, which we shall discuss later in this chapter. In addition to these more contemporary concerns, the genesis of the fear of crime debate also reflects the different strands of victimological thought discussed in Chapter 2 as well as the associated problems of measurement discussed in Chapter 3, both of which will be referred to again as this chapter unfolds.

Much of the contemporary exploration of the fear of crime has taken Giddens's (1991) notion of 'ontological security' as its starting point. As Valier (2004: 147) suggests, this concept 'commits blackmail against the future' by unwittingly tapping into versions of nostalgia (of there being some time past when things were better) and at the same time fails to engage in a fully differentiated understanding of fear (we do not fear all things with the same intensity: Mythen and Walklate 2006b). In addition, this more recent exploration overlooks the (potential) impact of the contemporary social condition of what has become to be known as the 'new' terrorism on an individual's expressions of fear. However, before we can consider these questions in any great detail it will be of value to present an overview of the different ways in which the relationship between criminal victimization and fear have been explored to date, and the assumptions within that debate as to who is and who is not harmed by the fear of crime, before we go on to consider how the horizons of this debate might be better framed. So, how might an understanding of the fear of crime be constructed?

Exploring the fear of crime: investigative issues

As Goodey (2005: 66) points out, 'fear is a concept with a long reach' and can be connected to a range of issues from the state of the nation and questions of security (Valier 2004) to the private domestic world of violence being 'just part of life' (Genn 1988). Moreover, Farrall *et al.* (2000: 399) observe that 'the fear of crime is now one of the most researched topics in contemporary criminology' and, what is more, they go on to state that 'it appears that the fear of crime is a social phenomenon of truly striking dimensions'. The question remains, however, how well this task has been completed: what kinds of questions are asked and of whom? It is important to remember that fears about crime are located within a wider tapestry of risk biographies (for example, lifetime experiences, structural and geographical location, cognitive abilities) that may also include fears about employment, the family, finances, consumption and so on (see also Tulloch and Lupton 2003). Furthermore, in the context of wider social processes, crime, disorder and incivilities can provide openings for a range of wider (potentially) sublimated concerns about (and challenges to) the certainty, order and security of everyday life (see Ewald 2000; Caldeira 2000; Kearon and Leach 2000). So, as Goodey (2005: 67–9) demonstrates, what is actually being measured in investigating the fear of crime is a key question. This is a question that becomes increasingly important in cross-cultural settings (see Pauwels and Pleysier 2005; see also below).

The fear of crime debate has been informed by the data generated by criminal victimization surveys. Generally criminal victimization surveys still operationalize the 'fear of crime' in relation to perceptions of 'risk from crime'. For example, respondents are asked how long they have lived in their area, their levels of satisfaction with their neighbourhood, and their views on the kind of neighbourhood they live in. These questions are then followed by others which focus on how safe they feel walking alone at night in their area, how safe they feel when they are alone in their own home, and how much they worry about different kinds of crime happening to them. The respondent is then moved on from discussing these 'fears' to their estimation of the chance of different crimes happening to them and the extent to which they think certain crimes in their area are common or uncommon. These are subsequently followed by questions which ask the respondent to recall their actual experience of criminal victimization during a given time period. Despite the increasing sophistication of the criminal victimization survey methodology with respect to these issues (see, for example, Gabriel and Greve 2003; Farrall and Gadd 2004; Sutton and Farrall 2005) there remains a commitment to operationalizing the 'fear of crime' in this way, and this commitment raises a number of issues.

As Maxfield (1984) pointed out some time ago in his analysis of the fear of crime based on British Crime Survey data, operationalizing the concept of fear is fraught with difficulties. From the summary offered above it is possible to see that in this process some effort is made to distinguish 'fears' from 'worries' – indeed, the questions asked in fact display an interesting preference for 'how *safe* do you feel?'. Individual levels of expressed safety are therefore used as indicators of levels of fear. Without entering into questions of semantics here, this does appear to be a little odd. The conceptual trans-formation from fear to safety is neither an easy nor a straightforward one to make, as the conceptual incursion of feminist work discussed below suggests. At a minimum it raises questions concerning what is actually being measured here, as Goodey (2005) observes, and a number of issues associated with this are worthy of further comment.

Whilst making the distinction between 'fears' and 'worries' might be useful, this distinction is often pursued with the respondent in the vacuum of criminal victimization. In other words, these data provide us with little sense of how these 'fears' and 'worries' measured in this way compare with other 'fears' and 'worries' that people might have and the extent to which those situational experiences might be a reflection of structural and/or material inequalities (Tulloch and Lupton 2003; Jackson 2004). This is an issue that is addressed in relation to other impacts of criminal victimization (see, for ex-ample, Mawby and Walklate 1994), but is noticeably absent in relation to the fear of crime. This observation becomes more acute in the context of the ICVS raising the spectre of occidentalism on the one hand and the failure to ap-preciate the importance of local socio-cultural settings on the other (see the related discussion on this in Chapter 3).

Moreover, the way in which fear has been operationalized traditionally within the criminal victimization survey reflects a narrow behavioural focus. For example, questions focus on when an individual is alone, reflecting an assumption that this is the behavioural condition in which fear is most likely to be experienced. Questions also make a distinction between outside the home and inside the home, as though in terms of fear these constitute se-parate and separable experiences. This is particularly problematic for under-standing women's expressed fear of crime, as Pain (1991) and Valentine (1992) have clearly demonstrated. Despite women's expressed fearfulness of the stranger, of the footsteps behind her (Morgan 1989), of being in public, the context of fear for many women is also the domain of the private, the safe haven of the home, when they are not alone but with their partner. Some of these dilemmas, especially the transgressive nature of the public and the private, and in understanding the role of the familiar in generating fear, are also increasingly coming to light in relation to questions of sexuality (see, for example, Brooks-Gardner 1995; Mason, 2005a, 2005b), and a failure to re-cognize the familial and familiar as arenas in which fear may be pertinent contributes to the inclusion and exclusion of some places and people being problematic and others not being so that arguably cuts across questions of gender alone.

Finally, though by no means least in importance, these are questions that are subsequently analysed in relation to both actual and perceived risk from crime. So what this process of operationalization does is to link fear, risk and behaviour together. In so doing, an equation is formulated between expressed worries and reported behavioural strategies for dealing with such worries which assumes a risk management view of human behaviour. This view sees individual behaviour as being constructed as a rational response to perceived situations of worry, threat or danger. Behavioural responses, however, can be constructed in response to a number of different processes, that may or may not be articulated (that is, spoken about), that may or may not be intuitive (he makes her 'feel' uncomfortable), or can be the result of a combination of factors. In other words, the risk management view is one that, empirically, and in relation to explanation, is only one possibility amongst several others (see, for example, the discussion of this in Skogan 1986). However, this risk management view is the favoured view because it proffers the opportunity for both prediction and control. In other words, it can offer practical policy advice (see, for example, Hagerty 2003; Campbell 2005) and presumes the primacy of a motivational world of risk avoidance that Douglas (1992) observed and, as Walklate (1997) argued, genders both risk-seeking and risk-avoiding behaviours yet fits with the inherent commitment to modernism that is embraced by both the disciplines of criminology and victimology.

To summarize, the pre-eminent position given to this risk management view of fear-related behaviour has resulted in a measurable and calculative operationalization of the concept of fear. The dominance of this interpretation of fear has persisted despite significant alternative conceptual incursions into the fear of crime debate that will be documented below, and despite Garofalo's (1981) incisive observation concerning whether or not fear, a feeling, could be measured at all! These problems notwithstanding, fear, and the fear of crime – or perhaps more accurately, in contemporary terms, the search for security – has climbed both the political and the policy agenda. For example, the United Nations has formed its own Commission on Human Security and, as that Commission justly notes, the demand for 'freedom from fear' has ascended the global political agenda (UN Commission on Human Security 2003: 4). Moreover, given the global focus on the potential impact of terrorist activity alongside that of natural disasters, the stakes are raised for an understanding of the impact of such events in relation to victims and victimization. Of course, much of this kind of conceptualization of the victim and victimization has been outside the remit of the criminal victimization survey, that work preferring to point to a much more conventional understanding of crime and fear, so it will be of value to have a flavour of the evidence that that approach has generated in the first instance.

Exploring the fear of crime: the evidence

First of all, it is important to note that, the work of the International Criminal Victimization Survey notwithstanding, few countries outside of the Anglo-American axis engage in the repeated use of criminal victimization surveys at a national level, with some European countries yet to participate in the international victimization survey itself (Greece, for example: Lambropoulou 2005). However, data from the various sweeps of the ICVS do suggest that the fear of crime, whilst present in different rates in different societies, is a problem that has international dimensions. Of course, when discussing the evidence associated with the fear of crime, in addition to the usual problems of comparison, there is not necessarily a comparable national database with which to work that would help make sense of the ICVS's general findings. This does not mean that some local survey data are not available, as in France, but does mean that extra care needs to be taken when endeavouring to set statistics relating to a particular context within an understanding of wider trends or concepts. So whilst British Crime Survey data consistently report high levels of fear and/or concern about crime in the face of declining crime rates (Dixon *et al.* 2006), similar trend statements cannot be made for other countries. However, Kara and Upson (2006) report that whilst the risk of being a victim of crime has declined to its lowest level since the British Crime Survey began, the proportion of adults expressing a high level of worry about crime has increased to 17% in relation to violent crime and 13% in relation to burglary. A similar disjunction between risk and fear is found in the statistics from the United States, lending weight to the views of Glassner (1999) and Furedi (2002) of a culture of fear in both countries.

The presence of such a culture of fear is not so readily ascribable to other countries, and findings in those places sometimes need to be framed a little differently. For example, in Poland the statistics on contemporary fears in relation to crime make little sense unless they are understood against the backcloth of the fall of communism in 1989 (Krajewski 2004), and similarly in Germany it is still pertinent to understand the available statistical evidence on public fear in relation to the differences between the western and the eastern parts of the country (Oberwittler and Hofer 2005). On the other hand, in France, for example, where a good deal of independent work has been done on the question of the fear of crime, that work is couched in quite different conceptual terms, with the equivalent French debate preferring to talk in terms of 'feelings of insecurity' (de Maillard and Roché 2004). In Belgium, Pauwels and Pleysier (2005) suggest that the term 'public safety' is pertinent, bringing to mind as it does the link between the general elections of 1991, 1995, 1999 and 2003, the rise of the extreme right and attention to the fear of crime (public safety). A study in Finland by Heiskanen and Piispa (1998) reports its findings in relation to fear of violence, with 52% of women being concerned about being assaulted in the street, 44% similarly concerned about being raped by a stranger, 14% concerned about being assaulted in the workplace and 11% sharing those concerns in relation to a violent family member, reflecting a different kind of agenda. These issues notwithstanding, there is some evidence to suggest that whilst the 'fear of crime' is differently constituted in these countries as an issue, it does have some salience as a 'perceived' social problem. However, it is clear that whilst the constitution of this social problem is differently framed, for example, by a history of Basque terrorist activity in Spain (Barbaret 2005) or by issues relating to xenophobia in Germany (Oberwittler and Hofer 2005), there is some agreement that the media bear some responsibility for its presence (de Maillard and Roché 2004; Lambropoulou 2005; Oberwittler and Hofer 2005; Smolej and Kivivuori 2005), and this is an issue to which we shall return. The purpose of this chapter is to explore the extent to which (if at all) studies in the fear of crime have properly and appropriately understood the relationship (if there is one) between criminal victimization in its broadest sense and the expression of fear – in other words, to examine the conceptual adequacy of this debate – and it is to those concerns that we shall now turn.

Exploring the fear of crime: conceptual issues

In an attempt to map the contours of discussions about the 'fear of crime', Walklate (1998a) offered a review of the development of that debate from the early 1970s concern with fear as the 'Other' through to the 1990s focus on fear as anxiety (Taylor 1996, 1997; Hollway and Jefferson 1997, 2000). That appraisal, whilst firmly rooted in the debates that have taken place in the UK, will provide a starting point for the discussion here.

In some respects, the growth in sensitivity to the fear of crime parallels the growth in sensitivity to the victim of crime more generally, as discussed in Chapter 1. That process was boosted in the early 1970s by the media coverage given to the so-called crime of 'mugging'. As Hall *et al.* (1978) documented, the social construction of the crime of 'mugging' left its indelible mark on the relationship between blackness, crime and criminal victimization. That process made a significant contribution to the construction of the 'blackness' of the criminal other, those to be feared. In the first articulation of the fear of crime, then, this was the fear of black crime, a couplet that has arguably never lost its symbolic power. In some respects it is a couplet that is now more starkly defined in its impact, as we shall see. Such social constructions notwithstanding, the 1970s also witnessed a rapid rise in the recorded crime rate. This, alongside the impetus provided by the piloting of the first criminal victimization survey to be conducted in England and Wales (Sparks *et al.*

1977), led to the adoption of that survey methodology by the Home Office in 1982, and out of this the fear of crime debate began. In its first form it constituted a debate between the more conventional victimological work of the Home Office and the work of the more radically oriented work of the left realists as to whether or not the fear of crime was rational or irrational.

This debate was one largely conducted in the 1980s between those who were referred to as 'administrative' criminologists and those who called themselves 'left realist' criminologists, each of whom had their different take on victimology (see Chapter 2). Both, however, shared in a common desire to link criminal victimization survey data on people's expressed fear or worry about crime to their actual risk from criminal victimization. The research emanating from the Home Office concluded that both women and the elderly were particularly 'irrational', given the disparity between their (high) levels of expressed fear and their (low) levels of actual risk. Presented in this way, this expressed fear of crime by women (and the elderly) lent weight to the view that women were indeed irrational creatures and by implication not capable of making 'proper' – that is, rational – sense of the real risks they faced, as opposed to their *perception* of the risks that they faced. Using the same methodology, left realists argued that if you conducted geographically focused and structurally informed surveys and then related people's expressed fears with their likely risk from crime then the disparity between these two measures (with the exception of young males) disappeared. Their expressed fears were therefore rational.

This debate appears to be paralleled by the work of Roché (1993) in France. His study, conducted in one urban and one rural location, suggested that people's fears (expressed insecurities) were largely a function of whether or not they were a part of what he called a uniplex or a multiplex social network. He suggested that when the nature of an individual's local network was controlled for – in other words, when the nature of their relationships and lifestyle was taken into account – the fears expressed by the elderly do not appear unreasonable. Indeed, their risk of criminal victimization looked very similar to that of younger people with different social networks and lifestyles, adding some weight to the left realist view of the need to understand the importance of local knowledge and local context in fuelling people's expressed fears.

However, connecting fear and risk in this way has become a perpetual and consistent feature of the criminal victimization survey industry. For example, it has become commonplace on the annual publication of crime statistics to spotlight the disparity between falling crime rates and rising public fears about crime. However, whether or not the 'fear of crime' is rational or irrational is a debate that was not – and arguably could not be – fully resolved. As Sparks (1992) asked some time ago, what would a rational fear look like anyway? Nevertheless, the perpetuation of this view, especially as it is articulated within international criminal victimization survey work and the standardized approach to the questions that that survey process asks, renders this understanding and approach to fear very powerful in denying the importance of local structural and cultural differences (see Walklate 2003b; Pauwels and Pleysier 2005).

The academic debate on the rationality or irrationality of the fear of crime was developed in a conceptual sidestep that emanated from feminist work. That conceptual sidestep introduced the notion of safety, or, as Stanko (1990) would prefer, 'climates of unsafety'. The introduction of this concept endeavoured to do three things: first, to challenge the view of women's expressed fears as irrational; second, to locate those fears within the lived reality of women's everyday lives; and third, given the empirical evidence from feminist work that fear was a normal condition for women (demonstrably connected to their experience of male violence and fear of sexual danger both in public and in private: see, for example, Warr 1985; Crawford *et al.* 1990; Stanko 1990; see also the discussion of feminism and victimology in Chapter 2) it might make better sense, for both men and women, to ask questions about the conditions under which people felt safe. The concept of safety then placed a gendered understanding of fear (and by implication risk) at the centre of the exploration of the fear of crime by asking questions about whose standards are used as a marker of what might count as a rational or reasonable fear.

Talking about safety rather than fear constituted a deep-rooted challenge to the production of empirical findings that presumed women as fearful (and thereby risk avoiders) and men as fearless (and thereby risk seekers) (Goodey 1997). Walklate (1997) argued that such presumptions were the result of the processes that had become embedded in the fear of crime debate that reduced both fear and risk to a measurable, calculable entity. Yet if the fear of crime (read fear of sexual danger for women) is a normal condition for women, a 'governing of the soul' (Stanko 1997; Campbell 2005), exploring the everyday lives of women (and men) utilizing the concept of safety would untangle what this looked like. Indeed, in the light of this feminist incursion in this debate, the criminal victimization survey industry made important efforts to take account of the differently structured relationship that women have with the experience of crime, especially within the questions asked (efforts were made to consider the question of domestic violence, for example) and the sample design (efforts have been made in exploring some issues with women-only samples). As a result, discussions of how, where and when people (women) feel safe are contemporarily much better informed (see also the discussion in Chapter 6).

The third academic shift in the fear of crime debate, building on the notion of 'ontological security', employed the concept of anxiety. This addressed the relationship between fear and risk in two quite distinct ways. The work of Taylor *et al.* (1996) and Taylor (1996, 1997) explored anxiety as an expression that was rooted in locally constructed and locally understood 'structures of feeling'. This approach argued that such structures of feeling are fuelled by perceptions, myths and folklore about what is known locally about crimes. These feelings act in a metaphorical capacity for concerns not just about crime in a locality but about other things going on in local areas, such as rising or falling house prices or the efficacy of the local job market (in some respects a view similar to that reported by French studies on this topic). This approach situated people in the context of the 'risk positions' in which they find themselves (see Tulloch and Lupton 2003, referenced earlier). Hollway and Jefferson (1997), on the other hand, adopted an explicitly psycho-analytical approach to the concept of anxiety. Using anxiety as the universal human condition, their concern was to map the extent to which people's expressed fear of crime (dis)connects with their mobilization of defence mechanisms against anxiety. They too situated this process of mobilization within the risk society thesis in which individuals seek biographical solutions to systemic problems (Bauman 2000) but very much as a process that de-mands the harnessing and embellishing individual defence mechanisms that again may or may not be differently expressed according to gender and/or other structural variables.

The implication from each of these different uses of the concept of anx-iety, given their differently constituted relationship with the risk society thesis, was to downplay the importance of understanding the fear of crime as a structured experience. This downplaying was in line with the risk society thesis as a whole (see Weaver *et al.*, 2000) that posits we are all equally exposed to the 'goods' and the 'bads' of the contemporary risk world. How-ever, contemporaneous with this work, other researchers were adopting more subtly and situationally nuanced understandings of the fear of crime that would also put the importance of structural variables in their place. This work drew on the concept of trust, developing the view that if risk constitutes one side of ontological security, trust and trust relationships comprise the other.

Work emanating from the feminist movement, especially radical femin-ism, had always been, both implicitly and explicitly, concerned to problem-atize the question of trust in relation to women's experiences of criminal victimization. That work rendered clearly problematic the notion of the safe haven of the home. Work on rape in marriage (Russell 1990), 'domestic' violence (see, for example, Dobash and Dobash 1979, 1992) and sexual har-assment (Stanley and Wise 1987) challenged the view that women need not fear men whom they know: work colleagues, boyfriends, partners and rela-tives. The recognition of the familiar and the familial as not being necessarily any more trustworthy than the stranger put a very different picture on the screen of who is and who is not to be trusted – a picture which, as feminist research demonstrated, routinely informs women's sense of 'ontological security' (see Stanko 1997).

The argument presented by Walklate and Evans (1999) also supported the usefulness of exploring the mechanisms of trust that underpin people's sense of ontological security, especially in high-crime areas. They suggested conceptualizing the fear of crime through an understanding of relationships of trust in which

> your place in relation to crime places you in a community of belonging and exclusion ... It is consequently important to recognise who is seen to be protecting you and how: for many people it is not the police or the council but local families and/or the Salford Firm. Moreover it is the absence of confidence in the formal agencies which creates the space for those other forces to come into play. (Evans *et al.* 1996: 379; see also Walklate 1998b).

This work placed the gendered (that is, male-dominated) nature of criminal gang activity, and its presence or absence in community relationships, at the centre of people's sense of 'ontological security'. Walklate and Evans's data suggested that the actual manifestation of trust relationships may be differently mediated by the nature of community relationships, age, gender, ethnicity and so on, thus suggestive of quite a complex relationship between crime, fear, trust, community and gender. The complex ways in which community networks fuel people's perceptions of their locality in relation to crime and their fear of it have been similarly articulated in the concept of collective efficacy in the work of Sampson *et al.* (1997) and Dekeseredy *et al.* (2003). The latter study was also concerned to reflect upon how such community processes facilitate (or otherwise) responses to violence against women. Moreover, in some European countries, trust in the criminal justice system in the post-communist era is still part of the issue that needs to be made sense of in relation to any statistics on crime and people's feelings in relation to this – for example, Krajewski (2004) reports only a 34% rate of reporting crime to the police in Poland, in comparison with a 51% rate for other European countries.

This work on the role of trust and trusting relationships, along with the work around questions of safety, clearly centred not only women's variable, problematic relationship with men, but also men's relationship with their sense of themselves as men. As a result the fear of crime debate reached a particular turning point under the influence of the developments of theoretical work on masculinity. This was a significant turning point, especially given victimology's failure to address men as victims (Newburn and Stanko 1994). Feminist work had already placed the problematic behaviour of men's violence towards women on the criminological agenda, and this precursor brought to the fore, for academics working in this area, the consistent finding of the criminal victimization survey data that whilst young males were the most at risk from crime, they expressed the least fear or concern about it (Stanko and Hobdell 1993; Goodey 1997). Indeed, some of the work conducted by Hollway and Jefferson (1997, 2000) also tried to address this conundrum. As Stanko and Hobdell (1993: 400) stated: 'Criminology's failure to explore men's experience of violence is often attributed to men's reluctance to report "weakness". This silence is, we are led to believe, a product of men's hesitation to disclose vulnerability.' As a result of observations such as these, there was a brief moment in which awareness of the gendered nature of the fear of crime debate became possible through exploring the value and applicability of concepts derived from masculinity theory.

According to Connell (1987), the ways in which men express their masculinity in contemporary society are connected to the powerful position held by the presumption of normative heterosexuality. In other words, it is expected and considered normal for men to see themselves as different from women and at the same time to desire women. This deep-rooted expectation of what it is to be a man is reflected in all kinds of social relations. So, for example, it is found in the idea of the man being the breadwinner, in the criminalization of homosexuality, and in making women the objects of pornography. Normative heterosexuality underpins all of these examples, and for Connell this presumption defines the structure and the form of manhood that any individual man is constrained to live up to. If the question of ethnicity is added to this framework, it indicates that it is the white, heterosexual male who is in a position of power and at the same time indicates that other forms of manhood are downgraded in relation to this (such as, the homosexual male or the ethnic minority male), as are forms of femininity.

This way of thinking about masculinity puts to the fore the maleness of crime and the criminal justice industry and has been used to facilitate an understanding of how men deal with victimization. This is an experience that men often struggle with since the demands of masculinity would suggest that being a victim is something highly contradictory for them. Whilst much victimological work leaves us with the impression that victims are not likely to be male, this is clearly empirically not the case. Much male violence is committed against other men, and in recent years there has been an increasing awareness that much of that male violence against other men is also sexual violence (see, for example, McMullen 1990; Lees 1997). Goodey (1997), in researching male reactions to violence, used the phrase 'big boys don't cry' to help explain how it was that young men struggled with being victimized. Put simply, it contradicted their understanding of themselves as men. The following quote from Etherington (2000) illustrates how one of his respondents felt about being abused by his mother:

Apart from being my mother, she was a woman. I'd been educated by my father that women were there for the cooking, cleaning and sex. They were put on earth for our benefit and every man should have several. They were not the abusers they were abused upon. So how could she abuse men when I was the man?

Of course, not all men will experience victimization in the same way. Criminal victimization survey data suggest the general unwillingness of men to identify themselves as victims and the greater likelihood of men reporting anger at being criminally victimized. This unwillingness to report victimization and the kinds of emotional response that men experience to it is only just beginning to be understood (see, for example, Coxell *et al.* 1999; Allen 2002) but may go some way to help us understand the relative invisibility of men in the patterning of reported criminal victimization alongside the way in which the fear of crime debate has consistently denied fear as a feeling.

This discussion really points to the way in which the fear of crime debate, in whatever form it has been articulated, fails to capture the lived reality of people's lives. In the latter example, it points to the way in which the cultural imperatives of what counts as the more legitimate behaviour for men and women have become embedded within this particular academic debate and in part explains why women who choose to engage in risk-taking activities (as opposed to risk-avoiding activities) – whether it be mountaineering, motor-cycling, crime, or being a victim of crime as a result of being inappropriately dressed or in the wrong place at the wrong time – receive such a bad press (see also Lois 2005). The same might also be said of men who express their fears. This is an issue that has latterly been taken up by those interested in refining the sensitivity of the criminal victimization survey instrument. The recent work of Sutton and Farrall (2005) discusses the social desirability effect that can be linked with women's (and by implication men's) survey responses in relation to the fear of crime. They argue that women's responses to survey questions can be understood, in part, as a result of them offering answers seen to be socially acceptable, and that this needs to be taken into account when making sense of data generated in this way, especially when compared with men's responses. They go on to suggest that men 'are suppressed by the perception that it is not socially acceptable to express one's fears' (Sutton and Farrall 2005: 222). Now there is a surprise!

The extent to which this debate, as outlined above, has either proceeded in quite the same way in different socio-cultural settings, or had any meaning for those socio-economic groups particularly vulnerable to the impact of crime (as discussed in Chapter 3), is of course a moot point. However, it is clear that there is contemporarily a more refined appreciation and under-standing of the nature and extent of the fear of crime and what kind of impact it is likely to have on whom. This is especially the case in understanding the impact that persistent exposure to victimization has, for example, in the case of women, in the case of people from ethnic minorities who live their routine daily lives exposed to racial harassment (see, for example, Hesse *et al.* 1992; Bowling 1998) or, as in the case of the elderly, subjected to routine abuse as a part of their institutional 'care' (Brogden and Nijhar 2000). Though this discussion also illustrates the conceptual fuzziness and lack of clarity in measurement by Ferraro and LaGrange (1987) found in much of this work. Yet it is also clear from the discussion above that the persistent commitment of the criminal victimization survey to linking fear with risk masks the possibility of a more subtly nuanced understanding of people's expressed fears that connects such expressions to other unsettling social processes, such as those alluded to for countries outside of the Anglo-American axis, that, in the world of 'new' terrorism, may be increasingly difficult to ignore.

Based on this overview, it is possible to make a number of general observations about both the state and the status of understanding the 'fear of crime'. In some respects this debate can be characterized as being sociologically overdetermined and sociologically underdetermined at the same time. Sociological overdetermination is reflected in the observation made by Farrell *et al.* (2000: 400) that this 'domination of the literature by sociologically informed theorizing has ignored important processes occurring at the individual level'. Embedded in this statement are two interconnected concerns. The first is the central focus given in the fear of crime debate to structural variables, whether they are age, sex, ethnicity or social networks, and exploring the available data through the lens of those structural variables. The second is the way in which the debate presumes that individual behaviour can be read from these structural variables, a problem referred to by Outhwaite (1987: 111) as 'reducing agents to the bearers of structures'. Sociological underdetermination reflects some of the concerns with which this chapter began. Where is an understanding of the global condition? Where is an appreciation of the macro condition of doubt and uncertainty and the way in which this might be translated to the local? Recognition of both of these problems offers some clues as to the kinds of questions that need to be asked in relation to contemporary social life, especially in a world that has been transgressed by global terrorism: how (if at all) are fears about crime perceived, negotiated and dampened down, and how (if at all) is the local–global interplay incorporated into individual risk biographies? Developing a framework of understanding that is oriented to questions such as these might also result in a better understanding of ontological (in)security of which expressed fears might be one manifestation.

Metaphorical fears and cultural processes

As has already been suggested, Taylor (1996) argued that the fear of crime had, for some, become a shorthand way, or a metaphor, for expressing their concerns about the changing nature of the socio-economic environment. Fear of crime acted in this kind of metaphorical capacity particularly in circumstances of economic insecurity – in other words, when life plans could either not be maintained or even contemplated. Such economic (and the concomitant social) precariousness has led some commentators such as Furedi (1997), whose work has been referred to elsewhere in this book, to posit that there has been a ground-shift away from risk taking as a positive emblem of progress towards a more negative 'morality of low expectation' in which we become fixated with the negative impacts of possible risks. As a result a 'culture of fear' has taken hold in which individuals are encouraged – most notably by soundbite politics and an uncritical mass media – to transform every human experience into a safety situation (Furedi 2002: 5). Everything, from the food we eat to the nature of our workplace and the utensils we might use in our homes, is classified as a potential site of danger. Guided by health and safety legislation and the threat of litigation, workers in all kinds of settings are required to conduct their business in the light of the 'what if' question (Mythen 2005). Extending Furedi's work, Tudor (2003) agrees that fear needs to be understood as indexed to social structures, culture and the environment which we inhabit. Thus, in order to properly understand fears about crime we need to attend to the cultural networks through which it is constructed and reinforced:

> If our cultures repeatedly warn us that *this* kind of activity is dangerous . . . then this provides the soil in which fearfulness may grow. Indeed, the very constitution of the ways in which we experience and articulate fear is significantly dependent upon the channels of expression made available to us by our cultures. That is particularly apparent where 'new' fears emerge and become widespread in relatively short periods of time. (2003: 249)

This point is well made and can be applied to the emergence of fears about all sorts of crimes, from terrorism to computer hacking. In addition, Tudor alerts us to the fact that, in contrast to a single 'culture of fear', we ought really to be talking about *cultures* of fear. This is a view that certainly has some legitimacy across different European countries, as the evidence cited earlier suggests.

Not too far removed from this kind of analysis is Garland's (2001) articulation of the 'culture of control'. Targeted more precisely at the processes that have occurred within the criminal justice system, Garland's analysis draws attention not only to the extent to which there is an increasing convergence between the USA and the UK in their respective responses to the crime problem, but also to the extent to which the victim of crime (in various guises) has been harnessed symbolically and practically in order to manage crime (see also Chapter 1). Whilst this analysis has not been without its critics (see, for example, Braithwaite 2003; Feeley 2003; Young 2003a; Walklate 2005a), what is beyond question is the current signification given to the victim of crime both in criminal justice policy and in the political rhetoric in support of criminal justice policy and in the media representations of both. Young (1999, 2003b) argues that this signification reflects the move from the inclusive to the exclusive society that is particularly characterized contemporarily by vindictiveness – in other words, the presence and articulation of very strong feelings towards those especially deemed 'not one of us'. Whatever aspects of this debate have the most appeal, it is without question that articulations of victimization have become an important cultural device that arguably masks the problems of real victimization. How and why this has happened is still open to debate, but what is clearly important is the need to understand the cultural context in which the notion of the victim in general, but the crime victim in particular, is being constructed and reconstructed, and, along with those processes, the fear of crime.

There are, however, several questions associated with these cultural articulations of risk. Those questions, especially in a world post 9/11, relate to the structural processes that underpin the cultural ones. Put simply, what is it that is defined as criminal, how is it that events are understood and articulated as criminal, and how, if at all, have these understandings been related to or impacted upon the fear of crime? The impact of global disasters, the transgression of health and safety legislation, and the horrors of the attacks on New York, Madrid and London might arguably supersede such niceties of intellectual argument; nevertheless the failure of criminology and victimology to embrace their relevance for how people might understand, and be encouraged to understand, the problem of crime and their associated fears, and maybe even their feelings of vindictiveness (Young 2003b), should not be disregarded. In addition to these cultural considerations, there are a set of harder-edged political questions about the social construction of criminality/ victimhood that has gone alongside these events. As Hudson (2003) argues, it is important to note the ways in which the categories of perpetrator and victim are politically manufactured. Hudson (2003: 65) points out 'suspect people do not have (actually) to commit crimes to be identified as criminal, nor do respectable people have to experience crime to identify themselves as (potential) victims'. In addition, returning to Taylor (1996), sight should not be lost of the potential role of economic processes in the expression of fear. If, then, we are to fully understand the harm done by the fear of crime it will be of value to consider some aspects of this socio-cultural and political construction of criminality and victimhood. These considerations will be developed in two related directions. First of all, we shall consider the role of the media in relation to these processes. Then we shall consider how some of these questions manifest themselves in relation to what has been called 'new' terrorism.

Cultural imaginings and teletechnologies

The intention here is not to consider what impact, if any, the media has on people's attitudes and/or behaviour, since this is a hugely contested arena covering a wide-ranging literature. It is important to note, however, that there is evidence to suggest that the media play an important role in influencing and shaping public perceptions of crime risks (de Maillard and Roché 2004; Banks 2005; Chadee and Ditton 2005), and this is a view that is endorsed by commentators in several different European countries (see, for example, de Maillard and Roché 2004; Oberwittler and Hofer 2005; Smolej and Kivivuori 2005). Indeed, in a study conducted in Finland, Smolej and Kivivuori (2005: 174) report that:

> Our main finding is that reading tabloid front pages is associated with both avoidance behaviour and higher levels of anxiety for becoming a victim of violence. We also found that people who are exposed to many sources of crime news are more likely to fear crime. These associations remain robust when violent victimisation and vicarious victimisation (of relatives and friends) are controlled.

They are careful to indicate that their findings do not necessarily constitute a causal relationship between media exposure and fear, since people predisposed to particular views may choose their reading material accordingly, but the point is well made nevertheless. The promotion and/or amplification of issues in the media can contribute towards setting the agenda on an issue or enhance a sense of threat or danger (Schlesinger *et al.* 1991; Kasperon and Kasperon 1996; Philo 1999). Cavender (2004: 346), in the context of assessing the media contribution to the emergence of a culture of control in the UK and USA over the last 25 years, states:

> The public had genuine concerns that reflected a changing social reality. But, the media reinforced and reproduced the public's attitudes. The media provided the organising frame, the narrative structure, the story line, and they kept it up for 25 years. Perhaps this is why the public's fear of crime has declined so little despite a decline in the crime rate. Crime has become an ever-present part of our symbolic reality.

Moreover, that ever-present part is also importantly visual, and this is a visual culture that plays upon people's feelings. It is now commonplace for the chief investigating officer at the conclusion of a trial in particularly gruesome or problematic cases to speak to awaiting reporters about the evil of the offenders and the road to recovery for the victim and/or victim's family, quite often drawing on a wide-ranging emotional repertoire. Moreover, as Valier (2004) points out, visual culture travels rapidly and can be viewed in locations and circumstances a long way from their point of production. For example, the widespread demonstrations across the Muslim world and elsewhere that followed the publication of contentious cartoons of the prophet Mohammed in Denmark in early 2006 stand as testimony to the power of such visual teletechnology. Moreover, media images of hostages, videotapes of beheadings, at-the-scene broadcasts of terrorist acts (such as the attacks of 11 September 2001) are all intended to move us, to encourage us to place ourselves next to the victim. The excavation of such feelings from newspaper headlines, television programmes, Internet websites and so on arguably has been a crucial component of the rise of penal populism in which the role of the media has yet to be fully articulated, Cavander's work notwithstanding. Nevertheless the excavation of such feelings has important purposes. As Valier (2004: 50) states, following Durkheim's view that there is an important link between shared sentiments and social solidarity: 'Anger, a passion excited by injury to the group's moral tenets, confirms membership of the group' – a process more than adequately illustrated by the Danish cartoon incident referred to above. Yet it must be remembered that anger is not an unusual feeling to express after criminal victimization, especially for men (see Ditton *et al.* 1999). What is important about understanding this anger, and other feelings that have been tapped in this process (Hodgson 2005), is the way that they are being harnessed.

This excavation of feelings has ensured a high public profile on sentiments about crime, especially those sentiments expressed by the victim. Moreover, this expression of sentiment has become increasingly politicized. As McMillan (2004: 383) states in the aftermath of 9/11: 'Suddenly, the national identity of each American was reappraised as inherently dangerous, an invitation for victimisation', with those same representations being used to endorse an imagery of the national hurt, or harm done, to the American body. Such representations have a multi-layered effect in appealing to moral notions of what a decent society should look like (Peelo and Soothill 2000; Cottle 2005). Such appeals not only potentially misrepresent the chances of victimization but also simultaneously maximize the harm done. In the UK this is increasingly expressing itself as a strategy of responsibilization in harnessing a culture of fear (Mythen and Walklate 2006a). As they argue, it is evidently the case that the 'war on terrorism' representational frame has become the means whereby the state has sought to extent its powers over us all

– what Innes (2002) has called 'control creep'; see also Head (2004) on Australia – and has resulted in the increased targeting of young Asian males as those to be feared not only by the media but also in criminal justice practice. For example, the rate at which young, Asian males have been stopped by the British Transport Police since the bombings in London in July 2005 has increased sixfold (*The Guardian*, 17 August 2005) thus supporting the views expressed by Hudson (2003) cited earlier. As Mythen and Walklate (2006a) state: 'In encouraging "us" to notice and report the unusual in "them", the socially acceptable targeting of "them" becomes vindicated.' However, what does this diversion into exploring the media and representations of terrorism lend to the fear of crime debate? Does it add to our understanding of the harm done by victimization?

It is clear that, if we accept the arguments of Furedi (1997, 2002) and Glassner (1999), in a culture already fearful of or even fascinated with risk, the terrorist events of 11 September 2001 transgressed a possible universal boundary (Jenks 2003). So much so that Worcester (2001) reported that 73% of people in England and Wales believed that the world would never be the same again, and whilst such a finding can be differently interpreted and might look quite different in different cultures, it nevertheless set a scene in which the fruits of fearfulness were further ripened in England and Wales. Whilst, as has already been intimated, fears of terrorism will be read through different cultural frameworks, the terrorist discourse as presented in media and policy talk invites fear at many different levels, from the construction of risky objects and activities (aeroplanes, the Underground, shopping, travel) through to the categorization of dangerous classes, creeds and countries. Yet, of course, as with crime in general, fears about terrorism will also be bound up in local understandings of place. Fear is not free-floating. It is related to self-resources, individual experiences and individual coping strategies (Salecl 2004). It is not an ever-present feeling or state of mind but burns differently in different contexts – see also Katz's (2001) general discussion of emotion. So managing the complex dynamics that constitute fear will be a messy business, as Burkitt's (2005) analysis of the public response after the Madrid bombings illustrates. Nevertheless articulations of anxiety that are extended and reinforced over a long period of time will take their toll, as the work of Oberwittler and Hofer (2005) suggests in relation to the presence of xenophobia in Germany or as Hughes's (2004) discussion of the merging of asylum seekers, economic migrants and issues relating to immigration in the British press intimates.

Conclusion

So in mapping the fear of crime debate, in some respects we have ended where we began, with the fear of crime being related to the fear of the Other. This Other was constituted by the media in the 1970s as the black mugger. In the twenty-first century it is the (Asian) terrorist. The harm done by the various articulations of fear that we have discussed here is in many ways immeasurable. For example, for those who can use their resources to create their own anxiety-free environments by living in closely monitored gated communities, the economic costs lie with how much they are prepared to pay for this, and the social costs lie in the further bifurcation of social relationships. Those without these kinds of resources may protect their homes and possessions as effectively as they can, they may keep a shotgun (as in the case of Tony Maitlii, the farmer from Norfolk who shot an intruder in his home), or they may just simply have other issues that concern them more. They do, however, arguably carry a disproportionate amount of this cost of the harm done by the fear of crime (Dixon *et al.* 2006). However, what it is very difficult for anyone to escape is the power and potential of the visual to tap into our sensibilities of the world.

There is arguably a different vision for the role of the state in the processes discussed above. Not one of extending control and surveillance, of fuelling people's fears, but one in which the coercive energies of the state, rather than being solely directed towards dangerous classes in dangerous places (Coleman 2005; Hall and Winlow 2005), might be directed to fulfil its promise of safety to the poor (Chevigny 2003: 91). As Loader and Walker (2004: 224) have argued, the state structures the processes of security both in its absence and in its presence. Unfortunately, the processes of neo-liberal conservatism that seem to have grasped the Anglo-American axis in recent decades have left many sections of people in those societies feeling the absence of the state's protection and its presence only in terms of rendering individual's responsible for their own security. It is within this lacuna that the fear of crime, whatever is being referred to by this phrase, will be perpetuated since there is little evidence of an alternative presence. We shall revisit this question and some of the themes that have been addressed in this chapter in the Conclusion of this book.

5 Responding to victims' needs or harnessing victims' rights?

Introduction

Chapters 3 and 4 clearly documented the range of harms it is possible to attribute to the experience of criminal victimization. From the data and the arguments presented in those chapters it is also possible to see that there are two not mutually exclusive but nevertheless competing images of the victim of crime that may inform the policy process in the light of the consideration of the harm done by crime. One is a structurally neutral image of the victim of crime. This is an image that may apply to all of us. The other image is structurally informed. This image implies that there are certain groups or sections of society for whom the harm done by criminal victimization is a differential experience and has a differential impact. In this chapter and the next we explore the different ways in which these different images of criminal victimization have informed the policy-making process. This chapter takes as its central focus a structurally neutral image of the victim that, on the one hand, seems to have informed debates and initiatives especially concerned to address the perceived needs of the victim within and from the criminal justice system, and, on the other hand, has endeavoured to translate those needs into formal rights. As in the other chapters in this book, we shall take the developments that have occurred within England and Wales as our primary reference point, contextualizing them when appropriate by reference to the influence of similar policy initiatives from other socio-cultural contexts.

But first, by way of setting the scene for the debates to follow, it will be useful to consider the following two statements intended to address the question of victims' needs and/or rights that have been made in recent years. The first refers to England and Wales, in which the government makes the following commitment:

> We will put victims and witnesses at the heart of the [criminal justice system] and ensure they see justice done more often and more quickly. We will support and inform them, and empower both victims and witnesses to give their best evidence in the most secure environment possible.
>
> (Home Office 2002: 19)

The second is taken from the Council of Ministers of the European Union. In 2001 they agreed a Framework Decision on the standing of victims in criminal proceedings, an agreement that is binding on all member states and came into force in March 2002. According to that Framework Decision, victims of crime should:

- be treated with respect
- have their entitlement to a real and appropriate role in criminal proceedings recognised
- have their right to be heard during proceedings, and to supply evidence, safeguarded
- receive information on: the type of support available; where and how to report an offence; criminal proceedings and their role in them; access to protection and advice; entitlement to compensation; and, if they wish, the outcomes of their complaints including sentencing and release of the offender
- have communication safeguards: [i.e. member states] should take measures to minimise communication difficulties in criminal proceedings
- have access to free legal advice concerning their role in the proceedings and where appropriate legal aid
- receive payment of expenses incurred as a result of participation in criminal proceedings
- receive reasonable protection, including protection of privacy
- receive compensation in the course of criminal proceedings
- receive penal mediation in the course of criminal proceedings where appropriate
- benefit from various measures to minimise the difficulties faced where victims are resident in another member state, especially when organising criminal proceedings.

(Victim Support 2002: 8)

Taken together, these two statements, one of intent and one having some legal status within Europe, identify a considerable policy agenda for those concerned with the role of the victim in the criminal justice system. The extent to which either of these statements necessarily or justifiably offers the victim of crime 'rights' within that system is a moot point, however, the legal status of the Framework Decision notwithstanding. In this chapter we shall consider the way in which contemporary policy initiatives within England and Wales might be viewed in the light of such broader international claims for improved participation for the victim of crime in the criminal justice system and the kinds of policy developments that have occurred within that international context that have influenced more local initiatives. It is important to note that the policies discussed in this chapter emerged out of a context that had already embarked on redefining the victim of crime as a consumer of criminal justice services (discussed in Chapter 1). That historical context sets significant parameters on how some of the issues that are discussed here and in the next chapter are understood and debated in the contemporary policy domain.

Charters, codes and the criminal justice process

The first Victim's Charter produced in 1990 arguably marked an incremental turning point in acknowledging the importance of the victim for the criminal justice process. However, as Mawby and Walklate (1994) argued, that first Victim's Charter was little more than a statement of good practice, reminding all parties that the victim was the consumer of the criminal justice process. Moreover, as Goodey (2005: 131) clearly argues, little changed with the 1996 Charter. In her view that charter 'not only failed to establish the victim as a consumer with incumbent rights but it also fails to establish the victim as a citizen with substantive rights, ... and therefore is misleading in terms of what it can deliver'. Yet the establishment of these charters characterizes one way in which efforts can be and have been made, to offer the victim of crime greater recognition within the criminal justice system and to take account of their respective needs and/or rights. However, as has already been suggested and as this chapter will go on to illustrate, what is meant by victims' needs and/or victims' rights is rather muddled. This is a muddle that is, in some respects, reflected in the differing conceptual starting points of victimology itself, as discussed in Chapter 2. Positivist victimology lends itself to a needs-based approach, whilst radical victimology lends itself much more to a rights-based approach. However, given the plethora of activity that this drive for the recognition of the victim has produced, it is not the intention here to offer a detailed account of it all but to offer the reader a way of making sense of these developments and, where appropriate, situating them within their international context. However, before doing so, it will be useful to reflect in just a little more detail on what imagery of the victim is embedded in the policy responses we shall discuss here.

As was demonstrated in Chapter 2, much mainstream victimological work has operated with a structurally neutral image of the victim of crime. This is an image that, until recently, ran in tandem with that to be found within many of the mainstream victim organizations. As has been argued elsewhere, the success of Victim Support during the 1980s can in part be understood by reference to the structurally neutral image of the victim that that organization (then) adopted: what Rock (1990) called the 'androgynous' victim. Their victims were just members of communities who might be better helped to feel that they still belonged in their community if someone else from that same community offered them a helping hand. In other words, all were individuals whose routine daily life had been interrupted by criminal victimization, and what was necessary was to enable such individuals to re-sume their normal day-to-day activities. It was only towards the end of the 1980s and into the 1990s that Victim Support began to set up more special-ized responses for victims of 'domestic' violence or racial harassment, but even then with an ostensibly politically neutral voice. It is this structural and political neutrality of the crime victim that lies behind many of the policy initiatives that have been at the forefront of the issues that will be discussed here. However, as is clearly implied by the statements with which this chapter began, there is a strong presumption contemporarily that such a (structurally neutral) image of the victim of crime can be used to claim rights from the criminal justice system. Therefore an important question to address is whe-ther or not victims have needs or rights at all, and, if they do, what these needs or rights might look like.

Do victims have needs or rights?

Understanding the nature of individual needs, connecting those needs to policy responses and, on the basis of those responses, making a case for in-dividual rights is neither an easy nor a straightforward process. Chapter 3 illustrated the complex relationship between the harm done by crime to in-dividuals and the extent to which that harm may or may not be connected to their own and/or collective vulnerability. For example, it is assumed that the harm done to children by criminal victimization may have a greater impact on them as a result of their vulnerabilities associated with their age, maturity and cognitive development; as a consequence their needs, both as individuals and as a group, from the criminal justice system will look somewhat different than adult needs. Indeed, much has been put in place within the criminal justice system to offer better protection for vulnerable victims and witnesses as a way of taking account of their different needs (see, for example, Hamlyn *et al.* 2004). However, even in the case of children, not all of those sharing the same levels of vulnerability will deal with a similar victimizing event in the same way. Their needs will vary according to their own personal coping skills and those of people around them. In other words, needs, even in the case of the vulnerable, are not fixed entities. Thus matching service delivery to needs in any service delivery context is fraught with difficulties, and the same is true in the context of victims of crime.

In Chapter 1 it was argued that the formation of the Criminal Injuries Compensation Board (as it was then) in 1964 was built on the principles of the postwar welfare state, and the subsequent formation of Victim Support in

England and Wales filled the remaining gap in reaching out to victims of crime. However, as that chapter also argued, these developments were put in place on the basis of very little knowledge about victims' needs. Moreover, as observed elsewhere in this book, these initiatives created the spaces in which the distinction between deserving and non-deserving victims of crime has been perpetuated, albeit largely as an unintended consequence of the policies themselves. As Goodey (2005: 124) states:

> Victims whose character, past conduct, or actions can be considered as undesirable or as somehow contributing to their victimisation, are unlikely to be responded to sympathetically by the criminal justice system as deserving victims with particular needs to be met.

But the question remains, what kinds of needs do victims have?

As many commentators have observed, and as was stated above, victims' needs vary quite considerably depending, for example, upon their personal resources, the nature of the crime that has been committed against them, and whether or not they knew the offender; they are different in the immediate aftermath of an event than some time later, or again depending on if and when they are called as a witness to court. Goodey (2005: 122–6) offers a very good, detailed summary of these issues. She also usefully lists the kinds of things that have been identified as victims' needs:

- Reassurance and counselling
- Medical assistance
- Financial and practical assistance to secure property
- Information about case progress
- Guidance about what to expect in court
- The chance to express how the crime has affected them
- Assistance with filling out a form for State compensation
- Information about the release date of their offender.

(Goodey 2005: 121–2)

Of course, who fulfils these needs will vary not only according to the individual victim, but also according to what is made available to them in the particular jurisdiction in which they live. For example, medical assistance is available through the National Health Service in the UK but is not available in the same way in the USA, and the opportunities to express how the crime has affected the victim (one of the policies to be discussed in detail in this chapter) have a different shape and form in the USA than in England and Wales. All of these needs may or may not be differently attended to by the different voluntary and statutory agencies working within the criminal justice system, and much research work has focused attention on the extent to which agencies within the criminal justice system respond to them (for a few notable examples, see Shapland *et al.* 1985; Maguire and Corbett 1987; Raine and Smith 1991; Hoyle 1998; Williams 1999), but there does seem to be some agreement that this kind of list constitutes a fair reflection of the kinds of things that victims would like to see working for them within the criminal justice system.

As Chapter 1 indicated, the processes that resulted in the victim of crime being placed much more at the centre of concern for criminal justice agencies, in England and Wales in particular, were largely related to the wider political initiative to recast citizens as consumers of services. Emanating from this change in emphasis, there has been a concern with ways in which victims might not only be responded to in terms of their needs but also further enfranchised within the criminal justice system in England and Wales (Dignan 2005). These efforts take a number of different forms, from re-orienting the work of the agencies of the criminal justice system (see, for example, Nettleton *et al.* 1997) to looking for ways in which to improve the participation of victims within the decision-making process of the criminal justice system, and ensuring that the question of impact on the victim is taken into account in dealing with the offender as in the case of parole decisions (see Dignan 2005: 83). Taken together, these kinds of developments move much more closely to offering victims rights, hence the claim made by Victim Support that was quoted at the beginning of this chapter. Yet what these rights might actually comprise remains a moot point. Nevertheless the question of victims' rights has become increasingly part and parcel of the way in which the role of the victim in the criminal justice system is discussed.

Since the election (1997) and subsequent re-election (2001, 2005) of the Labour Party to government in the UK, the political focus in terms of criminal justice policy has become preoccupied with 'rebalancing' the criminal justice system. This rebalancing, which, as Miers (2007) comments, is a suspect conceptual starting point, began with New Labour tasking the criminal justice system with implementing fast-track procedures from arrest to sentence, early intervention to divert young people from crime, improving services to victims and witnesses, enforcing court sentences more effectively, and ensuring that all the component parts of the system are performing to their maximum. Underpinning all these tasks has been New Labour's commitment to new managerialism dressed up as an agenda of modernization (McLaughlin *et al.* 2001). This modernization is the contemporary surface manifestation of processes that have been under way for some time, such as the shift from social democracy to neo-liberal democracy, to governance rather than Government, to the market rather than the state, and the vision of public services as being self-interested rather than the deliverers of public goods that were discussed in Chapter 1. Within these shifting processes the audit culture has emerged taking us above and beyond the processes of actuarial justice commented on by Feeley and Simon (1994). It is the power of the audit culture that underpins some of the initiatives that will be addressed in this chapter and the next. This audit culture, whilst appearing politically neutral, renders problematic what it is that policies are intended to address, whether it be the processes and possibilities of human agency or merely the outcomes that are associated with the intervention (see also Pavlich 2002).

In addition, this concern with 'rebalancing' marks a further twist in the politicization of the crime victim and it has taken the position of presuming that in reorienting attention towards the victim of crime it is necessary to encroach on the rights of defendants (see, for example, Garland 2001; Williams 2005). Indeed, as we shall see in the discussion on restorative justice, this rebalancing has had the effect of adding to the criminalization of some defendants, reaching a peak with the passing of the Domestic Violence, Crime and Victims Act in 2004. This piece of legislation (discussed again in the next chapter) introduces surcharges on fines and fixed penalties for motoring offences that will contribute to the funding of a new Victims Fund, it allows the Criminal Injuries Compensation Authority to recover payments made to victims from their offenders, it widens the opportunities for victims to provide and be given information in cases where the offender receives a prison sentence, it provides for a Commissioner for Victims and Witnesses and sets out a Code of Practice for Victims of Crime. The breadth of this legislation in relation to victims of crime is consequently without precedent in England and Wales, hence the claim that these developments constitute rights. Yet Rock's (2004) analysis of the policy development of victims' rights clearly argues that (at the time of his writing) there was no movement towards such rights within the Home Office policy-making process. Nevertheless a Code of Practice for Victims of Crime that makes claims for victims' rights is now in place.

The Code of Practice for Victims of Crime, published in October 2005 and effective from April 2006, codifies all the expectations and obligations that a victim might have of the criminal justice system and sets targets for how and when the criminal justice agencies need to have responded to and/or delivered services to victims of crime. It also lays out the procedures for complaint should these services not be delivered. In this respect it constitutes a stronger, more all-embracing document than either of the previous charters. However, it does not offer any legal redress for anyone who has a complaint with respect to service delivery. The question is still open, then, as to whether or not this document in reality does actually offer victims rights despite having been hailed as a victory for those making a case for victims to have rights. So, for some, the move from complainant within the criminal justice system, to consumer of criminal justice services, and on to an equal participant with rights would appear to be near completion. Indeed, this is a view that appears to be endorsed by the Home Office (2005). Yet is this the case?

In reviewing a range of international jurisdictions that claim to be victim-centred (some with the support of the legal framework, others not), Goodey (2005: 130) identifies what she calls a 'checklist of core rights'. These include:

- Compassion and respect
- Information on proceedings and rights
- Presentation of victims' views
- Legal aid
- Swift case processing
- Protection of privacy and identity
- Protection from retaliation and intimidation
- Compensation from the offender and the State
- Recognition of victims with special needs.

Many of these claims to rights within particular jurisdictions are clearly supportive of a range of United Nations and Council of Europe declarations and statements of intent that sometimes come with accompanying handbooks to enable practitioners to formulate appropriate legislation and service delivery. Of course, it is a moot point whether or not any particular jurisdiction enshrines all of the above list as victims' rights *per se*, that is, as rights claimable in law. Indeed, the Code of Practice for Victims of Crime, whilst touching upon a number of the 'core rights' listed above, even in its very title suggests an ambivalent relationship with the idea of constructing rights that are claimable in law (Rock 2004). As a consequence it can be seen that, despite political claims to the contrary, the case for victims' rights (that is, rights in law, though there are notable exceptions to this such as the protection of identity for female victims of rape) appears to be as patchy as the case for meeting victims' needs.

Despite the clear theoretical and evidential tensions articulated in these issues, the global dimensions to the development of victim-oriented policies are self-evident, and those global dimensions have had a discernible influence on the development of policy initiatives in the local context of England and Wales. In this chapter we shall consider under four headings the nature of this needs/rights debate and the different ways it has been articulated: perpetuating welfare; tinkering with adversarialism; moving towards allocation; and reorienting towards restorative justice. These headings are not intended to delineate discreet movements or initiatives but rather to represent points on a continuum as the move towards the greater participation of the victim in the criminal justice system has gained momentum.

Perpetuating welfare

A welfare approach to the victim of crime places victims' needs at the top of the agenda. As has been argued elsewhere, the formation of the Criminal Injuries Compensation Board in the 1960s was the last brick of the welfare state cemented with the principle of insurance (Mawby and Walklate 1994) and arguably mixed well with a welfare approach. Miers (2007) documents that since 1964 the government has paid out £3 billion to approximately 910,000 applicants. The role and nature of state compensation, however, remains a contested issue. Ashworth (1986), for example, suggested that the contractual assumption embedded within the CICB as initially formulated was misplaced since it gave no more than an individual might expect as their part of the social good called the criminal justice system. Arguably, this debate was partly resolved by placing the CICB on a statutory footing in 1995, thus making it a permanent and recognized part of the state delivery of compensation in relation to crime. De Greiff (2006) argues that the role and responsibility of the state in delivering such compensation comprises a public acknowledgement that an individual's life has been disrupted as a result of crime, crime that is a result of the failure of the criminal justice system to protect them. From this point of view state compensation is not only a contractual obligation but also a moral obligation in the face of the state's failure to ensure civic trust. This view is endorsed in some respects by the Home Office (2005) which in its consultation document on victims of crime says that a state financial award is one way of acknowledging the harm done to the victim. It is worth noting, however, that this document was prepared for consultation with a view to reviewing the speed at which compensation is delivered (amongst other issues) in the aftermath of the bombings in London on 7 July 2005. Nevertheless, state compensation is not without its difficulties, especially in its embrace of the distinction between the deserving and undeserving victim of crime in the form of the notion of innocence, or, as the Home Office (2005) says, 'blameless victims'. The difficulty of dealing with what Miers (2007) calls 'the delinquent victim', embedded as it is in traditional conceptions of welfare, remains.

In a related vein, the growth and development of Victim Support and associated self-help organizations can also be located with a welfare model of responding to victims' needs. This model was not intended as one of dependency but as one in which, after the offering of a sympathetic ear, the individual could be reintegrated into their local community. As such it gels quite well with a consumerist or responsibilized model of welfare (Clarke 2005) and, as was observed in Chapter 1, also gelled very well with the rising economic circumstances that were to herald a fundamental change in how the welfare state in England and Wales was to be understood. However, what is crucial to understanding these welfare-based initiatives, and their perpe-tuation within voluntary organizations working alongside the criminal jus-tice system (as with witness support schemes in the Crown and magistrates' courts, for example), is that they leave the workings of the criminal justice system intact. The welfare principle recognizes that crime has a differential impact upon individuals who have different abilities to cope with that im-pact. That implicit recognition of difference demands that in order to make good the harm done, that process occurs outside the process of justice. The same cannot be said for some of the other efforts that have been made to take account of the victim of crime that will be discussed below.

Tinkering with adversarialism

Mawby and Gill (1987: 229) argued that there were four aspects of victims' rights which could be improved: the right to play an active part in the criminal justice system; the right to knowledge; the right to financial help; and the right to advice and support. These were claims that acknowledged, as Dignan (2005: 65) has argued, the ways in which the criminal justice system had historically failed the victim of crime. As he says, it had failed to re-cognize the harm done by crime; it had treated the victim instrumentally; and had failed to offer financial redress. All of this led researchers to talk about 'secondary victimization', the victimization that occurs as a result of involvement in the criminal justice system (see also Chapter 3). Moreover, as the Audit Commission (2003) reported, out of 24 criminal incidents experi-enced, only half are reported to the police, only one-third are recorded as crimes, with less than one resulting in a guilty verdict. This report points to a huge attrition rate of victims and witnesses within the criminal justice system and endorses the view that a better response must be possible. Recognition of these shortcomings has resulted in an increasing preoccupation with how the conventional criminal justice response (to use Dignan's phrase) might do better. It is those responses that I have chosen to call 'tinkering with adver-sarialism', since it is the adversarial system of justice itself that is frequently the barrier to the ultimate success or failure of the kinds of policy initiatives to be discussed here.

Arguably two main strategies have been used to try to render the criminal justice system more responsive to the victim of crime: reorienting the work of criminal justice professionals and addressing such policies to the offender. In the case of the first, there is clearly some overlap with the welfare approach discussed above, but as some of the work to be carried out by criminal justice professionals is now required rather than discretionary I have chosen to dis-cuss them under this heading. Whilst all branches of the criminal justice profession have been increasingly encouraged to place the victim of crime nearer the centre of their routine daily work, that imperative has probably had its greatest impact on the Probation Service, so we shall discuss their changing role as an exemplar of this kind of system response.

Garland (2001:177) states that: 'For much of the twentieth century probation was a core institution of criminal justice. Extensively used, in the vanguard of penal progress, it was often regarded as the exemplary instance of the penal-welfare approach to crime control.' The extent to which either the public or the courts were ever convinced by probation as a mean of offender control is a moot point; however, the Probation Service no longer has as its central mission the goal of assisting, advising and befriending (deserving) offenders. The reorientation of probation work towards the victim of crime was put on a statutory footing by the Criminal Justice and Court Services Act 2000, though this focus was first introduced in the 1990 Victim's Charter. That charter obliged the Probation Service in England and Wales to contact the victims and/or families of life sentence prisoners prior to any consideration of their release. This task was widened in the 1996 Charter to include victims of serious violent or sexual offences. Under the Domestic Violence, Crime and Victims Act 2004, local probation boards have obligations to the victim of an offender who receives a sentence of imprisonment of 12 months or longer after conviction of a sexual or violent offence, and the victim of an offender convicted of a sexual or violent offence who receives a restricted (or other similar) hospital order. Consequently the Probation Service is now required to take reasonable steps to establish any victim representations about licence conditions or supervision requirements, subject to the offender's release from prison or hospital, and to ensure that those responsible for making such decisions are informed of the victim's wishes. They must also provide the victim with any information about the offender's release and any conditions that may be attached to it.

The early foray into this kind of work produced a mixed response from within the Probation Service. Whilst some commentators questioned the value of this change of direction (see, for example, Nellis 1995), others clearly embraced it. As James (1995: 346) states:

> It must be proper for the probation service to demonstrate concern for victims of crime by acknowledging the very real impact of victimisation upon individuals and in their direct work with offenders ensuring that offenders are cognisant of the impact of their crime upon victims.

However, the initial demands for partnership working and training which followed from this change in direction resulted in different practices being adopted in different areas (see Nettleton *et al.* 1997), and later evaluative work of probation involvement with victims (Crawford and Enterkin 2001), examined from the victims' point of view, pointed to similar issues of variation in local practice but also raised some other more disturbing concerns. Crawford and Enterkin pointed to the imbalance between what victims were permitted to know about their offender (and what the offender was entitled to know under human rights legislation) as compared with the information they were expected to give, and commented on the failure of the system as it then stood to guarantee victims' confidentiality. They concluded by saying that

> The findings from the research reported here suggest that the ambiguities and uncertainties surrounding the integration of victims in the post-sentencing process may generate expectations, demands, interests and unintended consequences which are difficult to control, rather like the contents of Pandora's box. (2001: 724)

The extent to which victims increasingly suffer from the problem of disappointed expectations will be referred to again. However, a survey conducted by MORI of victims' experiences of the Probation Service reported that half felt very or quite satisfied with the service they had received (higher than the police) and most were positive about the contact they had had with their victim liaison officer, especially with the emotional support they had been given, though the issue of information about the offender remained problematic (National Probation Service for England and Wales 2004). Moreover, some would say that it is mistaken to view probation involvement with victims as new since many of the early experiments with mediation, reparation and victim support had their origins in probation offices. In addition, recent policy initiatives have introduced joint police and Crown Prosecution Service witness care units under the government's No Witness, No Justice initiative. There were 165 such units across England and Wales by December 2005 (Home Office 2005) whose purpose is to ensure proper and effective communication of information to victims and witnesses in relation to the case in which they are involved.

The second strand of policies that tinker with adversarialism has looked to further the demands made on the offender with respect to the victim. There has been a long tradition within criminal justice policy of disposing the offender to pay compensation to the victim, and whilst there is some evidence to suggest that victims are in favour of this kind of disposition, historically they have been very difficult to implement. There are a number of reasons for this, but a prime one is the reluctance of the court to prioritize the victim in cases where compensation is appropriate. Cavadino and Dignan (1996) suggest that this is a result of the tensions that exist between the reparative principle implied by compensation and the more punitive impulse of the conventional criminal justice system. There are other difficulties, too, associated with the kind of information given to the court (which we shall discuss again below) and the offender's ability to pay. However, the invocation of ensuring that the offender 'pays' for their offence, whether that be in formal terms through a compensation order imposed by the court or through more rhetorical devices such as being seen to be involved in community work, raises the problematic issue of the extent to which paying attention to the victim results in the further penalization of the offender (this is a debate we shall return to at the end of this chapter and in the conclusion to this book). However, the ultimate barrier to tinkering with the adversarial system lies in understanding the nature of that system itself.

Conventional views of the adversarial system of justice start from the position that the central purpose of the criminal justice system is to ensure both the structure and the function of the criminal trial. The second of these is perhaps the most telling in its consequences for all participants, including the victim. McBarnett's (1988: 300) description of this relationship was quoted towards the end of Chapter 2. In principle, those who withhold evidence, or refuse to give evidence, or in any way try to subvert the course of justice may be prosecuted. In this interpretation of the function of the criminal justice system, neither complainants nor defendants have much of a voice at all, though defendants have clearly more 'rights' in this context than complainants. From this point of view, then, extending the participation of the complainant in the criminal justice process must always be balanced by the question of ensuring that the 'rights' of the defendant are not eroded. Ashworth (1993, 2000) has been a particularly vocal critic of enfranchising the victim with the introduction of victim (impact) statements. This particular policy move illustrates the next strategy for enhancing victim participation in the criminal justice system that I have called 'moving towards allocution'.

Moving towards allocution

Edwards (2004) suggests that there are four different ways in which the victim might participate within criminal justice decision making: in an expressive fashion through the offering of information or feelings; by being required to provide information; through consultation and as a result having an informal influence on decisions; and finally, by having control over the decision-making process. In summarizing the evidence on what it is that victims want from any role in the criminal justice decision-making process, Wemmers (2005: 130) suggests that the evidence is equivocal, though she does conclude, in reviewing the strengths and weaknesses of the various structural roles given to the victim in different European legal frameworks, that:

> Neither the victim impact statement, the adhesion procedure, the auxiliary prosecutor, nor a face to face meeting with the prosecutor give victims decision control ... Victims are largely in favour of the judge retaining full control over sentencing decisions.

Nevertheless moves have proceeded to offer the victim as 'a voice to be heard' within criminal justice systems of jurisdictions with very different legal traditions. (For a more detailed discussion of these different models of victim involvement in criminal justice, see, for example, Mawby and Walklate 1994.)

The introduction of victim impact statements is a measure that is largely associated with a 'victim allocution' model of the criminal justice system rather than a conventional model (Cavadino and Dignan 1996: 234). Put simply, the conventional model is one rooted in conceptions of just desserts in which the main victim measure is the compensation order and the role of the victim is considered minimal except when required as a witness. On the other hand, the victim allocution model is concerned with victim empowerment; the victim's wishes are considered paramount in prosecution and sentencing decisions. The difference between these two models is felt at its keenest over the question of victim impact statements. In practical terms, in England and Wales the controversy over whether or not to involve the victim in sentencing decisions has been avoided by not including that aspect of this kind of policy as part of the introduction of such measures. However, what cannot be avoided are the inevitable tensions that are generated by the introduction of a measure that presumes a very different mode of victim participation within the criminal justice system. Whilst, on the one hand, there is evidence to suggest that there is some therapeutic value in the involvement of victims in this way, the question remains as to how best to ensure this kind of victim participation. As we shall see, current policy in the UK falls short of offering the victim a say in the sentencing of an offender (though a number criminal justice systems do so internationally), though the UK scheme, discussed in more detail below, was given an added edge with the introduction of a pilot scheme of victims' advocates from April 2006, for cases in which a conviction of murder or manslaughter has been secured. It is proposed within these pilot schemes that the advocate will speak on behalf of the family so that the court can be told how the death and ensuing events have affected them. Given that a conviction must be secured for an advocate to speak, it must be assumed that their representations are intended to influence sentencing. Given the controversy that these statements appear to cause, it will be useful to consider what shape and form they take more generally.

Victim impact statements accept that there is space for the victim of crime to have what might be called 'procedural rights' within the criminal justice process. Governments frequently, however, have more obviously pragmatic reasons for moving in this direction. The need to secure the co-operation of victims, especially as witnesses, in the pursuit of the business of the criminal justice system counts as an important one. Moreover, evidence from British Crime Survey data (Mirrlees-Black 2001) increasingly suggests that lack of confidence in the criminal justice system is on the increase and successive governments have looked for policy initiatives that might militate against this trend. Victim impact statements have consistently cropped up as a policy that might fit this particular bill. So what is a victim impact statement, and where does a practice like this sit with these broader concerns for reintegration?

The Community Law Reform Committee of the Australian Capital Territory (1998: 1) defines a victim impact statement in the following way:

> A victim impact statement is a statement setting out the full effects – physical, psychological, financial and social – suffered by a victim as a result of a crime. The statement is prepared for placement before the court engaged in sentencing an offender for the crime in question so that the court may fully understand the effects of the crime on the victim.

This general definition gives no indication of whether or not such statements should be mandatory, nor does it say whether or not such statements should include recommendations for sentencing. Moreover, in some respects it is possible to argue that the opportunity for the full effects of a crime on the victim to be put before the court already exists in the legal system of England and Wales. This is possible, for example, in the context of a plea for compensation or, in the case of a violent crime, in the injuries caused as a result of the victimization put as evidence before the court. Yet nevertheless we have witnessed a slow but sure move towards putting in place more formal mechanisms to ensure the victim's voice is more clearly heard. With this in mind, pilot victim impact statement schemes were established in three police force areas in 1997 to encourage victims of all kinds of crimes to describe how the crime had affected them. These schemes went nationwide in 2001 and became what was called the Victim Personal Statement Scheme. This is discussed more fully below, but the then Home Secretary, Jack Straw, was reported as saying that this scheme would

> give victims a voice in a way that they have not had before. It will be a real opportunity to make their views known more formally to the police, crown prosecution service and the courts and to know they will be taken into account in the case. I want victims to feel they are at the heart of the criminal justice system.
>
> (*The Guardian*, 27 May 2000: 6)

So, victim statements appear to be a 'good' thing in so far as they constitute another step on the road to victims' rights at a maximum, and at least improved victim participation in the criminal justice system at a minimum. This road, however, marked by the politicization of the victim (Miers 1978), is now clearly part of any vote winning strategy. So are victim statements yet another ploy in the symbolic invocation of the victim on which politicians now so readily call? This is a question to which we will return, but first it is important to consider the extent to which such victim statements are considered to be controversial. Such statements raise some fundamental questions about conceptions of justice, about how they might be implemented and how victim participation might be secured. Drawing on the available international evidence, we shall discuss each of the questions in turn.

Victim (impact) statements used to inform sentencing raise serious alarm bells for those committed to the principle of the adversarial system. It is argued that this is a tactic that potentially can introduce a level of arbitrariness to the sentencing process above and beyond that which already exists, since, in essence, sentencing becomes reliant upon the persuasive powers of the victim's statement and the efficiency and accuracy with which it has been recorded. In other words, in principle it is a process that becomes subject to the potential influence of factors above and beyond the particular set of events to do with the crime committed that are before the court. If used in this way, the victim impact statement may erode the rights of the offender to a 'fair' trial, might result in the imposition of heavier penalties than would otherwise have been the case, and might as a consequence lead to an increase in sentencing disparity. The statement schemes introduced into England and Wales are not intended to influence sentencing, though this does not mean that the greater awareness of the impact of a crime put before a court would not result in some of these effects. Indeed, it would be very surprising if this were not the case. Moreover, as Ashworth (2000) also observes, if such statements are put before the court with any evidential status then presumably the defendant must have a right of cross-examination. Though, as Wemmers (2005) reports, in jurisdictions where this is permitted, it would appear that cross-examination rarely occurs as the prosecution tends to edit out those aspects of such a statement that might prove to be controversial, which rather defeats the object of them in the first place. In addition, it must also be remembered, of course, that victim impact statements are not the only source of arbitrariness in sentencing outcome. The potential for this already exists, the sentencing tariff systems notwithstanding. This leads to the second issue to be addressed here: what are the problems that emerge in practice?

It is frequently the case that issues of practice can and do overtake questions of principle. This is nowhere more so than when new measures are introduced into the repertoire of any organization, and the criminal justice system is no different in this respect. Victim impact statements can take various forms and can be implemented in a number of different ways. Examples of such variations can be found across international jurisdictions. So what kind of statements are collected, how, by whom, for what offences, at what juncture in the proceedings, are all issues for consideration. The practical response to each of these questions seems to vary dependent upon the purpose of collecting the statement. However, outside of Canada, there has been very little systematic research that has reliably evaluated schemes that have been implemented in different ways.

Canadian research suggests that there are two sets of purposes for collecting victim impact statements. The first is direct in its purpose. These schemes assume that such statements would provide an instrument to give information to the court, would provide direct input into the sentencing process by victims and would assist the court in arriving at an 'appropriate' sentence. The second is indirect in its purpose. These schemes would provide a means for victims to offer direct input about the effects of an offence, would increase the willingness of victims to co-operate with the criminal justice, would enhance victims' feelings of involvement and thereby improve victim satisfaction. That same research suggests that victims are more likely to participate in either kind of scheme if they are personally interviewed and were unlikely to participate if they thought the offence minor, if they wanted to put the incident behind them or if they were just too busy. Canadian schemes seem to lean towards the police collecting such statements because of the benefits that seem to accrue for all parties. In other words, the police would learn more about the crime and the victim would be more likely to feel that they were taken seriously. The actual use of the statements themselves seemed to vary with whether or not the Crown Counsel thought that the impact was significant and whether or not oral evidence had already covered the same material. Moreover, this research suggests that there was little difference in levels of satisfaction experienced by victims whether or not their statement was used in court. Indeed, the improved levels of satisfaction reported by all victims who participated in such schemes were not necessarily related to the victim impact statement itself, but to how they felt they had been treated, in general, by the criminal justice process.

Less systematic research conducted in other countries would seem to support these overall conclusions and also offers some evidence to allay the fears associated with the relationship between such schemes and sentencing. In this latter respect Erez (1999: 550), for example, reports that victim impact statements are more likely to underestimate the impact of a crime rather than overestimate it because 'stories are often constructed to suit the goals and objectives of the mediating agency'. Moreover, Erez and Rogers (1999: 234), reporting from an Australian study, assert:

The study reveals a rich and varied repertoire of strategies used by the legal profession to maintain their autonomous status, circumvent external demands to consider victim input and justify overlooking concrete presentations of harm. Built-in organisational incentives to exclude victims, or proceed with minimal input from them, maintain and reinforce the traditional criminal justice approach to victims as an 'extraneous party' if not sheer 'troublemakers'.

So it would seem that even where it is possible for victim impact statements to have an effect that is not necessarily the guaranteed outcome. Ashworth (2000) argues that raising victim expectations that are not met in this way might also be considered harmful, though it would seem that victims operate with quite a realistic set of expectations from their participation in the criminal justice system in this way. Hoyle *et al.* (1998), reporting on the evaluation of the pilot statement schemes in England and Wales, suggest that people had mixed motives for participating in them. Sixty per cent wanted to 'get things off their chest', 55% wanted to affect the sentence, and 43% wanted to give as much evidence as they could. Overall the majority felt satisfied with having participated, contributing to the view of Erez (1999) that there was a need for a 'therapeutic jurisprudence'. Or, as she states: 'Proceedings which provide victims with a voice or "process control" enhance their satisfaction with justice and sense of fair treatment' (1999: 551). Sanders (1999: 4) concludes that:

> Statement schemes are almost entirely unsuccessful in providing instrumental benefits for criminal justice agencies. Few victims feel more kindly disposed to the criminal justice system as a result of their participation, since many statement schemes take an extra statement and then ignore the victim as comprehensively as ever. The criminal justice system remains mysterious and unwelcoming to most victims.

If one takes a purely instrumental view of victim impact schemes and victim involvement in them, then such a conclusion is possible. However, despite the patchy and relatively unsystematic evidence available, this discussion has suggested that the picture might not be quite so straightforward for either the victim or the criminal justice system. There are clearly issues here for practitioners to consider that centre on such questions as to who takes the statement, how it is done, where it is done, and how it is brought to the attention of the court. However, these issues, and the patchy findings which have been referred to in this discussion, raise the more general question of how to manage victim participation in the criminal justice process, since such participation does seem to have a therapeutic effect, the presence or absence of victim impact statements notwithstanding.

An interesting variation to the victim impact statement was introduced to the criminal justice process in England and Wales in November 2000. This has been called the 'victim personal statement' scheme and follows the spirit, if not the actual practice, of victim impact statements discussed above. The purpose of a victim personal statement is twofold: to offer the optional opportunity to the victim of crime to relate to all the agencies how a crime has affected them, and to provide the criminal justices agencies with more information about the impact of a crime. As has already been stated, this is an entirely optional scheme and is not intended to be used by the criminal justice agencies to affect sentencing outcome. It is a two-stage process. The first stage involves taking a personal statement from the victim at the same time as a witness statement is taken. The second stage affords the opportunity for the victim to describe the impact of any longer-term effects of the crime. Both statements form part of the case papers for any trial and both are seen to be the responsibility of the police to collect. Whilst these statements provide an opportunity for the victim to raise any concerns that they may have about aspects of the crime and the offender not dealt with elsewhere by the criminal justice process (such as bail proceedings) and to provide all agencies within the criminal justice process with more information, this will only be the case in those cases where the victim chooses to make such statements and in which the police pursue such statements, leaving the space open for the deserving–undeserving distinction to appear. Indeed, Tapley (2005: 32) reports that 'Victim Personal Statements were not being offered to victims on a consistent and regular basis', echoing the finding of an earlier report by Her Majesty's Inspectorate of Probation (2003) that also found such statements were not being made generally available. Tapley (2005: 29) suggests that 'the redefinition of victims as consumers has resulted in the victims being denied the status of "active citizens" with rights and instead rendered them "passive consumers" of criminal justice services'. This lends further support to the view expressed by Padfield and Crowley (2003), quoted by Williams and Canton (2005: 4), that

> The reality of the service offered to defendants, victims and witnesses is not improved by simply passing yet more legislation. Indeed the gap between the theoretical protections offered by statute and the reality to be seen in practice seems in danger of growing ever wider.

Graham *et al.*'s (2004) qualitative evaluation of this scheme points to similar issues in victims' understanding of the scheme and the kind of information they had been given about it but overall is suggestive that those who participated felt that it had been a positive process. 'It was seen as "fair" that the extent, severity, and dominance of those impacts could be considered in sentencing an offender' (Graham *et al.* 2004: 49), though it is clear that the underlying issues of justice, implementation and participation remain. At the time of writing, the UK government was engaged in a consultation process on how better to include the families of murder and manslaughter victims in the criminal justice system above and beyond the facilities offered by the Victims Personal Statement Scheme that has resulted in the piloting of 'victim advocates' that were referred to above. This move may well lead to further controversy if it offers 'special' status to particular victims, thus returning us to the question of the structural relationship between the victim and offender (complainant and defendant) in the criminal justice system.

Sanders (2002: 220) argues that 'VIS [the victim impact statement] and its variants are probably more popular with people who have never used them that with those who have. They are good for idealised victims, rather than real victims', and goes on to suggest that these kinds of developments are characteristic of the exclusionary tendencies of contemporary criminal justice policy, whereby one is either a victim or an offender, that fail to recognize that quite often the individuals on either side of the witness box can be both victims and offenders at one and the same time. Some commentators argue that this problem is overcome by embracing the final strategy of victim participation in the criminal justice system to be discussed here – restorative justice.

The victim and restorative justice

It is now nearly 30 years since the first appearance of the essay by Christie in the *British Journal of Criminology* entitled 'Conflicts as property' (Christie 1977). In that essay Christie was keen to make the case that the law, and the emergence of the professions associated with the practice of law, in taking disputes out of people's own hands, had not only denied them the right to manage their own disputes but also, as a consequence, denied the development of more constructive and imaginative responses to such disputes. Whilst arguably this was primarily a polemical essay, its influence has nevertheless been significant in lending weight to what Pepinsky and Quinney (1991) called 'criminology as peacemaking'. This version of criminology is concerned to look for ways in which it might be possible to marry knowledge about crime and offending with a more constructive approach to the use of penalties for such behaviour. One of the themes in this work places emphasis on 'reintegration' – finding ways in which the offender is made aware of the consequences and impact of their offending behaviour yet simultaneously is reintegrated into (rather than ostracized from) the community.

More recently, Braithwaite (1989) has been influential in promulgating these ideas. His hypothesis is that in societies where there is a strong commitment to place collective interests over individual interests there are stronger incentives for people to conform and lower crime rates. The practical implication of Braithwaite's hypothesis is to establish mechanisms whereby offenders could be subjected to such collective processes, shamed by them, and subsequently reintegrated into the community with a stronger commitment to those community norms and values (that is, unlikely to reoffend). To date many examples of such practices have emanated from Australia and New Zealand in the form of 'community conferences' or 'family conferences'. The relative success or failure of such practices writ large is difficult to determine, though empirical evidence on different kinds of projects with different kinds of emphasis is plentiful. What is easy to establish is the impact that such ideas have had on contemporary criminal justice policy in England and Wales, especially when faced with the damning criticisms of the Audit Commission (1996) in relation to young offenders. That critique was contributory to the theme of getting the young offender to make good to their victim that was incorporated into the Crime and Disorder Act 1998. This theme rested on the hope that young people can be educated through the process of reparation on both the nature and the impact of their offending behaviour. It was hoped that as a consequence this would prevent reoffending and simultaneously repair some of the damage done to the victim of crime. In this way it was/is believed that both the victim and the offender can be reintegrated into the community and their conflict of interest resolved, to use Christie's phraseology. So how is this concern with restorative justice defined in contemporary policy and how does it manifest itself?

Miers *et al.* (2001: 8) define restorative justice in the following way:

> In broad and simple terms, 'restorative justice' signifies those measures that are designed to give victims of crime an opportunity to tell the offender about the impact of the offending on them and their families, and to encourage offenders to accept responsibility for, and to repair the harm they caused. Its general aims are to reduce reoffending to restore the relationship between the victim and the offender that was disturbed by the offence, and to improve victims' experiences with the criminal justice system.

The 1998 Crime and Disorder Act makes possible, at a number of different junctures, the introduction of restorative justice under this general rubric. For example, young offenders who receive warnings are referred to a Youth Offending Team, who may as a part of monitoring that offender require some sessions on victim awareness. Furthermore, those who come before the court may find themselves in receipt of a referral order which may include the prevention of reoffending through a youth offender contract. Such a contract may include direct and/or indirect reparation to the victim and/or the wider community. If a young offender is convicted of an offence they may find themselves in receipt of a 'community order'. Under the action plan that should flow from this order, the offender may be required to make reparation to the wider community or to the victim of the offence or anyone else affected by it, should they so wish it. The report by Miers *et al.* (2001) clearly indicates the problems facing researchers in trying to evaluate the effectiveness of these initiatives. They found that, for example, interpretations of what constituted reparation were somewhat elastic across the different schemes they were concerned with. Such problems notwithstanding, there are some issues of principle that are worth raising about the legislative move in this direction.

Such a policy commitment reflects a view that these strategies not only are workable but also will have the desired effect of reducing offending behaviour. It also reflects a presumption that such strategies constitute the preferred model of reparation, and make sense, for both the individuals involved in the process and the communities of which they are a part – in both instances this means those to be understood as the victims. Some of the issues that are generated by these presumptions draw attention to the tension between what might be expected from policy, what actually has been and can be delivered from such policy, and understanding what might already exist informally as ways of making amends between members of a community (see also Newburn and McEvoy 2003). But as Goodey (2005) has observed, restorative justice is more often than not represented as victim-centred justice, and the move to such a notion of justice has proceeded apace within England and Wales (see, for example, Home Office 2005). Some proponents of this way of doing business would point to United Nations resolutions and those passed by the Council of Europe as indications of a paradigm shift towards this way of conducting criminal justice work in support of moves in this direction. However, given the huge amount of activity that interest in restorative justice has generated over the last 20 years worldwide, my comments here will inevitably reflect how that activity has played itself out in England and Wales.

In a recent essay Miers (2004) documents and analyses some of the research conducted in the UK on restorative justice since the implementation of legislation in 1998 and 1999. Proponents of restorative justice heralded this legislation as constituting a sea change in criminal justice policy, especially in relation to responding to the criminal behaviour of young people. Restorative justice was seen as the means by which not only might the victim participate in the criminal justice system but also, through their participation, young people in particular could be made aware of the impact of their behaviour and take responsibility for it. As Miers (2004) observes, in the UK the importance of the victim of crime to the criminal justice system has been variously as-cribed to their being a supplier of information, a beneficiary of compensation, a partner in crime prevention, and a consumer of services. 'Restorative justice purports to take this relationship and these changes a step further – to one of victim participation in the system' (Miers 2004: 24) and 'has at its core the bringing together of victims and offenders' (Hudson 2003: 178). In the light of these efforts to shift criminal justice policy in the direction of such parti-cipation, much time and effort has been spent in the UK establishing whether or not this works and who it works for, without – and this is the nub of Miers's analysis – there being any consensus on what the question of what works actually means. Such issues notwithstanding, the focus of concern here is who the victim is in all of these developments, and how, if at all, this victim mirrors or challenges the victim of victimology or connects with the wider concerns of victims' needs and/or victims' rights with which this chapter began.

As Dignan (2005) has observed, many practitioners and advocates of res-torative justice have implicitly worked with the 'ideal type' victim that was identified by Christie (1986). Moreover, Dignan goes on to comment that questions on the concept of the victim rarely appear in the restorative justice literature, perhaps with the notable exception of the observations made by Young (2002) who also suggests that restorative justice works with a highly undifferentiated view of the victim. So exploring concepts of the victim within restorative justice is relatively uncharted territory. However, it is possible to trace three differently constructed images of the victim within restorative justice in the UK: the structurally neutral individual victim; the image of the socially inclusive community as victim; and the offender as victim. I shall say something about each of these and their relationship with victimology in turn.

For most people in the UK, their experience of crime is, as Goodey (2005: 229) suggests, home-grown, conventional and local. In other words, the ex-perience that people are likely to have of criminal victimization is more often than not the result of some petty act of vandalism or more serious burglary that has been committed by someone in their locality who is likely to have access to the same kinds of personal and social resources that they do. If we take this kind of experience of criminal victimization as given, then it is not surprising that the victim of restorative justice initiatives directed towards these kinds of offences, which for the most part reflect a desire to bring an individual victim face to face with their offender, would also take as given a structurally neutral image of the victim. This is the victim of positivist vic-timology discussed in Chapter 2. This is the victim who through lifestyle choices, proneness or their own precipitating behaviour had a part to play in what happened to them. So in restoring the harm done and reintegrating the behaviour of the offender, the focus of attention is on bringing the two parties to the event together, in the sense of an equal relationship, to make repairs for what has happened. This depiction captures some of Marshall's (1999) interpretation of the role of restorative justice in dealing with the aftermath of an event that may have much to commend it. However, what if we take another interpretation of people's routine experiences of criminal victimization that may also be characterized as home-grown, conventional and local?

What if we take that experience to be 'domestic' violence, child abuse or elder abuse? Here the victim imagery is not the structurally neutral victim of positivist victimology but implicated and embedded in the power relationships of a critical victimology and/or radical feminism. There are serious concerns about the efficacy of restorative justice in this context, some of which have been documented by Stubbs (1997), Gelsthorpe and Morris (2000) and Strang and Braithwaite (2002). These concerns point up the difficulty of how such individuals might be brought face to face to resolve their 'differences' in a process that assumes equality where none may exist. This view of restorative justice, by implication, raises the importance of more general questions. Whose agenda is being met by restorative justice, whose is being lost, how do restorative justice initiatives connect with other aspects of people's lives, and where do those people fit whose starting point is from a structurally less powerful position? As Goodey (2005) points out, it should not be assumed that the inequalities of the adversarial system cannot, or are not, reproduced in restorative justice.

The second depiction of the victim of restorative justice to be discussed here is that of the socially inclusive community. In this depiction of the victim, the offender is required to make amends not to the victim but to a rather more diffuse image of their community. As Goodey (2005) observes, community is frequently invoked as the third element that underpins successful restorative justice. However, as Crawford (2000) has cogently argued, there is a good deal of slippage between the political and policy rhetoric on which some restorative justice initiatives are built and the lived reality of communities. Parallel work on the role of informal justice in communities (see, for example, Walklate and Evans 1999; Feenan 2002; Newburn and McEvoy 2003) offers quite a different take on what restorative justice might look like in socially included communities whose dynamics are rooted in law-breaking behaviour rather than law-abiding behaviour. Nevertheless, some aspects of the restorative justice movement reflect a commitment to the idea of reintegrating the offender into their community and look to community-based options to facilitate this. Such a socially inclusive view of the relationship between the victim and the offender sees both categories as being 'just like us'. In other words, they challenge the view that you are either a victim or an offender taken by positivist victimology but raise other questions about what being 'just like us' means.

Sanders (2002) suggests that restorative justice used in this way is untenable since it assumes that the interests of both victims and offenders are always reconcilable. This, indeed, may not always be the case, or may only be possible where community and community relationships pre-existed in some meaningful, normative way. However, the normative invocation of some 'ideal' community that often permeates restorative justice discourse clearly elides the question of the role of the locally powerful, on the one hand (whether they comprise a locally powerful criminal gang or the locally powerful middle classes), and the relevance of such normative imagery in relation to constructions of the criminal Other, especially in the current social and political context that sees people as either victims or offenders, on the other hand. Following this line of argument, it is possible to suggest that both of the depictions of the victim discussed so far that are found in restorative justice within the criminal justice system in the UK, taken together, contribute to a view that restorative justice policy contrives to render the offender as victim. This is a view that can be discerned within the use of restorative justice for young offenders in the UK in particular. This returns us to some dimensions of the radical victimology proposed by Quinney (1972).

Pitts (2001) has argued that the 'new correctionalism' of New Labour is drawing less problematic young people in greater numbers into the criminal justice system, leading Muncie (2002) to talk about the 'repenalization' of youth offending. No wonder, if this is the case, that the Home Office can declare a 26.4% reduction in the reconviction rate for juvenile offenders (Jennings 2003). Indeed, a careful examination of these findings could lead one to conclude that the 'more serious' offenders have been excluded from this statistical picture to fit the political story. Further examination of the data by offence type shows considerable variation in reconviction rates, with both males and females having the highest rates for the 'other' category (motor vehicle related offences) and (whilst the numbers were small) there was no overall reduction in reconviction rates for offences of robbery, fraud and forgery. Moreover, as Burnett and Appleton (2004: 48) observe, with respect to the claims made by the Youth Justice Board (2002):

> it was reported that predicted reconviction rates for youth crime had been cut by nearly 15%. In making such claims it has been highly selective in utilising the findings of independent evaluations that the Youth Justice Board itself commissioned, thus conveniently drawing a veil over less encouraging findings.

So the question of which young people are being targeted and what aspects of their behaviour may be being changed by recent policy interventions, especially restorative justice interventions, appears to be very much a matter of conjecture and debate (echoing some of the observations also made by Miers

2004). According to Muncie (1999), in giving a prominent position to restorative justice, New Labour have established not only a 'new correctionalism' but also an 'institutionalized intolerance' of the young, which has been exacerbated by the anti-social behaviour legislation by which if an individual breaches an anti-social behaviour order they can find themselves incarcerated for what was not a substantive criminal offence! Pitts (2001: 189) argues that 'the prime target of New Labour's youth justice strategy is not about the criminal behaviour of a handful of young offenders, but the voting habits of a far larger and much older constituency'. In the space provided by these political processes restorative justice has developed an unprecedented swagger in the UK:

> Far from wilting in the face of controversy and resistance as so many other justice innovations of recent vintage have, restorative justice appears to be trading the temerity of cautious reform for a kind of *swagger*. Whether such self-confidence is justified, time will tell. It will however be very difficult to ignore. (McEvoy *et al.* 2002: 475; emphasis added)

This swagger is sustaining this policy for a range of different reasons, few of which connect with the victim of crime, but they do connect with the sociocultural processes emergent within the UK from the early 1990s that were commented on in Chapter 1 and that in this context are especially focused on young people. So it can be argued that there might be some features of the current political climate that, in promoting the 'cosmetic fallacy' (Young 1999) of restorative justice (being seen to address youth offending by using the victim), added to New Labour's persistent pursuit of the 'audit culture' and new managerialism, contribute to its swagger. Arguably, however, there are also other more fundamental processes in play here. These processes reflect deeper, structural concerns about the shifting contemporary relationship between the citizen and the state alluded to in Chapter 1. In the shift to neo-liberal governance, the question remains, what now constitutes the public interest, on the one hand, or a public good, on the other, in the arena of restorative justice?

As Williams (2003: 5) states:

> Although reparation orders were designed to be restorative, in many cases the pressure of work and practitioner cynicism have combined to create a production-line of mechanistic and unreflecting drudge-work which is of no benefit to victims and of little significance to offenders.

Such an observation might be made of many aspects of contemporary public service activity. What this does emphasize, however, is the dangers inherent in ignoring (denying?) the real context in which practitioners may be operating. This is a context in which, arguably, neither the needs of victims nor those of offenders are being met. Nor, one might add, is that of the public interest or the public good. The question remains as to whether the research being conducted in this arena is asking or, given the political climate, can ask these kinds of questions. Moreover, there is another issue, perhaps even more deeply hidden, here. That issue raises the spectre of gender in relation to the public interest. Hudson (2003) asks us to revisit the classic liberal dilemma of how much liberty should be traded for security, translated in the world of justice into the question of the extent to which justice can take account of the 'Other'. In the contemporary policy arena within England and Wales it is clear that the targeted 'Other' is increasingly young people as their behaviour is 'criminalized' and also 'penalized'. So, as both Muncie and Pitts have argued, drawing on the work by Cohen (1985), we have a situation presently in which the net is being widened and the mesh being thinned, all at the same time. It can be argued that restorative justice has become the policy means through which 'being tough on crime' and 'being tough on the causes of crime' has been articulated. In other words, restorative justice has been transformed from its image as a 'soft' option and co-opted as part of a 'tougher' stance on law and order. This is not the place to explore the politics of the re-gendering of this policy (though see Walklate 2004), but it is at this level too that we can catch part of the picture of the swagger of restorative justice. Questions such as this one, and their relationship with the restorative justice movement, are especially pertinent if one were to consider some of the inherent dangers (as well as some of the attractions) in the developing embrace of restorative justice to deal with, for example, 'domestic' violence. It may be within one interpretation of the public interest to redefine 'domestic' violence as 'relationship difficulty' (Cobb 1997), but the question remains as to what happens to gender issues within this interpretation. Nevertheless, as Snider (2003: 369) documents, feminist work has been used in the interests of an increasingly punitive society, and she goes on to say that what feminist (and other) work must continue to do is to 'challenge the punitive, cost cutting, agendas of the neo-liberal state'. Looking at the swagger of restorative justice is one way of contributing to this.

On the one hand, awareness of these policy processes draws attention to what Young (2001) has called the 'dynamic of essentialism': the repeated recreation of 'the Other', those problematic outsiders who are not 'us'. On the other hand, it leads us to revisit what Garland (2001) has characterized as the 'culture of control'; the increasingly expressed need in cultural and policy terms to control those who are not 'us'. In the 'culture of control', of course, our collective response to 'the Other' is not about tolerance but intolerance, not the least of which has been the targeting of young offenders in recent legislation. It is in this latter context that restorative justice initiatives have proved to be increasingly popular within contemporary criminal justice policy, and it is within this context that they have a swagger. From this point of view, the victim is the offender inexorably pushed upwards on the criminal justice ladder for offences that may not have previously received a formal sanction.

In many ways the previous discussion implies that whilst restorative justice initiatives have as their intent to repair the harm done to the victim of crime either through face-to-face contact with the offender or through the offender making amends to the community in some way, restorative justice as a movement has reflected little on how it has imagined the victim. This does not mean that some restorative justice initiatives do not work well at a local level, or that some victims who participate in such initiatives do not feel better about their participation, or that some proponents of restorative justice are not aware of the problematic status that results for the victim consequent to a commitment to restorative justice. However, in a socio-cultural process characterized by global doubt and uncertainty and a domestic preoccupation with control, the potential for sensitivity that the previous questions of res torative justice demand is lost. So is the potential for unpicking the imagery of the victim that is being employed, and thereby exploring the potential of thinking differently about that imagery. So the question remains, in a socio-cultural climate in which we are all potentially victims (see Chapter 1), are different imaginings of the victim in restorative justice possible and would these different imaginings contribute differently (better?) to the nature and extent of victim participation in the criminal justice process?

It is evident that some efforts have been made to extend the use of restorative justice to those victims of crime who were imagined in the critical victimology of Mawby and Walklate (1994). Young (2002), for example, makes a convincing case for the use of restorative justice between business corporations. Moreover, there are clear implications for the possibilities of restorative justice to be derived from Goodey's (2005) expansive victimological agenda that includes such activities as Internet crime, environmental crime, sex trafficking and genocide, some of which take victimology into the realm of human rights – this in an agenda that is not far from the one that was proposed by Elias (1986). Moreover, in the same collection of papers in which Young (2002) is to be found, there is clear support for an extended victimological agenda that takes the critical victimology of Miers (1990) a stage further introducing us, as it does, to the male victim of domestic violence (Grady 2002), the male victim of rape (Allen 2002), or indeed the male victim of paramilitary violence (Hamill 2002). All of these share in similar opportunities for restorative justice intervention including, in the case of the latter, peace and reconciliation work. So it would seem that different imaginings of the crime victim are possible, and indeed are being tried. However, despite these imaginings, there are structural, cultural and political limitations to their realization. Elsewhere I have called this the rhetoric of victimhood as a source of oppression (Walklate 2005a; see also Walklate 2006a) in which both restorative justice and victimology are implicated in being vehicles for contemporary state policy.

Conclusion

This chapter has covered an extensive policy ground. In it we have been concerned to explore the different ways in which the voice of, for the most part, a structurally neutral imagining of the victim of crime has been and is being taken account of in contemporary criminal justice policy in England and Wales. In the account that has been offered it is possible to discern the influence of policies from a number of other socio-cultural and legal settings, most notably from what in earlier chapters was called the Anglo-American axis. Within the development and implementation of this wide range of policy initiatives it is difficult to deny the increasing importance of victimhood, not just as a cultural process (Furedi 2002) but also as a claim to status. In this sense victimhood, whilst not a status to be recommended experientially, is nevertheless the status whereby the state through increasingly subtle and not so subtle global and local processes is reasserting its power over citizenship (see Chapter 1 and the Conclusion). It is in this sense that victimhood is harnessed as a source of oppression in the interests of the increasingly diverse and hegemonic (capitalist) state (Jessop 2002). (These are arguments that will be further developed in the next chapter.) These processes may not play themselves out in exactly the same way either globally or locally (though it would be of huge value to explore how such processes resemble or fail to resemble each other; see O'Malley 2002), but how they play themselves out does cumulatively contribute to not only the culture of control but also the maintenance of economic relationships.

Nevertheless, it is also important to remember that in the contemporary political and policy setting there are real divisions of inequality that have a real impact (Young 2003a; see also the discussion on the impact of crime in Chapter 3 above). As Hutton (2002: 84) has observed:

> It is not just a matter of accepting that the state can and should act to build an infrastructure of justice that diminishes inequality, equalises opportunity and tries to enlarge individual's capacity for self-respect. It is as the German philosopher Hannah Arendt argues about needing a public realm to allow the full flowering of our human sensibilities. For taken to its limits, a society peopled only by conservative 'unencumbered selves' jealously guarding their individual liberties and privacy, is a denial of the human urge for association and meaning.

It is within these processes that the real nature of oppression lies and the possibilities for change lie. The key concept in the quote above is respect, which returns us to the statements of intent in relation to what it is that victims want from their experience of the criminal justice process with which this chapter began.

Treating people with respect – that is, as individuals with personal resources – is key to ensuring that, traumatic circumstances notwithstanding, they are enabled to make use of their resources in order to make sense of what has happened in their lives. A number of implications can be derived from this position. Firstly and importantly, it challenges any presumed 'special' status associated with being a victim of crime. Victims are, after all, complainants in the criminal justice system as offenders are defendants. To use any other terminology prejudges the outcome of a case. This is perhaps a rather pedantic point to raise, but is nevertheless of crucial importance when endeavouring to introduce policies and practices designed to give the victim not only a voice in the criminal justice process but also a voice to be heard. This is an issue that raises particular difficulties with victim impact statement type policies discussed earlier in this chapter. Moreover, it is important to remember that victims are not necessarily the 'good' in opposition to the offender's 'bad'. This serves to remind us that whilst crime does impact upon people's lives, victims of crime are people too. So by implication, in this regard, it makes little sense to talk of people as victims or offenders, or indeed victims or survivors. They are people, and people need to feel OK about themselves, and sometimes need some help and support to achieve that. Whether male or female, whether a member of an ethnic minority, whether old or young, the maintenance of respect and the avoidance of contempt sustains a sense of well-being and contributes to people feeling OK (Harré 1979).

The macro-political context of criminal justice policy has led some commentators to conclude that the global nature of late modern societies (or risk societies) is resulting in comparable ways of managing social problems, including crime. However, as O'Malley (2002) argues, it should not be assumed that globalization is taking its toll in the criminal justice arena in the same way everywhere. His analysis, which interestingly uses examples from Australia and New Zealand, whence it has been argued here that restorative justice has travelled, points to the important impact that local socio-economic conditions might have on the fruits born of policy. So it is possible to theorize that some socio-economic conditions might facilitate restorative justice or any other policy that has 'travelled', and others might not be so welcoming (see also Jones and Newburn 2002). Yet it is important questions such as these that may facilitate and/or inhibit the production and reproduction of respect, that are largely being overlooked within those policies that invoke a structurally neutral image of the victim of crime. As Ashworth (2000: 590) states: 'Penal history yields plenty of examples of apparently benign policies resulting in repressive controls.' And although the ever rising tide of imprisonment in England and Wales must be seen as part of the context in which many other political claims are being made about contemporary criminal justice policy, it is also within that context that policies, and in this case policies invoking the victim of crime, have particular stories attached to them. As Daly (2002: 33) remind us:

> If we want to avoid the cycle of optimism and pessimism (Matthews, 1988) that so often attaches to any justice innovation, then we should be courageous and tell the real story of restorative justice. But in telling the real story, there is some risk that a promising, fledgling idea will meet a premature death.

For the purposes of this chapter (and the next), part of telling that 'real story' means exposing the political context and its influence on policy, its influence on the associated research processes, and what the other stories might look like. In the context of restorative justice, for example, it means telling some of the other stories of justice, especially those associated with the socially excluded, who may have their own means of social control that have restorative elements (see, *inter alia*, Walklate and Evans 1999). It means taking on board the 'democratic principle' of restorative justice espoused by Braithwaite (2002) not just for the participants of restorative justice but for the rest of us – the 'all of us' for whom many of the policy initiatives discussed in this chapter are intended – and thinking critically about what those democratic implications might be. After all, if the criminal justice system remains a public good, then it must work in all our interests: victims and offenders.

6 Crime, victims and justice

Introduction

The data discussed in Chapter 3 clearly illustrated that the victim of crime, rather than being the structurally neutral being embedded in the policy initiatives and responses to the victim of crime addressed in Chapter 5, is in fact a highly structured being shaped by class, gender, ethnicity, race, age and sexuality. The purpose of this chapter is the explore how criminal justice systems have responded to and tried to deal with an increased awareness of this structured victim who, as Chapter 3 suggested, appears to have features in common across different cultures. In order to do this, this chapter will focus on three main areas of activity: women as victims of male violence, people from ethnic minorities as victims of racially motivated crime, and hate crime (though, as we shall see, these last two issues have become somewhat intertwined especially in the aftermath of 11 September 2001). As with the previous chapter, the policy activity that has been generated around these issues in England and Wales will be situated within the wider global context as appropriate.

Feminism, violence and policy

As Chesney-Lind (2006) has observed, much of the intellectual and policy activity that has taken place over the last 25 years, which has had as its focus tackling the issue of violence against women, needs to be understood by reference to what is known as second-wave feminism. That movement, largely located at its inception within the Anglo-American–European axis, took for granted the gains that women had made in relation to civil rights but recognized that there were many areas of women's lives in which they still suffered as a result of their unequal relationship with men. That focus of concern drew attention to women's experiences of, amongst other things, violence at the hands of men in general, but domestic violence and sexual violence in particular. It is possible to suggest that much has changed since those early campaigning days of the 1960s and 1970s in respect of these experiences, but arguably much has also remained the same. Here we shall discuss what the parameters of those changes might look like, what the role of the feminist movement and 'feminist' victimology has been in informing those changes, and what issues remain unresolved within the contemporary picture. This discussion will link with some of the theoretical questions raised in Chapter 2 and will also reflect some of the same processes of politicization and consumerism of the victim that have emerged elsewhere in this book but especially in Chapters 1 and 5.

Charting the nature and extent of violence against women

Charting the nature and extent of violence against women is fraught with difficulties. Moreover, it is perhaps self-evident that this particular topic highlights the significant gap between positivist victimology and feminist-informed work discussed in Chapter 2. This gap is at its most obvious in their respective use and understanding of the concept of lifestyle. The tensions that those uses generate, between understanding lifestyle as a series of incidents and lifestyle as a process, is well illustrated by the quote from Genn (1988) that criminal victimization for her female informant in Bleak House was 'just part of life'. The feminist acceptance of this different view of lifestyle results in a range of difficulties with what to measure, incidence (events that happen during a particular time period) or prevalence (events that happen over the course of a lifetime), and how to separate out what is to be measured. This second difficulty relates to the awareness that under some circumstances it is very difficult to separate physical violence from sexual violence since any particular event may entail both. Moreover, at the level of experience such categories may not be very meaningful. Kelly (1988) and Lundgren *et al.* (2002) express this in terms of a 'continuum' of violence. This is a concept that recognizes the nature, extent and experience of women's violence, from lethal violence (for example, murder and 'honour' crimes) to sexual harassment. For example, the homicide statistics for England and Wales indicate that on average two women are murdered by their partner or former partner every week, a pattern that has some international dimensions (see Wilson and Daly 1998; and for a detailed analysis of 'honour' crimes, see Welchman and Hossain 2005), and on the question of sexual harassment Lundgren *et al.* (2002) report Swedish levels at 16% in the previous year (see also Stanley and Wise 1987). As we shall see, this broad remit of concerns means that care needs to be taken when endeavouring to chart the nature and extent of violence against women, especially when referring to the data from criminal victimization surveys.

As Chapters 2 and 3 suggested, the recognition that the experience of criminal victimization varies according to structural variables has led to a good deal of development and innovation in the data gathering process associated with the criminal victimization survey. Some of those developments have been usefully documented by Walby and Myhill (2001). They point to a range of improvements that have been made to such survey techniques – among them interviewer practices, mode of inquiry, how the concept of violence is operationalized, and the nature of the sampling frame – all of which, taken together, have resulted in greatly improved measurement of the nature and extent of violence against women. How changes such as these particularly informed survey work in this area in Finland is documented by Piispa (2003). Moreover, various countries, following the lead of Statistics Canada, have engaged in their own national surveys of violence against women – see, for example, Schroettle and Müller (2004) on Germany and Fougeyrollas-Schwebel (2005) on France. As a consequence, violence against women has a much higher profile and much more is known about the nature and extent of such violence than was the case in the early 1970s. So what do these data suggest?

It has already been shown that the strongest predictors of victimization by violence were being young, male and single and that these predictors are mediated by whether or not the person knew the offender. It is generally agreed that domestic violence is the only category of violence for which the risks for women are substantially higher that those for men, and the findings from the USA (Catalona 2005) and the UK (Walby and Allen 2004) reported in Chapter 3 seem to reflect a pattern that is repeated in other countries. For example, in Canada, 'One-half of all women have experienced at least one incident of violence since the age of 16', with male on female violence accounting for 46.5% of all violent crime in Canada (Ministry of Community Services n.d.). Lundgren et al. (2002: 8) report from a Swedish survey that 'Almost every second woman i.e. 46% has been subjected to violence by a man since her fifteenth birthday', with Heiskanen and Piispa (1998: 3) reporting that in Finland '40% of adult women have been victims of male physical or sexual violence or threats after their 15th birthday, 14% in the course of the past twelve months'. Mouzos and Makkai (2004), reporting on the Australian component of the International Violence Against Women Survey, suggest that over a third of women in their sample who had a current or former intimate partner had experienced at least one form of violence in their lifetime. Barbaret (2005: 358) reports that 'intimate partner violence is as prevalent and serious in Spain as in other countries', and in a more detailed offering O'Donnell (2005) reports a sharp upward trend in the recorded number of sex crime in the Republic of Ireland, though he attributes much of this to improved recording practices and also comments on the diminishing power of the stigma attached to reporting such victimization.

Clearly embedded in these findings and the way in which they are reported are some of the problems alluded to above. These different findings reflect the different ways, and the extent to which, violence against women is recognized as a problem, and most importantly it should be remembered that these findings are not always measuring like events, in terms of both what is understood by violence and what is defined as violence by the law in these respective legal contexts. For example, Swedish law enacted an offence of 'gross violation of a woman's integrity' in 1998, defined as follows:

> If a man engages in certain criminal acts such as assault, threatening behaviour or coercion, sexual or other molestation, or sexual exploitation against a woman to whom he is, or has been married, or with whom he is, or has been cohabiting, and the acts are such as may seriously damage the victim's self confidence, he is to be sentenced for gross violation of the woman's integrity, rather than for the individual offences that each act comprises.
>
> (Lindström 2004: 225)

In 2000 this law was amended to require that the 'acts must have constituted part of a repeated violation' (Lindström 2004: 225). As will be illustrated below, this kind of all-embracing legal framework sounds somewhat different from that found in England and Wales and illustrates admirably some of the problems of data comparison discussed in Chapter 3. Such difficulties notwithstanding, the data presented are generally supportive of Newman (1999) who suggests that these kinds of patterns have global dimensions.

There are, however, a number of issues that are hidden by statistical snapshots such as those presented above. First of all, they mask the question of vulnerability that was discussed in Chapter 3, but they also mask the changing nature of that vulnerability. For example, whilst some of the reports quoted from above also refer to men's experiences of violence, their *visibility* as victims of sexual violence and/or domestic violence is much higher now than it was 30 years ago. Why this might be the case raises all kinds of political and policy questions, some of which are discussed more fully below.

Second, these figures need to be understood in relation to a wider changing social – and, it would appear, international – context that has increasingly viewed the use of violence by men against women as unacceptable, certainly at the level of agenda setting (see, for example, United Nations 2004). These wider social/global changes, and the policy responses that have accompanied them, arguably fuel the criminal victimization figures themselves. In other words, events and incidents are now reported and recorded that were once not recognized as being problematic. These changes in behaviour are suggestive of far less complicity on the part of the victim than might have been the case some years ago. In this respect the issue of violence against women in particular might be an indicator of more a positive change in attitudes and values than that implied by the 'morality of low expectation' analysis offered by Furedi (1997, 2002). In other words, the culture of victimhood that he raises might also be a reflection of changing sensibilities towards interpersonal violence between men and women. However, that view does possibly depend on which side of the gender divide an individual finds him/herself. Nevertheless there are some empirical data that connect this question of complicity with rates of women's experience of violence. A report on Finland by Savolainen (2005: 171), for example, indicates that

> the rate of decline in family violence in the population of Finnish women is strongly related to actual reductions in the incidence of violence against women living in family settings with male partners. The research suggests that this decline cannot be explained in terms of changes in the behaviour of Finnish men towards women. ... Finnish women have become more selective in their decision to reside with male partners. They are less likely to agree to live with a violent man.

This clearly points to a decline in complicity as suggested above, and to the importance of situating specific statistical findings with their socio-cultural and economic environment.

Third, and most obviously, charting the nature and extent of a problem reveals little about how that problem has been addressed and how effective such initiatives may be. This is the main focus of the discussion here. For the purposes of that discussion it will be of value to deal with responses to domestic violence and sexual violence (rape) separately in the first instance. Both will be presented primarily in relation to England and Wales.

Responding to 'domestic' violence

Raising the profile of women's experience of violence at the hands of men whom they know, usually their partner, has been a key feature of feminist campaigning, from the formation of the first women's refuge in Chiswick, London, in 1977 to the zero tolerance campaigns supported by many local authorities in the 1990s. Whilst the difficulties that women face in recognizing and reporting the criminal nature of their experiences are now more widely acknowledged, it is worthwhile remembering that such an acknowledgement is a relatively recent one and, moreover, as we shall observe, much remains to be achieved in this respect. As the following data from ESRC (2002) illustrate:

- From Home Office data for 2001 there are an estimated 150,218 incidents of domestic assault a year.
- The U.K. police receive the equivalent of one call every minute asking for assistance with domestic violence.
- Only 5% of these incidents include men as victims.

- Half of young men aged 14–21 think it is acceptable to hit a woman or force her to have sex, as did a third of young women in the same age group.

Moreover, the murder figures for 2003–4 indicate that there were 858 deaths recorded as homicide (murder and manslaughter), one-third of which were female, with 60% of that one-third being killed by their partner – about one murder every 2 days. In addition, Toren (2004) reports on behalf of the Women's Aid Federation of England that, during 2003–4, 18,569 women and 23,084 children were accommodated in refuges.

If these figures and the increased awareness of the nature, extent and cost of this problem (each murder now costs the state about £1.5 million at 2003 prices) are taken together, it is understandable that one arena in which much effort has been made to appreciate the nature of domestic violence, and to develop more appropriate responses to such incidents, has been the criminal justice system. This effort began by challenging the police perception that dealing with domestic incidents was 'rubbish work' (Radford and Stanko 1991) and has proceeded to look at more effective civil and criminal law interventions. It is worth exploring these two avenues in a little more detail.

The cumulative effect of campaigning, the drive for value for money and effectiveness to which the police had become subjected, and the increasing recognition of victims as consumers of criminal justice services (Mawby and Walklate 1994; Williams 1999) combined to produce Home Office circulars in 1986 and 1990 that gave the clear signal that domestic violence was to be treated as seriously as violence between strangers. Reiterated in 2000, these circulars have resulted in a marked change of direction for not only policing (though arguably the police have been the most responsive to their content) but also the criminal justice system as a whole. In particular, these circulars formed the backcloth against which a 'presumption to arrest the offender' practice has emerged. Despite the ambivalent supportive evidence for arresting the offender in these circumstances, this practice follows the North American model of mandatory arrest – another example of a policy with a global reach. Yet as the researchers who first proposed this pro-arrest stance later pointed out, the short-term gains for the victim often resulted in long-term losses (in other words, the violence worsened), especially for women from ethnic minorities (see Sherman *et al.* 1991). In addition, it is important to note that evaluation of such strategies rarely compares women who have sought legal help with those who have not, rendering understanding the effectiveness of intervention problematic (Sherman and Smith 1992). Moreover, as Chesney-Lind (2006) documents, the implementation of the mandatory arrest stance has frequently resulted in unintended consequences, including the increasing arrest of women for their use of violence in fighting back, which in her view has contributed to the rising statistics on female violence and the raised visibility of male victims of such violence, some of which is now reflected in official statistics (see, for example, Ministry of Community Services n.d.).

Alongside a presumption-to-arrest stance, police forces have been active in developing specialist units to deal with domestic violence whose key task is to support the victim. It would appear that women who are supported through the work of such units have at their disposal a better service than existed prior to their implementation, though problems clearly remain as to the extent to which the needs of women from ethnic minorities are under- stood and met (Patel 1992), whether or not such service delivery meets with notions of victim empowerment (Hoyle and Sanders 2000) and the extent to which many women still feel patronized and stereotyped by the police (Women's National Commission 2003). Problems such as these were com- pounded by the findings of a report by Her Majesty's Inspectorate of Con- stabularies and Her Majesty's Crown Prosecution Service Inspectorate (2004) which pointed to the fact that these agencies still did not share in a common definition of what counted as 'domestic' violence and evidenced that of 463 incidents to which the police were called, 118 were recorded as a crime and 90 people were charged with an offence, of whom 45 were convicted at court. These findings more than adequately illustrate the attrition rate in such cases.

Nevertheless the commitment to responding to and dealing with do- mestic violence has continued, with more recent policy interventions fo- cusing on the courts. In 2003 the Crown Prosecution Service established five specialist, fast-track, domestic violence courts. The evaluation of these courts reports that they enhanced the effectiveness of court and support services for victims, made advocacy and information sharing easier and improved victim satisfaction with and confidence in the criminal justice system (Cook *et al.* 2004: 6). It was announced in October 2005 that on the basis of this success this scheme was to be extended to 25 courts throughout England and Wales. Furthermore, the Domestic Violence, Crime and Victims Act 2004 extended the reach of the criminal justice system in tackling domestic violence by making common assault an arrestable offence for the first time. Of course, it is too soon to say to what extent this continued criminalization of domestic violence is likely to result in long-term effects. However, an Australian study on the effectiveness of legal protection from domestic violence for young women suggests that the impact of legal protection was not straightforward and varied according to whether or not the young women had sought the help of the police and the courts and also varied with the severity of the violence that they had experienced (Young *et al.* 2000). This study concludes that a 'co-ordinated approach which systematically links court protection orders with police intervention may be the best way to protect young women from violence' (2000: 6), thus lending weight to the power of a 'threat to arrest' stance. A report on effective intervention in the context of domestic violence by Hester and Westmarland (2005) offers a series of much wider-ranging recommendations that includes partnership working between the different branches of the criminal justice, educational programmes, and other more 'socially' rather than criminal focused interventions, and whilst some of these kinds of initiatives may exist in local areas, to date much national energy in England and Wales has paid central attention to the criminalization of the offender – a process that is echoed in a *Guardian* newspaper headline, 'Domestic attackers escaping with a fine' (15 April 2006). Whilst the disposition of the offender is not of key concern here, such coverage is clearly indicative of the spirit in which policies on domestic violence are being approached.

Embedded in the policy responses outlined here (and in the next section) is a belief in the symbolic power of the law both in criminalizing behaviour that a short time ago was (and by many still is) seen to be acceptable and at the same time vindicating feminists who campaigned for the private experiences of women to be taken seriously. Indeed, this focus on the law appears to have a degree of international consensus attached to it (see, for example, United Nations 2004). However, behind this symbolism problems remain. As Chesney-Lind (2006) comments, these developments place advocates for victims in an uneasy alliance with criminal justice professionals that may have unintended consequences in which the voices of the women themselves, and what they might want from the criminal justice system (if anything), are disregarded (see also Hoyle 1998) – though, as Lewis (2004) reports, all may not be lost. She considers that the legal system can provide some protection for women in violent relationships, but obviously only for that small proportion whose cases reach the courts. In addition, she points to the importance of the fact that 'As a result of broad social and cultural changes, women may now have a greater sense of entitlement to safety and quality of life' (Lewis 2004: 221). There is a further danger here, though, that in all of this activity the question of what women want and what the organizations that represent women campaign for are co-opted in the interests of the state, as the securing of confidence in the criminal justice system constitutes the overriding concern. Moreover, as Lundgren *et al.* (2002: 10) state, 'it is impossible to regard violence to women as a marginal isolated problem that can be dealt with separately from discussion of relations between men and women in society as a whole'. Yet the struggle remains to recast discussions in this kind of direction. Similar issues emerge when we consider policy responses to sexual violence.

Responding to sexual violence

Rape crisis centres also emerged during the 1970s in England and Wales as a parallel development to the women's refuge movement. In a similar vein to the refuge movement, rape crisis centres were established with the central purpose of supporting women without any presumption that this required their involvement with the criminal justice system. Indeed, many individuals working within the rape crisis movement had rather prickly relationships with criminal justice systems, to say the least. However, it was not until the early 1980s in England and Wales that the poor response of the criminal justice system in general, and the police in particular, to women who had been victims of sexual violence came to the attention of a wider audience, largely through the impact of a 'fly on the wall' style television programme covering the work of the Thames Valley Police with a woman complainant of rape. The public outcry that this programme produced added considerable weight to the existing voices campaigning against violence against women, resulting in a reorientation of policing policy responses at that time in the form of the development of the 'rape suite'. These 'rape suites' were intended to offer a much more supportive environment for female complainants in an atmosphere that did not compromise the need to gather evidence. However, as Kelly (2001) reports, issues relating sexual violence were largely sidelined until the late 1990s in the face of the focus on domestic violence, and did not really reappear until the problem of attrition in cases of rape reappeared. However, before we go on to consider this issue, it will be useful to say something about the nature and extent of this kind of sexual violence.

Measuring the nature and extent of sexual violence is fraught with difficulties (see the discussion in Chapter 3 and above), with some of these difficulties seriously compounded when trying to engage in such measurement in cross-cultural settings or across criminal justice systems. As a result, it is important to understand that the figures that follow may in fact be measuring quite different things. With that caveat in mind, efforts have been made to offer pictures of women's experiences of sexual violence in different countries. The 2000 International Criminal Victimization Survey (van Kesteren *et al.* 2002), for example, reports that 'Women in Sweden, Finland, Australia, and England and Wales were most at risk of sexual assault. Women in Japan, Northern Ireland, Poland and Portugal were least at risk' (though it does concede that these risk differences were quite small: they amount to about one in a hundred women in this report). The report also goes on to say that women knew their assailant in about half of the incidents reported: a third were known by name, and a sixth by sight. In the Australian study conducted by Mouzos and Makkai (2004) referred to above, 10% of women reported experiencing at least one incident of physical or sexual violence in the previous 12 months, though they were more likely to report the physical rather than the sexual violence. The 1993 Violence Against Women Survey carried out by Statistics Canada found that four in ten women were victims of sexual assault (Ministry of Community Services, Government of British Columbia n.d.), and the study conducted by Lundgren *et al.* (2002: 8) in Sweden reports that one woman in three has been subjected to sexual violence at least once since turning 15 with 7% having had such experiences in the last year. Myhill and Allen (2002), reporting on British Crime Survey data, indicate that 0.9% of women aged 16–59 said that they had been subject to some form of sexual victimization, including rape, during the previous year, with 0.4% of women saying that they had been raped during that period. So the picture can vary enormously (for a good comparative review, see Kelly 2001), yet despite these variations there seems to be one common problem: the attrition rate.

In reviewing responses to rape in a European context, Regan and Kelly (2003) show that, with the exception of the Czech Republic, Germany and Latvia, conviction rates for rape have declined in all European jurisdictions since 1977, with the greatest rate of decline being in Hungary at 27% closely followed by England and Wales at 22%. (The current conviction rate for case of rape stands at 5.6% in England and Wales: Kelly *et al.* 2005.) This is despite the fact that 11 countries during that same time period have either made rape a gender-neutral offence or included men within it, have removed the exemption of rape in marriage, and have extended the definition to include other forms of penetration (Regan and Kelly 2003: 16). This leads Regan and Kelly (2003: 13) to suggest that 'legal reforms and changes in the investigation and prosecution of rape have had little, if any, impact on convictions'. Yet, as in the case of domestic violence, campaigns have continued to be focused on the law as constituting a mechanism for change. This focus on the law resulted in the Sexual Offences Act 2003 in England and Wales that came into force in May 2004.

This legislation confirmed the gender-neutral nature of the act of rape and extended the definition to include the mouth as another orifice of penetration, though the object of penetration remains the penis. This legislation also endeavoured to codify an understanding of reasonable belief and the steps that the accused had to take to ascertain whether or not the complainant had consented. So in many ways this legislation can be seen as a landmark in addressing many of the historical complaints that radical feminism in particular had of the legal framework for rape in England and Wales. As Jones (2004) testifies, whilst the 2003 Sexual Offences Act might stand as a monument to the achievements of the Rape Crisis Federation – an organization formed in 1996 to provide the rape crisis movement with a national voice which secured Home Office funding in 2001, thus enabling it to be heard at national level – the closure of that organization that resulted from the withdrawal of its funds just before the Sexual Offences Act received the Royal Assent is more than suggestive of the problem of incorporation that is faced when dealing with what Hudson (2006) has called 'white man's justice'. The problem of 'white man's justice' will reappear when we go on to consider responses to ethnic minorities as victims of racially motivated crime.

Of course, it should also be remembered that changes in the law, which may have some symbolic resonance, are not necessarily accompanied by changes in public attitudes, as was illustrated by an ICM opinion poll conducted on behalf of Amnesty International's 'Stop Violence Against Women' campaign (ICM 2005). That poll revealed that 26% of those asked thought that a woman was partially or totally responsible for being raped if she was wearing sexy or revealing clothing and more than one in five held the same view if a woman had had many sexual partners, with 30% 'blaming the woman' if she was drunk. Moreover, a widely reported case in 2005 in which a female complainant of rape admitted in the witness box to being unable to remember whether or not she had consented to sexual intercourse because of the amount she had drunk, has opened up the debate on the legal relationship between drunkenness and consent, echoing a range of problematic issues in trying to legislate for consent – so much so that the safest legal position for males embarking on a sexual relationship might be to have consent in writing for such activities.

The problem of the attrition rate in cases of rape and associated public attitudes led the government to issue a consultation paper, *Convicting Rapists and Protecting Victims*, in March 2006 (Office for Criminal Justice Reform 2006). That document puts a number of proposals on the policy agenda, including the use of expert witnesses to put evidence before the jury on the psychological impact of rape on victims; to allow adult victims of rape to give video-recorded evidence; to consider whether or not the law with regard to drunkenness in cases of rape needs further definition; and to consider whether or not evidence of complaints should be admissible in a trial irrespective of when the alleged incident occurred. Proposals such as these say much about the continuing perceived problem of rates of attrition in such cases both in England and Wales and elsewhere, and what might be considered to be the appropriate policy response to them. However, as 'successful' as these legislative changes may or may not prove to be, it is at this point in time too early to judge what their impact might be on the attrition rate. In the interim, other issues concerning (sexual) violence against women have climbed their way up the policy agenda, in particular, the (sexual) trafficking of women and children.

The (sexual) trafficking of women had a particularly high profile in the UK at the beginning of 2006 in the aftermath of some police activity in relation to this issue, with some politicians calling for any man who had sex with a women who was known to be 'trafficked' to be liable to prosecution for rape. Interestingly enough, this issue constitutes one of the areas that Goodey (2005) considers lost to victimology, despite its connections with human rights abuse and potential links with radical victimology. Situating her concern with this issue as a concern for victimology within European and United Nations protocols on the smuggling and trafficking of people, she argues that the particular trafficking of women is of concern for two reasons: first, because it is a crime of violence by men against women; and second, because it is a human rights issue. There is also a third issue here, and that lies within the links that this kind of activity has with organized crime, and Goodey (2005) points to the fact that in the case of trafficking, women have been criminalized by default as a result of their status as illegal immigrants. Of course, the presumption of victimhood on behalf of such women points to an elision of categorizations between victimization, migration and illegal immigration that is commonly found in media, and other, coverage of these issues. A similar elision is to be found in our next area of analysis in relation to the structurally informed image of the victim of crime: ethnicity.

Taking account of ethnicity: racially motivated and hate crime

The data presented in Chapter 3 illustrated that the chances of suffering criminal victimization are structured not only along gender lines but also along ethnic lines. Threats, verbal abuse and harassment often constitute 'just part of life' for people from ethnic minorities in much the same way as for women – part of the lived reality of their everyday lives, presenting similar problems of measurement between incident and process discussed above. For example, Home Office data indicate that during 2003/4 racist incidents recorded by the police rose by 7%, with an increase of approximately 12% in offences that were racially or religiously aggravated during that same time period. As incident measures these figures are likely to constitute a significant underestimate of the extent to which such routine harassment constitutes the backcloth of the lives of people belonging to ethnic minority groups, as the studies conducted in England and Wales by Hesse et al. (1992) and Bowling (1998) clearly showed. Increasing awareness of this level of routine harassment and its impact on the quality of life experienced by those from ethnic minorities has clearly influenced the policy agenda in England and Wales on this issue. However, there has been a growing elision between what is known about the experiences of people from ethnic minorities in relation to criminal victimization and what has come to be called 'hate' crime, and it will be useful to reflect upon the relationship between the two.

Lawrence (1999) suggests that there are two defining characteristics of hate crime: that the victims are interchangeable and merely need to share a common characteristic; and that there is little prior relationship between the victim and the offender. However, as Lawrence (1999) acknowledged, there are problems with each of these defining characteristics of hate crime. The studies conducted by Ray and Smith (2001) and Mason (2005a), for example, point out that the presumption of a lack of relationship between victim and offender is highly problematic. Nevertheless the presumption of these characteristics can be found in legal frameworks that have endeavoured to take this kind of criminal victimization seriously.

In the UK there is no legislative status that delineates hate crime from other kinds of crime, although the Association of Chief Police Officers does have an operational definition of such crime which states that it is 'a crime where the perpetrator's prejudice against an identifiable group of people is a factor in determining who is victimised'. However, whilst there have been in recent years several amendments to the law in England and Wales relating to race (Crime and Disorder Act 1998) and religion (Anti-terrorism and Security Act 2001) to deal with situations where it can be demonstrated that acts have been committed gratuitously, at present hate crime *per se* is not a meaningful legal category. The legal ambiguity of hate crime in England and Wales contrasts with the position in the USA. In the USA the FBI defines hate crime as offences that are 'motivated in part or singularly by personal prejudice against others because of a diversity – race, sexual orientation, religion, ethnicity/national origin, or disability'. Its report for 2003 states that racial bias accounted for 51.4% of single-bias hate crime incidents, with religious bias accounting for 18%, ethnic or national bias 13.7%, and sexual orientation bias nearly 17%. Despite these differences in legal status of this crime (some of the problems with which are discussed below), it is nevertheless a label that inspires media headlines. For example, on 4 August 2005 the BBC reported that 'hate crimes soar after bombings' and went on to assert that there were '269 religious hate crimes [in London] in the three weeks after 7 July, compared with 40 in the same time period in 2004'. Indeed, the Home Office figures reported above for a different time period are suggestive of an overall increase in this kind of victimization. As Mason (2005a: 839) states: 'In terms of incidents against members of the Asian and black communities, qualitative research, victimisation studies, and police statistics collectively paint a picture of verbal abuse, graffiti, property damage, threats and physical violence that is widespread and consistent.' A European monitoring report on racism and xenophobia reports that the groups most vulnerable to racist violence in 15 European member states are illegal immigrants, Jews, Muslims, North Africans, people from the former Yugoslavia, refugees, Roma/Sinti/gypsies, with the perpetrators most likely to be young males either affiliated or not affiliated to extremist political groups (European Monitoring Centre on Racism and Xenophobia 2005), thus lending some support to the argument developed by Tomsen (2001) of the links between 'hate crimes' and masculinity.

'Hate crime' is not only perpetrated against ethnic minority or religious minority groups, as some of the statistics reported above indicate. Gay and lesbian people are also the target of 'hate crime', though assessing the nature and extent of this in England and Wales is not easy, as Spalek (2006) observes. Mason (2005b) reports that the Metropolitan Police recorded 754 homophobic incidents in the first 6 months of 2001, and Moran and Skeggs (2004) report on similar kinds of low-level harassment and more serious attacks experienced by the gay and lesbian community to those experienced by ethnic minority groups. GALOP (a gay, lesbian and transgender community safety charity operating in London) conducted a survey of gay and lesbian people's experiences in 2001 and reported that one in ten people surveyed had experienced homophobic physical abuse, with 4% having experienced homophobic sexual abuse. Differences in reporting and recording practices, and differences in experiences of lifestyle, as with the experiences of women and members of ethnic minorities, will all feed into what is seen to be the size of this kind of problem. There are, however, a number of problems associated with the emergence of 'hate' crime on the victimological, criminological and legal agendas, some of which are worth reiterating here.

The first problem worth reflecting on has already been mentioned in passing and has been picked up on in recent research. That problem lies in the presumption that it is the stranger who is a danger to the potential victim of hate crime. As has already been observed in the work of Ray and Smith (2001) and Mason (2005b), this is far from straightforward empirically. Associated with this problem is also the tendency to elide all criminal victimization experiences of those belonging to minority groups as though they are all constituted and motivated in a similar way. It is important to remember that crime is not only most likely to be committed by someone familiar to us, but also an experience that is intra-class, intra-ethnic and intra-sexual. In other words, it is likely to be committed on us by someone very like us. This was one of the important interventions made by left realist victimology in the wider debate on criminal victimization in the late 1980s, and there is little to suggest that this pattern has changed very much. This does not mean to say that other forms of crime do not affect minority groups, but it is offered as a careful reminder as to how the experience of criminal victimization is likely to be structured.

The second problem, linked with the first, lies with the actual behaviour that is labelled as 'hate' crime. It is evident that this behaviour may be just the same as other kinds of crime, that is, vandalizing property or violence against the person. This leads Tomsen (2001: 1) to suggest that ' "hate crime" is a problematic label that may narrowly represent criminal motive and simplify the interpretation of victimisation and offending' and that for him masks the perennial problem of how to deal with disaffected young males. This is a view of hate crime that is endorsed, for different reasons, by Perry (2003). She argues that this catch-all phrase has little of social scientific value since it masks the distinct experiences of different minority groups. It is also important to try and locate an understanding of the emergence of this kind of phenomenon within a wider socio-economic and political setting. This is the kind of analysis that is also offered by Ray and Smith (2001: 213) who state that:

> We are arguing that the appearance of 'hate crime' as a public issue is related to the social movement activity around identity and victim politics and that these have emerged in a context in which juridical rights have been the focus of new forms of regulation and integration.

In other words, as in the discussion of responses to women as victims of violence, there has been a recourse to the law and wider institutional responses as the means by which this kind of victimization is to be recognized and responded to, looking to the relationship between what Spalek (2006: 143–7) calls 'hate crime, identity politics, and victimisation'. In order to get a feel for some of the issues that this relationship poses in making sense of the complexities of this kind of criminal victimization in England and Wales, we shall briefly consider first of all the institutional responses in the aftermath of the Macpherson (1999) report and secondly the recourse to the power of the law more generally in relation to 'hate' crime.

Institutional racism and the murder of Stephen Lawrence

There is a history to both understanding the nature and extent of criminal victimization within ethnic minority groups within England and Wales, and the way that they feel they are treated by the criminal justice process more generally, that dates back at least to the Scarman Report (1982). However, the murder of Stephen Lawrence in 1993 and the Macpherson (1999) report that followed in its wake reignited and added a further dimension to the debate on the relationship between ethnic minority groups, criminal victimization and the criminal justice process. In particular, that report opened up a continuing debate on the nature and extent to which 'institutional racism' constitutes an additional dimension to the processes of victimization that were already experienced by people from ethnic minorities. Put simply, it brought to the fore, in a very focused way, the extent to which people from ethnic minority groups feel that they are under-policed and over-policed at the same time. Much of the focus of this debate has been concerned with policing and the disproportionality argument. For example, Home Office data for 2004 indicate that black people were 6.4 times more likely to be stopped and searched in 2003–4 than white people, with Asian people twice as likely to be so targeted. Figures such as these, of course, mask huge regional variations, and as has been reported elsewhere in this chapter, were certainly higher for young Asian males in London in the aftermath of 7 July 2005. However, it is not only in relation to policing that people from ethnic minority groups feel victimized. The disproportionality argument also applies to their rate of imprisonment as compared with the white populations, for example. This is also a pattern of experience that bears some comparison with other countries. In the USA, for example, Catalona (2005) reported that in 2002 six out of every ten people in local gaols were members of an ethnic minority group. Moreover, a report by Martens and Holmberg (2005: 76) on crime among Swedes and immigrants points to 'immigrants being registered in connection with crime more often than others raising the question of discriminatory practices of the criminal justice system'. In the context of England and Wales this disproportionality argument has resulted in much effort being made to try to change institutional practices through recruitment programmes, diversity educational initiatives and fundamental changes to police training programmes – initiatives that echo much of the effort that has been made to address women's experience of criminal victimization and the criminal justice response to it. Alongside these efforts, attempts have also been made to use the power of the law to address racist crime and religiously motivated crime. It is at this juncture that the criminal victimization experiences of people from ethnic minorities have become intertwined with the experiences of other minority groups who are targeted because of their difference.

The politics of identity and the power of the law

The recourse to the law in the context of crime targeted against people from ethnic minority or any other minority group has become more acute in the UK since the election of the Labour Party to power in 1997. The Crime and Disorder Act 1998 and the Anti-terrorism Crime and Security Act 2001 both offered the victim of racial or religious hatred crime more protection under the law. Moreover, in practice the problems faced by other minority groups from (violent) victimization have increasingly achieved some recognition (for example, the problem of homophobic violence). However, the use of the law for these kinds of problems raises a number of questions.

The first question is to consider the limits of the law itself. As Moran (2001: 333) states: ' "Hate" and "bias" give new significance to particular questions of legal doctrine; the mental element of crime, intention (mens rea)'. Indeed, a good deal of legal debate has been dedicated to considering the relationship between hate, bias and intention. It is Moran's view that the resultant effect of this debate has been to focus attention on the perpetrator and the abnormality or otherwise of their violence, at the expense of understanding the ordinariness and everyday nature of the victim experience. He expresses it this way: 'The hate crime perpetrator jurisprudence tends to leave the institutional perpetrator out of the frame of concern' (2001: 335). This leads to a second problem with this recourse to the law. In this context the institutional perpetrator is the law itself both in contributing to the construction of the offender on the one hand and in the way in which recourse to the law buys into essentialist thinking: this is either a racist attack or it is something else, thus denying the lived reality of the victim. Moreover, in so doing the law also contributes to the view that the perpetrator is a stranger (see also Mason 2005a), not neighbours and/or local school children (Stanko 2004). The third problem that comes to light here is in respect of the role of the state as an institutional perpetrator – a state which in Garland's (2001) terms has utilized the law to perpetuate a criminology of the Other and at the same time has rendered the question of day to day security as something for which we are all responsible.

Interestingly this discussion returns us to the inherent critique of the law posed by Hudson's (2006) phrase 'white man's law' and raises many dilemmas for feminists who appeal to the law as both a symbolic referent and as a mechanism for real change. As Ray and Smith (2001: 213) state: 'Whilst "hate crime" legislation is offered as a form of rights based protection for vulnerable groups, there is considerable uncertainty as to its appropriateness and effectiveness.' They go on to raise a range of questions that are pertinent for those interested in an analysis of the relationship between criminal victimization, victimology and wider social processes. For example, does social integration require universal, content-neutral rights or particular rights that address the diverse and unequal nature of social membership? Does hate crime empower or does it cultivate a view that to be a victim or potential victim become a defining marker of identity? Does recognition of this kind of problem extend freedom through equal treatment or further extend the powers of the state for misuse (2001: 213–14)?

This recourse to the law notwithstanding, there has been another identifiable story in responses to this structurally informed victim of crime. That story has emerged as a consequence of the Crime and Disorder Act 1998 that required all local authorities to engage in a local crime audit and, on the basis of that, produce a crime reduction plan. Within this legislative framework the community safety industry has grown – an industry which, as de Lint and Virta (2004: 466) comment, constitutes the ever increasing 'securitisation of social life ... the command to think security instead of full employment, public education or the good society'. This command to think security has, in their view, resulted in the 'depoliticisation of crime prevention and community safety'. Yet in this space many local crime and disorder reduction strategy documents have foregrounded issues relating to domestic violence, hate crime, and/or other associated 'quality of life' indicators. However, what has this story achieved? Whose safety is this?

The community safety story: but whose safety is it?

The community safety story has a number of threads associated with it. For the purposes of this discussion we shall focus on the storylines that relate to the issues addressed in this chapter. For example, Her Majesty's Inspectorate of Constabularies and Her Majesty's Crown Prosecution Service Inspectorate (2004) indicated that 86% of community safety strategies had prioritized domestic violence, though only 7% of them in their review had targets associated with this. This might not be considered to be too surprising given that the Deputy Prime Minister's Office, which oversees the work of local authorities, also had domestic violence as one of its priorities for 2003–5. So it can be seen that some policies develop a political 'life of their own'. However, in addition, pertinent questions can be asked about what policies on community safety can be reasonably expected to achieve, given the tensions between the policies themselves and the nature of domestic violence, the nature of the victimization experienced by people from ethnic minorities and the notion of community safety itself. It is important to remember that the kind of victimization that is under discussion here occurs, as the previous discussion has indicated, more often than not in the context of a *relationship*, and relationships do not lend themselves easily to incident-oriented policy responses. In the context of this chapter, for example, this implies recognizing that what women want, that is, what they want to be kept safe from (or for that matter what men want or want to be kept safe from, or what people from ethnic minorities want or want to be kept safe from) in the context of their relationships may not be what the policy intervention has in mind. Kirkwood (1993) and Hoyle (1998, 2000) both document the tensions for the women in their samples in relation to this. As far as policy priorities are concerned, this kind of questioning raises a much more philosophical one (Hudson 2003): how much liberty should be traded for security, or, rather more prosaically, whose community and whose safety is being prioritized here, and why?

The inclusion of domestic violence, or hate crime, as a *priority* in many crime and disorder reduction strategy documents raises a number of questions. Who decided on the priorities? What kind of community consultation took place? What is the evidence that there was support for such prioritization, or was this a case of the experts knowing best, given the need to comply with service agreements? Similar questions are also raised in a different way by the empirical work of Whyte (2004). Whyte examined the targets of all crime reduction strategies in the north west of England for 2001 and found that they reflected a remarkable commonality with the list of priorities made by the Home Office: 26 listed vehicle crime as a priority, 24 burglary, 15 drug-related crime, 15 violent crime, 12 anti-social behaviour, 12 youths causing a nuisance, 11 road safety/speeding, 8 domestic violence, 8 robbery, and 7 the fear of crime. This is in some respects a rather unremarkable list until it is considered that the same region, as Whyte (2004: 58) reports, 'is, by a long way, the most concentrated site of carcinogenic production in the UK, if not Europe. Just two plants ... between them release around four tonnes of factory-produced cancer-causing chemicals (40 per cent of the UK total)'. It is no great surprise, then, to note that Widnes, an area in close proximity to this industrial site, has one of the highest incidents of cancer per head of population in England and Wales. Yet, as reported by Whyte (2004), the Environment Agency instituted only 98 prosecutions in 2001–2 in this region: 1 for industrial process offences, 2 for radioactive substance offences, 62 for waste offences and 32 for water quality offences. He concludes that:

> To the extent that the CDA [Crime and Disorder Act] actually represented an opportunity for imagining new possibilities for crime control beyond its traditional preoccupations with relatively powerless groups of offenders, it appears on the evidence here to have failed. . . . The criminological industry, in the midst of this remarkable boom period, trundles on, all but ignoring some of the greatest threats to the safety of our communities. (2004: 60)

A cursory glance through any of the iterations of the crime reduction strategies produced so far would confirm such a pessimistic conclusion. Moreover, it is hard to find any that have critically evaluated the success or otherwise of the rather conventional agendas they have set for themselves, let alone moving towards the challenge of what kinds of crimes communities need to be kept safe from that is implicit in Whyte's (2004) analysis and so usefully reminds us of the other dimensions to victimization that so often impact on the least powerful in society (as well as the crime of violence discussed in this chapter) and that are so readily hidden by contemporary policy agendas.

So the work by Whyte (2004) raises slightly different, though related, questions to those of domestic violence and hate crime: who decided that these kinds of issues of safety were to be excluded from or included in crime and disorder partnership agendas, whose interests are served by such exclusion or inclusion, who was consulted or not in that process, whose liberty has been prioritized here, and what concept of justice does that reflect? These are contentious questions indeed, but the point of making them draws attention to the importance of understanding the structure of communities, and all its multi-layered facets, and the relationship between that structure, the structure of community safety agendas, and the image of the victim that is presumed in the policy responses that have been constructed under the guise of community safety.

To summarize: this discussion has intimated that the community safety turn in policy responses to crime has operated with very conventional images of both the nature and structure of communities and notions of what it is that communities need to be kept safe from in relation to crime. Those images reflect multi-faceted assumptions about victimhood, from the nature of communities that need intervention to the kinds of crimes that worry people (for a fuller development of this argument, see Walklate 2006b). So whilst there is another story, another arena of activity, that makes contemporary policy claims about the victim of crime as a structurally informed image, that imagery is not only limited, but also highly questionable about what it is actually achieving when writ large. This is not to say that particular local authorities might not be making headway in particular areas and locales where issues that bother people have been seriously taken into consideration as part of a meaningful consultation process. However, the contemporary audit culture has meant that much of the intervention work that is conducted under the rubric of community safety is subject to the vagaries of short-term funding mechanisms. In other words, it may be that it is the political rhetoric that is more real here, rather than changes on the ground.

Conclusion

This chapter has taken as its focus of concern the policies that have taken as their starting point a structurally informed image of the crime victim. In reviewing those policies it has become apparent that whilst much energy has been focused in this respect on the criminal justice system and the law, similar issues emerge to those identified in Chapter 5 as standing in the way of their success. Those issues variously point to the structure and the function of the criminal justice system, what its role is as a mechanism for social change, the extent to which the law can act as a vehicle for change, and the struggles that ensue when energy is focused in this way. As in the previous chapter, the issues that have been raised clearly point to the ways in which it is possible to see that the policy responses discussed here, whilst taking a different form of crime victim as their starting point, nevertheless can be understood as part of a continuum of the same processes that were discussed in Chapter 5. Those processes lead inexorably to the politicization of this crime victim too. However, this politicization process has arguably also resulted in the co-option of groups and their interests on behalf of the state as competing pieces of legislation take over and potentially redefine what the problem looks like. For example, the Crown Prosecution Service has trained 520 specialist rape prosecutors to ensure that all rape cases are prepared by experts, and yet in

November 2005 the government also announced a pilot scheme to 'allow prosecutors to speak to victims and witnesses before a trial (drawing on prosecution practice in Australia, Canada and Northern Ireland), and enabling the prosecutor to make a better-informed decision about whether to prosecute or to continue with the prosecution of an offence' (Home Office 2005). How well these two practices sit together is a moot point, but what they both potentially point to is the incessant drive to be seen to be doing something, in the face of whether or not that something results in an improved service. It seems it is enough to claim that it will. Thus returning us not only to the questions of the politicization of the victim of crime but also to the bigger questions of justice that that move in this direction implies.

The policy responses discussed in this chapter reflect an ongoing commitment by some feminists, politicians and policy makers, both in the UK and elsewhere, to persist with the arena of the law as a mechanism of social change, despite the evidence that, as Hudson (2006: 30) states, 'Feminist and race-critical criminologies have produced countless examples of the maleness and whiteness of criminal justice' and that 'It has long been argued that law in modern western societies reflects the subjectivity of the dominant white, affluent, adult male' (see also MacKinnon 1989; Smart 1989; Naffine 1990). The law cannot redress social inequalities; relationships of power that are socially and economically constructed. Despite these problems, Hudson (2003, 2006) does suggest that the law can act as a catalyst for change but only if it embraces a logic of discourse (that people can make claims in their own terms not in accommodation to dominant discourses), is relational, and is reflective. Hudson (2006) goes on to consider these principles in the context of the likely success or otherwise of restorative justice to grapple with 'white man's law'. Yet the dilemmas posed for restorative justice are similar to the dilemmas inherent in the recourse to law discussed in this chapter. One key dilemma is universalism – the tensions between the search for what might be in the interest of all of us as compared with what might be in your or my interest. This dilemma alone would suggest that the search for effective responses in law and/or the criminal justice system (that is, responses that make a difference for the people who want those differences made) is likely to be met perpetually with the problem of attrition, especially in the context of societies committed to and embraced by the (global) hegemonic capitalist state.

Conclusion: Criminal victimization, globalization and cosmopolitanism

Introduction

There have been two main interconnected themes running through this book. The first has been concerned to address how victimology, as a discipline, might be utilized and/or developed to make sense of the contemporary global condition. The second has been concerned to offer some useful insights into the question of how and why we have reached the contemporary policy position in relation to the victim of crime in England and Wales. Both have drawn more or less implicitly on a notion of a critical victimology that was outlined in Chapter 2. In these final pages an attempt will be made to render these themes somewhat more explicit. In so doing we shall revisit and draw on what has already been covered in this book, and our starting place will be with the recourse to the law that has such a strong presence in the policy responses discussed in Chapters 5 and 6.

The state of law or the state and the law?

As has been documented in Chapters 5 and 6, recourse to the law as a vehicle for change is not impossible but is fraught with difficulties. The difficulties that can result range from the unintended consequences of how the law is used (Smart 1989), to the problems in facing 'white man's law' (Hudson 2006), the potential for co-option in the service of the state (Chesney-Lind 2006), and the interests of the victim potentially overriding those of the offender (Williams 2005). Such difficulties, and the practice issues that may ensue from changing the law, have not prevented continued energy and emphasis being placed on the symbolic power of legal reference. Yet as the discussion on hate crime in Chapter 6 illustrates, and the current reaction to the attrition in rape cases intimates (also discussed in Chapter 6), much of the change that might make a difference to these respective victim voices lies in facilitating social and cultural change, not just legal change. It is not just campaigning and/or pressure groups that persist in this legal reference point.

The government itself uses the same reference point. At this point it is apposite to return to the quote from McRobbie (2006: 82) used earlier, but at this juncture it will be of value to quote her more fully.

> The necessity of adhering to legal procedures is frequently responded to by Ministers with some obvious degree of irritation to the extent that, in the U.K. over the last four years, antagonistic relations between government and judiciary have come to occupy a centre stage in political life. The shoot to kill policy introduced suddenly in the aftermath of July 7th and without due discussion across the departments of government, only to be seemingly re-invoked following the killing of an innocent young Brazilian man on his way to work, reflects this cavalier relation to existing law. Law is downgraded and is even seen to be an impediment to the success of the fight against terrorism.

Thus she points to, by implication, the relationship between the state and the law, a relationship that, in the particular example with which she is working, can be considered to be more or less defensible depending upon an individual's political stance on this issue. Such possibilities notwithstanding, this relationship between the state and the law, does not shift over much in relation to the issue under consideration. So there is a clear link between the state of the law and the relationship between the state and the law. In the context of criminal victimization this relationship can be seen in the way in which recourse to the law has resulted in pitting the victim against the offender. This relationship has been illustrated in Chapter 5, for example, by strategies designed to give the victim a voice in the criminal justice process and, in Chapter 6, in the use of the law to further criminalize behaviours deemed unacceptable. O'Malley (2004: 325) expresses some of these concerns in this way:

> Certain persons are defined primarily in terms of their purely negative and dangerous status as threats to others (victims) and accordingly are incapacitated. Therapeutics are abandoned or become subordinate to a regimen of risk reduction. Risk avoidance negativity has been taken as the hallmark of risk in criminal justice, just as it has in critical and liberal analysis of government more generally.

And in the context of the criminological response to this he goes on to say that:

> They assume that risk can only be imagined and operationalised as a zero-sum: a game between potential victims and potential offenders, in which the risks to one party are created by the other.

Indeed, this zero-sum relationship can also be seen in much victimological thought (see Chapter 2). For O'Malley one of the problems that this relationship poses is that it sets a boundary on how risk is understood on the one hand and how risk might be responded to on the other, resulting in a lack of imagination on both counts. He goes on to argue that whilst instituting devices such as Megan's Law may say much about morality, there is little evidence that these kinds of strategies reduce the risk of sexual victimization but rather 'allows security to be defined in terms of rotten apple theory' (2004: 335). He further observes that:

> If the risk is defined as a social problem in terms of society that is culturally and socially saturated with sexual violence, then neither the victim–offender binary nor the exclusionary response appear adequate or even productive. (2004: 335)

This is a view that shares some similarity with the harm done/social justice approach of Hillyard *et al.* (2005). However, the view that has been taken here is that these other choices are not made, not because they may not provide meaningful alternatives, or solely because of the power of actuarial justice, but because of the myriad ways in which the hegemonic capitalist and, it has to be said, masculine state, operates to maintain its interests. Some of the complexity of this operation is captured again by McRobbie (2006: 82) when, in discussing the value of Butler's work, she states:

> In addition the existence of roaming officials, policy advisors, so-called tsars, and unelected Ministers with senior responsibilities of state reflects the extent to which the Blair government has emulated lessons learnt from the think tanks of the Bush administration and has a governmental infrastructure already in place which facilitates dispersed sovereignty. Butler opens up for discussion the ongoing transformation and re-emergence of sovereign power as a series of tactics, widely dispersed across social and cultural life, with the effect of calling into question key elements of democratic process.

Of course, we have seen in some of the processes mapped in Chapter 1 how these tactics are reflected in the changing emergent voice of the victim of crime – who is listened to about what, parliamentary democracy notwithstanding. However, these tactics, as McRobbie (2006) implies, constitute somewhat more than recognizing the processes of governance, they call into question the bigger issue of power – power not just to influence but to institute and to control. Arguably, the use of power in that way – for example, proceeding with policy changes in spite of the evidence rather than because of it – runs through some of the problems faced by the contemporary criminal justice system's preoccupation with 'rebalancing' – writ small in some respects in relation to the victim of crime, but writ large when it comes to questions of terrorism, questions which we are told are now of global proportions.

Terrorism and the contemporary global condition

Beck (2002) talks of a post-terroristic world society, and whilst questions remain as to who such a condition actually exists for outside of the Anglo-American–European axis, the processes of globalization, including those associated with terrorist activity, have made themselves felt in a wide range of arenas, including criminal justice policy. This influence we have seen in the pages of this book from the development of the International Criminal Victimization Survey, to the wide range of policy initiatives that have travelled from other societies to be tried out in England and Wales, often with little real consideration of what kind of policy might work when and under what conditions. Moreover, such processes are also evident in the role of tele technologies that Valier (2004) discussed. In all of the effects there has been an implicit presumption of a unitary victimhood that has rarely been rendered visible or questioned. Though as Wole Soyinka observed, in comparing responses to a terrorist related aeroplane crash in Niger with one in Scotland that took place at around the same time:

> Even in death, where all victims are surely considered equal, some continue to die more equally that others. Dying over Scotland, no matter what your pedigree, enhances your value over dying over African soil. (BBC 2004)

Nevertheless, some might argue that in the aftermath of terrorist activities, which take no account of national boundaries and have no militaristic imperative, we are all victims now. This is a view reflected in the simplistic duality of international politics according to which you are either with us, or against us (the 'us' in this case, of course, being the USA). As Mythen and Walklate (2006a: 129) argue, this duality

> relates to a potentially disparate collection of ideas, about – amongst other things – foreign policy, national security, warfare, electronic systems of monitoring and crime prevention. Thus, in the UK the 'war against terrorism' metaphor is not simply extending into national policies about immigration, detention, identity cards, policing and surveillance, it actually appears to be driving them.

Thus rendering problematic not only individuals, whereby 'In encouraging "us" to notice "them", the socially acceptable targeting of "them" becomes acceptable' (2006a: 136; see also Hudson 2003), but also nation states, countries and creeds. And, of course, in these processes victims are created by both the action and the inaction of the state in the interests of security. Beck (2006: 146) suggests that:

> The 'war' on terror has no declared beginning and no declared end. The separation between war and peace is cancelled in both space and in time. The goals of transnationally operating terrorists are non-negotiable. Conversely violations of the human rights of terrorists (torture, indefinite imprisonment without trial etc.) are often not viewed as illegal. There are no valid demarcations between criminal, enemy and terrorist. The label 'terrorism' empowers and justifies states to free themselves from the constraints of the laws of war which are in any case weak and pliable.

Whilst this is a view that is open to dispute – as Freedland (2006) points out, 'Faced with terrorists, states can either class them as warriors, who would then be held as prisoners of war, with all the Geneva protection. Or they can decide they are criminals to be treated by the normal process of law . . . rather than be held to constitute a whole new category – "unlawful combatants" – and then duly plunged into a legal black hole' – it is also equally the case that the events of the last five years raise all kinds of questions for criminology and victimology, in relation to who is the criminal and who is the victim. Each discipline has the opportunity to embrace these questions and has at its disposal some theoretical armoury with which to make sense of them (see, for example, Mythen and Walklate 2006b). Victimology has a legacy from the work of Elias (1985) with which to make claims about such concerns, though it has been remarkably quiet on the theoretical front as to how to progress such claims, beyond the agenda setting of European conventions or the United Nations. Both forums are, however, settings in which, global and/or transnational standards overlook the problems and possibilities of the local context. The importance of understanding local conditions was particularly apposite in considering the fear of crime in Chapter 4.

There is, however, a further issue here that, interestingly, is alluded to by Freedland (2006) in the quote above. This issue raises the spectre of how to manage difference. In the context of global terrorism, difference appears to have been managed by the creation of a third category, the 'unlawful combatant'. Opting for a middle way (in Beck's terminology), or what in the UK has come to be called the Third Way, seems to have a currency above national politics. Yet in this middle way, it is possible to see the rise and rise of cosmopolitanism.

Cosmopolitanism and difference

Beck (2006) argues that cosmopolitanization is multi-dimensional and demands multiple loyalties and it is its multi-faceted character that makes it different from globalization. He goes on to state that cosmopolitanism 'basically means the recognition of difference, both internally and externally' (2006: 57). It is a view of the contemporary social world that regards the either/or principles of sameness/difference debates as constituting false alternatives, preferring to deal with 'the both/and principle' (2006: 137). So, for example, 'cosmopolitan realism rests on a twofold negation: it negates both the universalism of and the essentialist insistence on ethnic difference' (2006: 61). In some respects these are exactly the tensions that we have observed in efforts to respond to the victim of crime. Chapter 5 documented those policy possibilities that have been engendered from a (universal) structurally neutral image of the victim. Chapter 6 documented those policy possibilities that have been engendered from an (essentialist) structurally informed image of the victim. They co-exist in the policy domain, but still with the either/or principle, not on the 'both/and principle'. You are either victim or an offender. You are either with us or against us. Arguably, this unhappy co-existence is largely a product of the politicization of the victim that has facilitated the maintenance of the state and has been well documented in this book and elsewhere. However, there is another victim here. That victim is justice: for both the victim and the offender.

The cosmopolitan turn and the search for justice

The discussion above clearly intimates that some of the struggles and tensions that exist in endeavouring to respond to the victim of crime are located in wider social processes. One of the central purposes of pursuing a critical stance towards victimology and its concerns is to locate those interests within that wider social context. Such a framework has been more or less explicit throughout this book and has taken us on a tour from the emergence of the criminal victimization survey to responses to hate crime. The first in its origins largely assumes an undifferentiated victim. The second assumes a highly differentiated victim. The increasing tendency to take account of difference, whatever form that difference takes, whilst arguably possible in the local domain of the wide range of support work that exists to help people in difficult circumstances, when writ large hits the brick wall of a criminal justice system rooted in the modernist principles of 'white man's justice' (Hudson 2006). Those modernist principles reflect principles of justice that assume a majoritarian worldview. In other words, justice is in the interests of all of us, and we can all agree on what that might look like. Interestingly this kind of majoritarian view is also to be found in the work of Beck. It is a view that McRobbie (2006: 85) suggests is 'based on an assumption that we can somehow learn to understand each other and on this basis conduct a global politics so as to minimize catastrophe and conflict'. In some respects it is a view that is also possible to trace in the restorative justice movement and Braithwaite's (2003) call for the embrace of democratic principles therein. In the face of cooption, silence and silencing, and the complex management of sovereignty in the interests of the hegemonic capitalist state, what is possible, if anything, in this cosmopolitan turn is a moot point. It might help if victimology took a little more note of the problems and possibilities that these debates raise.

References

Allen, S. (2002) Male victims of rape: responses to a perceived threat to masculinity. In C. Hoyle and R. Young (eds) *New Visions of Crime Victims*. Oxford: Hart Publishing.

Anderson, S., Kinsey, R., Loader, I. and Smith, C. (1994) *Cautionary Tales: Young People, Crime and Policing in Edinburgh*. Aldershot: Avebury.

Armstrong, D., Hine, J., Hacking, S., Armaos, R., Jones, R., Klessinger, N. and France, A. (2005) *Children, Risk and Crime: The On Track Young Lifestyles Surveys*. London: Stationery Office.

Ashworth, A. (1986) Punishment and compensation: victims, offenders and the state. *Oxford Journal of Legal Studies*, 6: 86–122.

Ashworth, A. (1993) Victim impact statements and sentencing. *Criminal Law Review*, 498–509.

Ashworth, A. (2000) Victims' rights, defendants' rights and criminal procedure. In A. Crawford and J. Goodey (eds) *Integrating a Victim Perspective within Criminal Justice: International Debates*. Aldershot: Gower.

Audit Commission (1996) *Misspent Youth: Young People and Crime*. London: Audit Commission.

Audit Commission (2003) *Victims and Witnesses*. London: Audit Commission.

Banks, M. (2005) Spaces of (in)security: media and fear of crime in local context. *Crime, Media, Culture: An International Journal*, 1(2): 169–89.

Barbaret, R. (2005) Country survey: Spain. *European Journal of Criminology*, 2(3): 341–68.

Bauman, Z. (2000) *Liquid Modernity*. Oxford: Polity.

BBC (2004) Reith Lecture 1: The changing face of fear. http://www.bbc.co.uk/radio4/reith2004/lectures.shtml.

Beck, U. (1992) *The Risk Society*. London: Sage.

Beck, U. (2002) The terrorist threat: world risk society revisited. *Theory, Culture and Society*, 19(4): 39–55.

Beck, U. (2006) *Cosmopolitan Vision*. Cambridge: Polity.

Bottoms, A.E. (1983) Neglected features of the contemporary penal system. In D. Garland and P. Young (eds) *The Power to Punish*. London: Heinemann.

Bowling, B. (1998) *Violent Racism, Victimisation, Policing and Social Context*. Oxford: Clarendon.

Box, S. (1983) *Crime, Power and Mystification*. London: Tavistock.

Braithwaite, J. (1989) *Crime, Shame and Reintegration*. Cambridge: Cambridge University Press.

Braithwaite, J. (2002) Setting standards for restorative justice. *British Journal of Criminology*, 42(3): 563–77.

Braithwaite, J. (2003) What's wrong with the sociology of punishment? *Theoretical Criminology*, 7(1): 5–28.

British Journal of Criminology (1995) Symposium on repeat victimisation. *British Journal of Criminology*, 35(3): 327–99.

Brogden, M. and Nijhar, P. (2000) *Crime, Abuse and the Elderly*. Cullompton: Willan.

Brooks-Gardner, C. (1995) Men of steel: gay men and the management of public harassment. In S. Edgell, S. Walklate and G. Williams (eds) *Debating the Future of the Public Sphere*. Aldershot: Avebury.

Burkitt, I. (2005) Powerful emotions: power, government and opposition in the 'war on terror'. *Sociology*, 39(4): 679–95.

Burnett, R. and Appleton, C. (2004) Joined-up services to tackle youth crime: a case study in England. *British Journal of Criminology*, 44(1): 34–54.

Cain, M. (1990) Towards transgression: new directions in feminist criminology. *International Journal of the Sociology of Law*, 18: 1–18.

Cain, M. (2000) Orientalism, occidentalism and the sociology of crime. *British Journal of Criminology*, 40(2): 239–60.

Caldeira, T. (2000) *City of Walls: Segregation and Citizenship in Sao Paulo*. Berkeley: University of California Press.

Campbell, A. (2005) Keeping the 'lady' safe: the regulation of femininity through crime prevention literature. *Critical Criminology*, 13: 119–40.

Carrabine, E., Iganski, P., Lee, M., Plummer, K. and South, N. (2004) *Criminology: A Sociological Introduction*. London: Routledge.

Catalona, S.M. (2005) *Criminal Victimization 2004*. Washington, DC: Bureau of Statistics, US Dept of Justice.

Cavadino, M. and Dignan, J. (1996) Reparation, retribution and rights. *International Review of Victimology*, 4: 233–53.

Cavender, G. (2004) Media and crime policy: a reconsideration of David Garland's Culture of Control. *Punishment and Society*, 6(3): 335–48.

Chadee, D. and Ditton, J. (2005) Fear of crime and the media: assessing the lack of relationship. *Crime, Media, Culture: An International Journal*, 1(3): 322–32.

Chambers, G. and Millar, A. (1983) *Investigating Sexual Assault*. Edinburgh: HMSO.

Chambers, G. and Tombs, J. (1984) *The British Crime Survey: Scotland*. Edinburgh: Home Office.

Chesney-Lind, M. (2006) Patriarchy, crime and justice: feminist criminology in an era of backlash. *Feminist Criminology*, 1(1): 6–26.

Chesney-Lind, M. and Pasko, L. (2004) *The Female Offender*. London: Sage.

Chevigny, P. (2003) The populism of fear: politics of crime in the Americas. *Punishment and Society*, 5(1): 77–96.

Choudry, S. (1996) *Pakistani Women's Experiences of Domestic Violence in Great Britain*, HORS Research Findings 43. London: HMSO.

Christie, N. (1977) Conflicts as property. *British Journal of Criminology*, 17: 1–15.

Christie, N. (1986) The ideal victim. In E.A. Fattah (ed.) *From Crime Policy to Victim Policy*. London: Macmillan.

Clarke, J. (2005) New Labour's citizens: activated, empowered, responsibilised, abandoned? *Critical Social Policy*, 25(4): 447–63.

Clarke, J, Gewirtz, S., Hughes, G. and Humphrey, J. (2000) Guarding the public interest? Auditing public services. In J. Clarke, S. Gewirtz and E. McLaughlin (eds) *New Managerialism: New Welfare?* London: Sage.

Cobb, S. (1997) The domestication of violence in mediation. *Law and Society Review*, 31: 397–440.

Cohen, S. (1985) *Visions of Social Control*. Oxford: Polity.

Coleman, R. (2005) Surveillance in the city: primary definition and urban spatial order. *Crime, Media, Culture: An International Journal*, 1(2): 131–48.

Community Law Reform Committee of the Australian Capital Territory (1998) *Victims of Crime*, Report No. 6. http://www.jcs.act.gov.au/eLibrary/lrc/r06/Report6r3.html.

Connell, G. W. (1987) *Gender and Power*. Oxford: Polity.

Cook, D., Burton, M., Robinson, A. and Vallely, C. (2004) Evaluation of specialist domestic violence courts/fast track systems. Crown Prosecution Service/Department of Constitutional Affairs, London.

Cottle, S. (2005) Mediatised public crisis and civil society renewal: the racist murder of Stephen Lawrence. *Crime, Media, Culture: An International Journal*, 1(1): 49–71.

Coxell, A., King, M., Mezey, G. and Gordon, D. (1999) Lifetime prevalence, characteristics and associated problems of non-consensual sex in men: cross sectional survey. *British Medical Journal*, 318: 846–9.

Crawford, A. (2000) Salient themes and the limitations of restorative justice. In A. Crawford and J. Goodey (eds) *Integrating a Victim Perspective within Criminal Justice*. Aldershot: Ashgate.

Crawford, A. and Enterkin, J. (2001) Victim contact work in the Probation Service: paradigm shift or Pandora's box. *British Journal of Criminology*, 40(4): 707–25.

Crawford, A., Jones, T., Woodhouse, T. and Young, J. (1990) The Second Islington Crime Survey. Centre for Criminology, Middlesex Polytechnic.

Daly, K. (2002) Restorative justice: the real story. *Punishment and Society*, 4(1): 55–80.

de Greiff, P. (2006) Justice and reparations. In P. de Greiff (ed.) *The Handbook of Reparations*. Oxford: Oxford University Press.

de Lint, W. and Virta, S. (2004) Security and ambiguity: towards a radical security politics. *Theoretical Criminology*, 8(4): 465–89.

de Maillard, J. and Roché, S. (2004) Crime and justice in France: time trends, policies and political debate. *European Journal of Criminology*, 1(1): 111–52.

Dekeseredy, W.S., Schwartz, M., Alvi, S. and Tomaszewski, A. (2003) Perceived collective efficacy and women's victimization in public housing. *Criminal Justice*, 3(1): 5–27.

del Frate, A. (1998) Victims of Crime in the Developing World. UNICRI No. 57: Rome.

del Frate, A. and van Kesteren, J.N. (2004) *Criminal Victimisation in Urban Europe: Key Findings of the 2000 International Crime Victim Survey.* Turin: UNICRI. http://www.unicri.it/icvs.

Dignan, J. (2005) *Understanding Victims and Restorative Justice.* Maidenhead: Open University Press.

Dingwall, G. and Moody, S. (1999) *Crime and Conflict in the Countryside.* Cardiff: University of Wales Press.

Ditton, J., Farrall, S., Gilchrist, E. and Pease, K. (1999) Reactions to victimisation: why has anger been ignored? *Crime Prevention and Community Safety: An International Journal,* 1(3): 37–54.

Dixon, M., Reed, H., Rogers, B. and Stone, L. (2006) *CrimeShare: The Unequal Impact of Crime.* London: IPPR.

Dobash, R.P. and Dobash, R. (1979) *Violence against Wives: A Case against Patriarchy.* New York: Free Press.

Dobash, R.P. and Dobash, R. (1992) *Women, Violence and Social Change.* London: Routledge.

Dobash, R.P. and Dobash, R. (1998) *Rethinking Violence against Women.* London: Sage.

Douglas, M. (1992) *Risk and Blame: Essays in Cultural Theory.* London: Routledge.

Economic and Social Research Council (2002) *Taking Stock.* Egham: ESRC Violence Research Programme, Royal Holloway University of London.

Edwards, I. (2004) An ambiguous participant: the crime victim and criminal justice decision-making. *British Journal of Criminology,* 44(6): 946–67.

Elias, R. (1985) Transcending our social reality of victimisation: towards a new victimology of human rights. *Victimology,* 10: 6–25.

Elias, R. (1986) *The Politics of Victimisation.* Oxford: Oxford University Press.

Elias, R. (1993) *Victims Still.* London: Sage.

Erez, E. (1999) Who's afraid of the big bad victim? Victim impact statements as victim empowerment and enhancement of justice. *Criminal Law Review:* 545–56.

Erez, E. and Rogers, L. (1999) Victim impact statements and sentencing outcomes and processes: the perspectives of legal professionals. *British Journal of Criminology,* 39(2): 216–39.

Etherington, K. (2000) When the victim is male. In H. Kemshall and J. Pritchard (eds) *Good Practice in Working with Victims of Violence.* London: Jessica Kingsley.

European Monitoring Centre on Racism and Xenophobia (2005) *Racist Violence in 15 EU Member States.* Vienna: EUMC.

Evans, K., Fraser, P. and Walklate, S. (1996) Whom can you trust? The politics of grassing on an inner city housing estate. *Sociological Review,* 44(3): 361–80.

Ewald, U. (2000) Criminal victimisation and social adaptation in modernity. In T. Hope and R. Sparks (eds) *Crime, Risk and Insecurity.* London: Routledge.

Farrall, S. and Gadd, D. (2004) Research note: The frequency of the fear of crime. *British Journal of Criminology*, 44(1): 127–33.

Farrall, S. and Maltby, S. (2003) The victimisation of probationers. *Howard Journal of Criminal Justice*, 42(1): 32–54.

Farrall, S., Bannister, J. Ditton, J. and Gilchrist, E. (2000) Social psychology and the fear of crime. *British Journal of Criminology*, 40(3): 376–99.

Farrell, G. (1992) Multiple victimisation: its extent and significance. *International Review of Victimology*, 2(2): 85–102.

Farrell, G. and Pease, K. (eds) (2001) *Repeat Victimization*. Monsey, NY: Criminal Justice Press.

Fattah, E. (1991) *Understanding Criminal Victimisation*. Scarborough, Ontario: Prentice Hall.

Fattah, E. (ed.) (1992) *Critical Victimology*. London: Macmillan.

Feeley, M. (2003) Crime, social order and the rise of the neo-Conservative politics. *Theoretical Criminology*, 7(1): 111–30.

Feeley, M. and Simon, J. (1994) Actuarial justice; the emerging new criminal law. In D. Nelken (ed.) *The Futures of Criminology*. London: Sage.

Feenan, D. (ed.) (2002) *Informal Justice*. Aldershot: Ashgate.

Ferraro, K. and LaGrange, R. (1987) The measurement of fear of crime. *Sociological Inquiry*, 57(1): 70–101.

Flynn, R. (2006) Health and risk. In G. Mythen and S. Walklate (eds) *Beyond the Risk Society: Critical Reflections on Risk and Human Security*. Maidenhead: Open University Press.

Foresight (2000) Crime Prevention Panel: Just around the corner. http://www.foresight.gov.uk.

Fougeyrollas-Schwebel, D. (2005) Violence against Women in France: The context, findings and impact of the Enveff survey. UN Division for the Advancement of Women, Expert Group Meeting, Geneva, April.

Freedland, J. (2006) No, international law doesn't have to be dumped because of al-Qaida. *The Guardian*, 5 April.

Fry, M. (1951) *Arms of the Law*. London: Gollancz.

Furedi, F. (1997) *Culture of Fear: Risk Taking and the Morality of Low Expectation*. London: Cassell.

Furedi, F. (2002) *Culture of Fear: Risk Taking and the Morality of Low Expectation*, revised edition. London: Continuum.

Furedi, F. (2005) Terrorism and the politics of fear. In C. Hale., K. Hayward., A. Wahidin and E. Wincup (eds) *Criminology*. Oxford: Oxford University Press.

Gabriel, U. and Greve, W. (2003) The psychology of fear of crime: conceptual and methodological perspectives. *British Journal of Criminology*, 43(3): 600–15.

Garland, D. (1996) The limits of the sovereign state. *British Journal of Criminology*, 36(4): 445–71.

Garland, D. (2001) *The Culture of Control*. Oxford: Polity.

Garland, D. and Sparks, R. (2000) Criminology, social theory, and the challenge of our times. *British Journal of Criminology*, 40(2): 189–204.

Garofalo, J. (1981) The fear of crime: causes and consequences. *Journal of Criminal Law and Criminal Policy*, 72: 839–57.

Gelsthorpe, L. and Morris, A. (2000) Re-visioning men's violence against female partners. *Howard Journal*, 39(4): 412–28.

Genn, H. (1988) Multiple victimisation. In M. Maguire and J. Pointing (eds) *Victims of Crime: A New Deal?* Milton Keynes: Open University Press.

Geis, G. (1973) Victimisation patterns in white collar crime. In L. Drapkin and E. Viano (eds) *Victimology: A New Focus vol. V.* Lexington, MA: D.C. Heath.

Giddens, A. (1984) *The Constitution of Society.* Oxford: Polity.

Giddens, A. (1991) *Modernity and Self Identity.* Oxford: Polity.

Glassner, B. (1999) *Culture of Fear.* New York: Perseus Book.

Goodey, J. (1997) Boys don't cry: masculinities, fear of crime and fearlessness. *British Journal of Criminology*, 37(3): 401–18.

Goodey, J. (2005) *Victims and Victimology.* Harlow: Longman.

Grady, A. (2002) Female on male domestic violence: uncommon or ignored? In C. Hoyle and R. Young (eds) *New Visions of Crime Victims.* Portland, OR: Hart.

Graham, J., Woodfield, K., Tibble, M. and Kitchen, S. (2004) Testaments of harm: a qualitative evaluation of the Victim Personal Statement scheme. National Centre for Social Research, May.

Hagerty, K. (2003) From risk to precaution: the rationalities of personal crime prevention. In R. Ericson and A. Doyle (eds) *Risk and Morality.* Toronto: University of Toronto Press.

Hale, C. (1996) Fear of crime: a literature review. *International Review of Victimology*, 4: 79–150.

Hall, R. (1985) *Ask Any Woman.* Bristol: Falling Wall Press.

Hall, S. and Winlow, S. (2005) Anti-nirvana: crime, culture and instrumentalism in the age of insecurity. *Crime, Media, Culture: An International Journal*, 1(1): 31–48.

Hall, S., Cricher, C. and Jefferson T. (1978) *Policing the Crisis.* London: Macmillan.

Hamill, H. (2002) Victims of paramilitary punishment attacks in Belfast. In C. Hoyle and R. Young (eds) *New Visions of Crime Victims.* Portland, OR: Hart.

Hamlyn, B., Phelps, A., Turtle, J. and Sattar, G. (2004) *Are Special Measures Working? Evidence from Surveys of Vulnerable and Intimidated Witnesses*, Research Study 283. London: Home Office.

Hamner, J. and Saunders, S. (1984) *Well Founded Fear.* London: Hutchinson.

Harding, S. (1991) *Whose Science? Whose Knowledge?* Buckingham: Open University Press.

Harré, R. (1979) *Social Being.* London: Basil Blackwell.

Head, M. (2004) Australian government uses Madrid bombings to justify further police-state powers. http://www.wsws.org/articles/2004/apr2004/terr-a07.shtml.

Heiskanen, M. and Piispa, M. (1998) *Faith, Hope, Battering*. Helsinki: Statistics Finland.

Her Majesty's Inspectorate of Constabularies and Her Majesty's Crown Prosecution Service Inspectorate (2004) *Violence at Home*. London: CPSI.

Her Majesty's Inspectorate of Probation (2003) *Valuing the Victim: An Inspection into National Victim Contact Arrangements*. London: Home Office.

Hesse, B., Rai, D.K., Bennett, C. and McGilchrist, P. (1992) *Beneath the Surface: Racial Harassment*. Aldershot: Avebury.

Hester, M. and Westmarland, N. (2005) *Tackling Domestic Violence: Effective Interventions and Approaches*. Home Office Research Study 290. London: Home Office.

Hillyard, P., Pantazis, C., Tombs, S., Gordon, D. and Dorling, D. (2005) *Criminal Obsessions: Why Harm Matters More Than Crime*, Monograph 1. London: Crime and Society Foundation.

Hindelang, M.J., Gottfredson, M.R. and Garofalo, J. (1978) *Victims of Personal Crime: An Empirical Foundation for a Theory of Personal Victimization*. Cambridge, MA: Ballinger.

Hodgson, C. (2005) Angry or what? Experiences of being a victim of crime. *British Journal of Community Justice*, 3(3): 50–61.

Hollway, W. and Jefferson, T. (1997) The risk society in an age of anxiety. *British Journal of Sociology*, 48: 255–66.

Hollway, W. and Jefferson, T. (2000) The role of anxiety in the fear of crime. In T. Hope and R. Sparks (eds) *Crime, Risk and Insecurity*. London: Routledge.

Holstein, J.A. and Miller, G. (1990) Rethinking victimisation: an interactional approach to victimology. *Symbolic Interaction*, 13: 103–22.

Home Office (2002) *Justice for All*, Cm. 5563. London: Stationery Office.

Home Office (2005) *Rebuilding Lives: Supporting Victims*. London: Stationery Office.

Hope, T. and Sparks, R. (eds) (2000) *Crime, Risk and Insecurity*. London: Routledge.

Hope, T. and Walklate, S. (1995) Repeat victimisation: differentiation or structuration? Paper presented to the British Criminology Conference, Loughborough, July.

Hough, M. and Mayhew, P. (1983) *The British Crime Survey: First Report*. London: HMSO.

Hough, M. and Mayhew, P. (1985) *Taking Account of Crime: Key Findings from the Second British Crime Survey*. London: HMSO.

Howarth, G. and Rock, P. (2000) Aftermath and the construction of victimisation: 'the other victims of crime'. *Howard Journal of Criminal Justice*, 39: 58–78.

Hoyle, C. (1998) *Negotiating Domestic Violence*. Oxford: Clarendon.

Hoyle, C. (2000) Being a nosey bloody cow. In R. King and E. Wincup (eds) *Doing Research on Crime and Justice*. Oxford: Oxford University Press.

Hoyle, C. and Sanders, A. (2000) From victim choice to victim empowerment. *British Journal of Criminology*, 40(1): 14–36.

Hoyle, C., Cape, E., Morgan, R. and Sanders, A. (1998) *Evaluation of the One Stop Shop and Victim Statement Pilot Projects. A Report for the Home Office Research and*

Development Statistic Directorate. Bristol: Department of Law, University of Bristol.

Hudson, B. (2006) Beyond white man's justice: race, gender and justice in late modernity. *Theoretical Criminology*, 10(1): 29–47.

Hudson, S. (2003) *Justice in the Risk Society*. London: Sage.

Hughes, G. (2004) Community safety and 'the stranger': challenges for radical communalism. Paper presented to the New Directions in Community Safety Conference, Birmingham, December.

Hutton, W. (2002) *The World We're In*. London: Little Brown.

ICM (2005) *Sexual Assault Research. Summary Report*. http://www.amnesty.org.uk/uploads/documents/doc_16619.doc.

Innes, M. (2002) Control creep. *Sociological Research Online*, 6(3). http://www.socresonline.org.uk/6/3/innes.html.

Jackson, J. (2004) Experience and expression: social and cultural significance in the fear of crime. *British Journal of Criminology*, 44(6): 946–66.

James, A. (1995) Probation values for the 1990s – and beyond? *Howard Journal of Criminal Justice*, 34(4): 326–43.

Jenks, C. (2003) *Transgression*. London: Routledge.

Jennings, D. (2003) *One-Year Juvenile Reconviction Rates: First Quarter of 2001 Cohort*, Home Office Online Report 18/03. London: Home Office.

Jessop, B. (1991) State theory. Paper presented to the Dept. of Politics, University of Manchester, May.

Jessop, B. (2002) *The Future of the Capitalist State*. Cambridge: Polity.

Jefferson, T., Sim, J. and Walklate, S. (1992) Europe, the left and criminology in the 1990s: accountability, control and the construction of the consumer. In D. Farrington and S. Walklate (eds) *Victims and Offenders: Theory and Policy*. London: British Society of Criminology and the Institute for the Study and Treatment of Delinquency.

Johnson, H. (2005) Crime victimisation in Australia: Key results of the 2004 International Criminal Victimisation Survey. Research and Policy Papers Series No. 64. Australian Institute of Criminology, Canberra.

Johnson, J.H., Karper, H., Hayes, D. and Killenger, G. (1973) *The Recidivist Victim: A Descriptive Study*. Hunstville, TX: Institute of Contemporary Corrections and the Behavioural Sciences, Sam Houston State University.

Jones, H. (2004) Opportunities and obstacles: The Rape Crisis Federation in the U.K. *Journal of Interdisciplinary Gender Studies*, 8(1/2): 55–69.

Jones, T. and Newburn, T. (2002) Policy convergence and crime control in the USA and the UK: streams of influence and levels of impact. *Criminal Justice*, 2(2): 173–203.

Kara, M. and Upson, A. (2006) *Crime in England and Wales Quarterly Update*. London: HMSO.

Karmen, A. (1990) *Crime Victims: An Introduction to Victimology*. Belmont, CA: Wadsworth.

Karstedt, S. (2002) Emotions and criminal justice. *Theoretical Criminology*, 6(3): 299–318.

Kasperon, R. and Kasperon, J. (1996) The social amplification and attenuation of risk. *Annals of the American Academy of Political and Social Science*, 545: 116–25.

Katz, J. (2001) *How Emotions Work*. Chicago: Chicago University Press.

Kauzlarich, D., Matthews, R.A. and Miller, W.J. (2001) Toward a victimology of state crime. *Critical Criminology*, 10: 173–94.

Kearon, T. and Leach, R. (2000) Invasion of the body snatchers: burglary reconsidered. *Theoretical Criminology*, 4(4): 451–73.

Keat, R. and Urry, J. (1975) *Social Theory as Science*. London: Routledge & Kegan Paul.

Kelly, L. (1988) *Surviving Sexual Violence*. Oxford: Polity.

Kelly, L. (2001) *Routes to Injustice: A Research Review on the Reporting, Investigation and Prosecution of Rape Cases*. London: Crown Prosecution Service Inspectorate.

Kelly, L., Lovett, J. and Regan, L. (2005) *A Gap or a Chasm? Attrition in Reported Rape Cases*, Home Office Research Study 293. London: Home Office.

Kershaw, C., Budd, T., Kinshott, G., Mattinson, J., Mayhew, P. and Myhill, A. (2001) *The 2000 British Crime Survey*. London: Home Office.

Kinsey, R., Lea, J. and Young, J. (1986) *Losing the Fight against Crime*. Oxford: Basil Blackwell.

Kirkwood, C. (1993) *Leaving Abusive Partners*. London: Sage.

Krajewski, K. (2004) Crime and criminal justice in Poland. *European Journal of Criminology*, 1(3): 377–408.

Lambropoulou, E. (2005) Crime, criminal justice and criminology in Greece. *European Journal of Criminology*, 2(2): 211–48.

Lawrence, F.M. (1999) *Punishing Hate: Bias Crimes under American Law*. Cambridge, MA: Harvard University Press.

Lee, M. (2006) *Inventing Fear of Crime: Criminology and the Politics of Anxiety*. Cullompton: Willan.

Lees, S. (1997) *Ruling Passions*. Buckingham: Open University Press.

Lewis, R. (2004) Making justice work: effective legal intervention for domestic violence. *British Journal of Criminology*, 44(2): 204–24.

Lindström, P. (2004) Violence against women in Scandinavia: a description and evaluation of two new laws aiming to protect women. *Journal of Scandinavian Studies in Criminology and Crime Prevention*, 5: 220–35.

Loader, I. and Walker, N. (2004) State of denial? Rethinking the governance of security. Review of L. Johnston and C. Shearing (2003) Governing Security: Explorations in Policing and Justice. *Punishment and Society*, 6(2): 221–8.

Lois, J. (2005) Gender and emotion management in the stages of edgework. In S. Lyng (ed.) *Edgework: The Sociology of Risk-Taking*. London: Routledge.

Lundgren, E., Heimer, G., Westerstrand, J. and Kalliokoski, J. (2002) *The Captured Queen: Men's Violence against Women in 'Equal' Sweden: A Prevalence Study*. Stockholm: Fritzes Förlag.

MacIntyre, A. (1988) *Whose Science? Which Rationality?* London: Duckworth.

MacKinnon, C. (1989) *Toward a Feminist Theory of the State*. Cambridge, MA: Harvard University Press.

Macpherson, Sir William (1999) *The Stephen Lawrence Inquiry*, Cm 4262. London: Stationery Office.

Maguire, M. (1982) *Burglary in a Dwelling*. London: Heinemann.

Maguire, M. and Corbett, C. (1987) *The Effects of Crime and the Work of Victim Support Schemes*. Aldershot: Gower.

Maguire, M. and Kynch, J. (2000) *Victim Support: Findings from the 1998 British Crime Survey*, Home Office Research Study 117. London: HMSO.

Marshall, T. (1999) *Restorative Justice: An Overview*. London: HMSO.

Martens, P. and Holmberg, S. (2005) *Crime Amongst Persons Born in Sweden and Other Countries*. Stockholm: National Council for Crime Prevention.

Mason, G. (2005a) Hate crime and the image of the stranger. *British Journal of Criminology*, 45(6): 837–60.

Mason, G. (2005b) Being hated: stranger or familiar? *Social and Legal Studies*, 14(4): 585–605.

Matthews, N. (1994) *Confronting Rape*. London: Routledge.

Matthews, N. (1988) *The Feminist Anti-rape Movement and the State*. London: Routledge.

Matthews, R. and Young, J. (eds) (1992) *Issues in Realist Criminology*. London: Sage.

Mawby, R. and Gill, M. (1987) *Crime Victims: Needs and Services*. London: Tavistock.

Mawby, R. and Walklate, S. (1994) *Critical Victimology*. London: Sage.

Mawby, R. and Walklate, S. (1997) The impact of burglary: a tale of two cities. *International Review of Victimology*, 4(4): 267–95.

Mawby, R., Gorgenyi, I., Ostrihanska, Z., Walklate, S. and Wojcik, D. (1999) Victims' needs and the availability of services. *International Criminal Justice Review*, 9: 18–38.

Maxfield, M. (1984) *Fear of Crime in England and Wales*, Research Study 78. London: Home Office.

Mayhew, P. (1993) *The 1992 British Crime Survey*. London: HMSO.

Mayhew, P. and Hough, M. (1988) The British Crime Survey: origins and impact. In M. Maguire and J. Pointing (eds) *Victims of Crime: A New Deal?* Milton Keynes: Open University Press.

Mayhew, P., Elliott, D. and Dowds, L. (1989) *The 1988 British Crime Survey*. London: HMSO.

Mayhew, P., Mirrlees-Black, C. and Aye-Maung, N. (1994) *Trends in Crime: Findings from the 1994 British Crime Survey*. London: HMSO.

McBarnett, D. (1988) Victim in the witness box – confronting victimology's stereotype. *Contemporary Crises*, 7: 279–303.

McEvoy, K., Mika, H. and Hudson, B. (2002) Introduction: Practice, performance and prospects for restorative justice. *British Journal of Criminology*, 42(3): 449–75.

McLaughlin, E, Muncie, J. and Hughes, G. (2001) The permanent revolution: new

Labour, new public management and the modernisation of criminal justice. *Criminology and Criminal Justice*, 1(3): 301–18.

McMillan, N. (2004) Beyond representation: cultural understandings of the September 11 attacks. *Australian and New Zealand Journal of Criminology*, 37(3): 380–400.

McMullan, R.J. (1990) *Male Rape: Breaking the Silence on the Last Taboo*. London: Gay Men's Press.

McRobbie, A. (2006) Vulnerability, violence and (cosmopolitan) ethics: Butler's 'Precarious Life'. *British Journal of Sociology*, 37(1): 69–86.

Mendelsohn, B. (1956) A new branch of bio-psychological science: la victimology. *Revue Internationale de Criminologie et de Police Technique*, 2.

Mendelsohn, B. (1974) The origins of the doctrine of victimology. In I. Drapkin and E. Viano (eds) *Victimology*. Lexington, MA: Lexington Books.

Mezey, G. and King, M. (eds) (1992) *Male Victims of Sexual Assault*. Oxford: Oxford University Press.

Miers, D. (1978) *Responses to Victimisation* Abingdon: Professional Books.

Miers, D. (1989) Positivist victimology: a critique part 1. *International Review of Victimology*, 1(1): 1–29.

Miers, D. (1990) Positivist victimology: a critique part 2. *International Review of Victimology*, 1(3): 219–30.

Miers, D. (2004) Situating and researching restorative justice in Great Britain. *Punishment and Society*, 6(1): 23–46.

Miers, D. (2007) Looking beyond Great Britain: the development of criminal injuries. In S. Walklate (ed.) *The Handbook of Victims and Victimology*. Cullompton: Willan.

Miers, D., Maguire, M., Goldie, S., Sharpe, K., Hale, C., Netten, A., Uglow, S., Doolin, K., Hallam, A., Enterkin, J. and Newburn, T. (2001) *An Exploratory Evaluation of Restorative Justice Schemes*, Crime Reduction Research Series Paper 9. London: Home Office.

Ministry of Community Services, Government of British Columbia (n.d.) Fact Sheet: Violence against Women. http://www.mcaws.gov.bc.ca/womens_services/stopping-violence/facts.htm (accessed on 17 March 2006).

Mirrlees-Black, C. (1999) *Domestic Violence: Findings from a New British Crime Survey Self Completion Questionnaire*, Home Office Research Study 191. London: Home Office.

Mirrlees-Black, C. (2001) *Confidence in the Criminal Justice System: Findings from the 2000 British Crime Survey*. Home Office Research Findings 137. London: Home Office.

Mirrlees-Black, C., Mayhew, P. and Percy, A. (1996) *The 1996 British Crime Survey*. London: HMSO.

Mirrlees-Black, C., Budd, T., Partridge, S. and Mayhew, P. (1998) *The 1998 British Crime Survey*. London: HMSO.

Mooney, J. (1993) The North London Domestic Violence Survey. Middlesex University, Middlesex.

Moran, L. (2001) Affairs of the heart: hate crime and the politics of crime control. *Law and Critique*, 12: 331–44.

Moran, L. and Skeggs, B. with Tyrer, P. and Corteen, K. (2004) *Sexuality and the Politics of Violence and Safety*. London: Routledge.

Morgan, J. and Zedner, L. (1992) *Child Victims: Crime, Impact and Criminal Justice*. Oxford: Oxford University Press.

Morgan, R. (1989) *The Demon Lover*. London: Mandarin.

Mouzos, J. and Makkai, T. (2004) *Women's Experiences of Male Violence*, Research and Public Policy Series No 56. Canberra: Australian Institute of Criminology.

Muncie, J. (1999) *Youth and Crime*. Buckingham: Open University Press.

Muncie, J. (2002) Policy transfers and 'what works': some reflections on comparative youth justice. *Criminal Justice*, 1(3): 27–35.

Myhill, A. and Allen, J. (2002) *Rape and Sexual Assault: Its Nature and Extent*. Home Office Research Study 237. London: Home Office.

Mythen, G. (2005) From goods to bads? Revisiting the political economy of risk. *Sociological Research Online*, 10(3). http://www.socresonline.org.uk/10/3/mythen.html.

Mythen, G. and Walklate, S. (2006a) Communicating the terrorist risk: harnessing a culture of fear? *Crime, Media, Culture: An International Journal*, 2(2).

Mythen, G. and Walklate, S. (2006b) Criminology and terrorism: which thesis? Risk society or governmentality? *British Journal of Criminology*, 43(3): 379–98.

MVA Consultancy (2000) *The 2000 Scottish Crime Survey*. Edinburgh: Scottish Executive.

Naffine, N. (1990) *Law and the Sexes*. London: Allen & Unwin.

National Board for Crime Prevention (1994) *Wise After the Event: Tackling Repeat Victimization*. London: Home Office.

National Probation Service for England and Wales (2004) Views of the probation victim contact scheme. *National Probation Service Briefing*, 20 (September).

Nelken, D (2002) Comparing criminal justice. In M. Maguire, R. Morgan and R. Reiner (eds) *The Oxford Handbook of Criminology*. Oxford: Oxford University Press.

Nellis, M. (1995) Probation values for the 1990s. *Howard Journal of Criminal Justice*, 34(1): 19–44.

Nettleton, H., Walklate, S. and Williams, B. (1997) *Probation Service with the Victim in Mind*. Keele: Keele University Press.

Newburn, T. and McEvoy, K. (eds) (2003) *Criminology, Conflict Resolution and Restorative Justice*. London: Macmillan.

Newburn, T. and Stanko, E.A. (eds) (1994) *Just Boys Doing Business*. London: Routledge.

Newman, G. (ed.) (1999) *Global Report on Crime and Justice*. New York and Oxford: Oxford University Press.

Nicholas, S., Povey, D., Walker, A. and Kershaw, C. (2005) *Crime in England and Wales 2004/5*. London: Home Office.

Oberwittler, D. and Hofer, S. (2005) Crime and Justice in Germany: An analysis of recent trends and research. *European Journal of Criminology*, 2(4): 465–508.

O'Donnell, I. (2005) Crime and justice in the Republic of Ireland. *European Journal of Criminology*, 2(1): 99–131.

O'Donnell, I. and Edgar, K. (1998) Routine victimisation in prisons. *Howard Journal of Criminal Justice*, 37(3): 266–79.

Offe, C. (1984) *Contradictions of the Welfare State*. London: Macmillan.

Office for Criminal Justice Reform (2006) *Convicting Rapists and Protecting Victims – Justice for Victims of Rape*, Ref. 274404. London: Office for Criminal Justice Reform.

O'Malley, P. (2002) Globalizing risk? Distinguishing styles of 'neo-liberal' criminal justice in Australia and the USA. *Criminal Justice*, 2(2): 205–22.

O'Malley, P. (2004) The uncertain promise of risk. *Australian and New Zealand Journal of Criminology*, 37(3): 323–43.

Outhwaite, W. (1987) *New Philosophies of Social Science: Realism, Hermeneutics and Critical Theory*. London: Macmillan.

Padfield, N. and Crowley, R. (2003) Procedural and evidential protections in the English courts. In M. Tonry (ed.) *Confronting Crime: Crime Control Policy under New Labour*. Cullompton: Willan.

Pain, R. (1991) Space, sexual violence and social control: integrating geographical and feminist analyses of women's fear of crime. *Progress in Human Geography*, 15(4): 415–31.

Painter, K. (1991) Marriage, wife rape and the law. Department of Social Policy, University of Manchester.

Patel, P. (1992) Plenary address. Violence Against Women Conference, Manchester Metropolitan University, Manchester, May.

Pauwels, L. and Pleysier, S. (2005) Assessing cross-cultural validity of fear of crime measures through comparison between linguistic communities in Belgium. *European Journal of Criminology*, 2(2): 139–60.

Pavlich, G. (2002) Towards an ethics of restorative justice. In L. Waldgrave (ed.) *Restorative Justice and the Law*. Cullompton: Willan.

Pawson, R. (1989) *A Measure for Measures*. London: Routledge.

Pearce, F. and Tombs, S. (1998) *Toxic Capitalism*. Aldershot: Ashgate.

Pease, K. (1998) *Repeat Victimisation: Taking Stock*, Crime Prevention and Detection Series Paper 90. London: Home Office.

Peelo, M. and Soothill, K. (2000) The place of public narratives in reproducing social order. *Theoretical Criminology*, 4(2): 131–48.

Pepinsky, H. and Quinney, R (eds) (1991) *Criminology as Peacemaking*. Bloomington: Indiana University Press.

Percy, A. and Mayhew, P. (1997) Estimating sexual victimisation in a national crime survey. *Studies in Crime and Crime Prevention*, 6: 125–50.

Perry, B. (2003) Where do we go from here? Researching hate crime. *Internet Journal of Criminology.* http://www.internetjournalofcriminology.com.

Philo, G. (1999) *Message Received: Glasgow Media Group Research 1993–1998.* New York: Addison Wesley Longman.

Phipps, A. (1988) Ideologies, political parties and victims of crime. In M. Maguire and J. Pointing (eds) *Victims of Crime: A New Deal?* Milton Keynes: Open University Press.

Piispa, M. (2003) Violence against women as conveyed by surveys – the Finnish case. *Journal of Scandinavian Studies in Criminology and Crime Prevention,* 3: 173–93.

Pitts, J. (2001) *New Politics of Youth Crime.* Basingstoke: Macmillan.

President's Task Force on Victims of Crime (1982) *Final Report.* Washington, DC: US Government Printing Office.

Quinney, R. (1972) Who is the victim? *Criminology,* 10: 309–29.

Radford, J. (1987) Policing male violence. In J. Hamner and M. Maynard (eds) *Women, Violence and Social Control.* London: Macmillan.

Radford, J. and Stanko, E. (1991) Violence against women and children: the contradictions of crime control under patriarchy. In K. Stenson and D. Cowell (eds) *The Politics of Crime Control.* London: Sage.

Raine, J. and Smith, R.E. (1991) *The Victim/Witness Support Project.* London: Victim Support.

Ray, L. and Smith, D. (2001) Racist offenders and the politics of 'hate crime'. *Law and Critique,* 12: 203–21.

Regan, L. and Kelly, L. (2003) Rape: still a forgotten issue. Child and Woman Abuse Studies Unit, London Metropolitan University.

Reiman, J. (2001) *The Rich Get Richer and the Poor Get Prison.* New York: Allyn and Bacon.

Rhodes, R.W. (1997) *Understanding Governance.* Buckingham: Open University Press.

Roché, S. (1993) *Le Sentiment d'Insecurité.* Paris: PUF.

Roché, S. (2002) Towards a new governance of crime and insecurity in France. In A. Crawford (ed.) *Crime and Insecurity. The Governance of Public Safety in Europe.* Cullompton: Willan.

Rock, P. (1986) *A View from the Shadows.* Oxford: Oxford University Press.

Rock, P. (1990) *Helping Victims of Crime.* Oxford: Clarendon Press.

Rock, P. (1998) *After Homicide.* Oxford: Clarendon Press.

Rock, P. (2002) On becoming a victim. In C. Hoyle and R. Young (eds) *New Visions of Crime Victims.* Oxford: Hart.

Rock, P. (2004) *Constructing Victims' Rights: The Home Office, New Labour, and Victims.* Oxford: Clarendon Press.

Rumgay, J. (2005) *When Victims Become Offenders: In Search of Coherence in Policy and Practice.* London: Fawcett Society.

Russell, D. (1990) *Rape in Marriage.* New York: Collier.

Salecl, R. (2004) *On Anxiety.* London: Routledge.

Salisbury, H. and Upson, A. (2004) *Ethnicity, Victimisation and Worry about Crime: Findings from the 2001/2 and 2002/3 British Crime Survey*. London: Stationery Office.

Sampson, R.J., Raudenbush, W. and Felton, E. (1997) Neighbourhoods and violent crime: a multilevel study of collective efficacy. *Science*, 277: 918–24.

Sanders, A. (1999) *Taking Account of Victims in the Criminal Justice System: A Review of the Literature*, Social Work Findings No. 32. Edinburgh: Scottish Office Central Research Unit.

Sanders, A. (2002) Victim participation in an exclusionary criminal justice system. In C. Hoyle and R. Young (eds) *New Visions of Crime Victims*. Portland, OR: Hart.

Savolainen, J. (2005) The decline in family violence against Finnish women. In R. Sirén and P. Honkatukia (eds) *Victimisation to Violence in Finland 1980–2003*. Helsinki: National Research Institute of Legal Policy.

Sayer, A. (2000) *Realism and Social Science*. London: Sage.

Scarman, Lord (1982) *The Scarman Report*. Harmondsworth: Penguin

Schafer, S. (1968) *The Victim and His Criminal*. New York: Random House.

Schlesinger, P., Humber, H. and Murdock, G. (1991) The media, politics of crime and criminal justice. *British Journal of Sociology*, 42(3): 397–420.

Schroettle, M. and Müller, U. (2004) *Gesundheit, Wohlbefinden und persönliche Sicherheit von Frauen in Deutschland* [Health, Well-Being and Personal Safety of Women in Germany]. Berlin: Federal Ministry for Family Affairs, Senior Citizens, Women and Youth (BMFSFJ). http://www.bmfsfj.de.

Sebba, L. (2001) On the relationship between criminological research and policy: the case of crime victims. *Criminology and Criminal Justice*, 1(1): 27–58.

Shapland, J., Willmore, J. and Duff, P. (1985) *Victims and the Criminal Justice System*. Aldershot: Gower.

Sherman, L. and Smith, D. (1992) Crime, punishment and stake in conformity: legal and informal control of domestic violence. *American Sociological Review*, 57: 670–90.

Sherman, L., Schmidt, J., Regan, D., Gartin, P. and Cohn, E. (1991) From initial deterrence to long-term escalation: short custody arrest for ghetto poverty violence. *Criminology*, 29(4): 821–49.

Simmons, J. and Dodd, T. (2003) Crime in England and Wales 2002/2003. London: Home Office.

Skogan, W. (1986) The fear of crime and its behavioural implications. In E.A. Fattah (ed.) *From Crime Policy to Victim Policy*. London: Macmillan.

Slapper, G. and Tombs, S. (1999) *Corporate Crime*. Harlow: Longman.

Smart, C. (1989) *Feminism and the Power of Law*. London: Routledge.

Smart, C. (1990) Feminist approaches to criminology: or postmodern woman meets atavistic man. In L. Gelsthorpe and A. Morris (eds) *Feminist Perspectives in Criminology*. Buckingham: Open University Press.

Smith, D. (1987) *The Everyday World as Problematic*. Milton Keynes: Open University Press.

Smolej, M. and Kivivuori, J. (2005) The association between crime, media and fear of violence. In R. Sirén and P. Honkatukia (eds) *Victimisation to Violence in Finland: Results from 1980–2003 National Surveys*. Helsinki: National Research Institute of Legal Policy.

Snider, L. (2003) Constituting the punishable woman: atavistic man incarcerates post-modern woman. *British Journal of Criminology*, 43(2): 354–78.

Spalek, B. (2006) *Crime Victims: Theory, Policy and Practice*. London: Palgrave.

Sparks, R. (1992) Reason and unreason in left realism; some problems in the constitution of the fear of crime. In R. Matthews and J. Young (eds) *Issues in Realist Criminology*. London: Sage.

Sparks, R., Genn, H. and Dodd, D. (1977) *Surveying Victims*. London: Wiley.

Squires, P. (ed.) (2006) *Community Safety: Critical Perspectives on Policy and Practice*. Bristol: Policy Press.

Stanko, E. (1985) *Intimate Intrusions: Women's Experience of Male Violence*. London: Virago.

Stanko, E. (1988) Hidden violence against women. In M. Maguire and J. Pointing (eds) *Victims of Crime: A New Deal?* Milton Keynes: Open University Press.

Stanko, E.A. (1990) *Everyday Violence*. London: Virago.

Stanko, E.A. (1997) Safety talk: conceptualising women's risk assessment as a technology of the soul. *Theoretical Criminology*, 1(4): 479–99.

Stanko, E.A. (2004) Reviewing the evidence of hate: lessons from a project under the Home Office Crime Reduction Programme. *Criminal Justice*, 4(3): 277–87.

Stanko, E.A. and Hobdell, K. (1993) Assaults on men: masculinity and male victimisation. *British Journal of Criminology*, 33(3): 400–15.

Stanley, L. and Wise, S. (1987) *Georgie, Porgie: Sexual Harassment in Everyday Life*. London: Macmillan.

Strang, H. and Braithwaite, J. (eds) (2002) *Restorative Justice and Family Violence*. Cambridge: Cambridge University Press.

Stubbs, J. (1997) Shame, defiance and violence against women. In S. Cook and J. Bessant (eds) *Women's Encounters with Violence: Australian Experiences*. London: Sage.

Sumner, C. (1990) *Censure, Politics and Criminal Justice*. Buckingham: Open University Press.

Sutton, R. and Farrall, S. (2005) Gender, socially desirable responding and the fear of crime: are women really more anxious about crime? *British Journal of Criminology*, 45(2): 212–24.

Tapley, J. (2005) Public confidence costs – criminal justice from a victim's perspective. *British Journal of Community Justice*, 3(2): 39–50.

Taylor, I. (1996) Fear of crime, urban fortunes and suburban social movements: some reflections on Manchester. *Sociology*, 30: 317–37.

Taylor, I. (1997) Crime, anxiety and locality: responding to the condition of England at the end of the century. *Theoretical Criminology*, 1(1): 53–76.

Taylor, I., Evans, K. and Fraser, P. (1996) *A Tale of Two Cities*. London: Routledge.

Tombs, S. (2005) Workplace harm and the illusions of law. In P. Hillyard *et al.* (eds) *Criminal Obsessions: Why Harm Matters More Than Crime*. London: Crime and Society Foundation.

Tombs, S. and Whyte, D. (2006) Risk and work. In G. Mythen and S. Walklate (eds) *Beyond the Risk Society: Critical Reflections on Risk and Human Security*. Maidenhead: Open University Press.

Tomsen, S. (2001) Hate crimes and masculinity: new crimes, new responses and some familiar patterns. Paper presented to the 4th National Outlook Symposium on Crime in Australia.

Toren, A. (2004) *2004 Survey of Domestic Violence Services (England) Findings*. http://www.womensaid.org.uk.

Tseloni, A. and Pease, K. (2003) Repeat personal victimisation: boosts or flags? *British Journal of Criminology*, 43(1): 196–212.

Tudor, A. (2003) A (macro) sociology of fear? *Sociological Review*, 51(2): 238–56.

Tulloch, J. and Lupton, D. (2003) *Risk and Everyday Life*. London: Sage.

United Nations (1999) *Handbook on Justice for Victims*. New York: United Nations Office for Drug Control and Crime Prevention, Centre for International Crime Prevention.

United Nations (2004) *Violence against Women: Report of the Secretary General*. New York: United Nations.

United Nations Commission on Human Security (2003) *Human Security Now*. New York: United Nations.

Valentine, G. (1992) Images of danger: women's sources of information about the spatial distribution of male violence. *Area*, 24: 23–9.

Valier, C. (2004) *Crime and Punishment in Contemporary Culture*. London: Routledge.

van Kesteren, J.N., Mayhew, P. and Nieuwbeerta, P. (2002) *Criminal Victimisation in Seventeen Industrialised Countries: Key Findings from the 2000 International Crime Victims Survey*, Onderzoek en Beleid, no. 187. The Hague: Ministry of Justice, Wetenschappelijk Oderzoek- en Documentatiecentrum.

Victim Support (2002) *New Rights for Victims of Crime in Europe*. London: Victim Support.

von Hentig, H. (1948) *The Criminal and his Victim*. New Haven, CT: Yale University Press.

Walby, S. and Allen, J. (2004) *Domestic Violence, Sexual Assault and Stalking: Findings from the British Crime Survey*, Home Office Research Study 276. London: Home Office.

Walby, S. and Myhill, A. (2001) New Survey methodologies in researching violence against women. *British Journal of Criminology*, 41(3): 502–22.

Waldron, J. (1993) *Liberal Rights: Collected Papers 1981–91*. Cambridge: Cambridge University Press.

Walklate, S. (1989) *Victimology: The Victim and the Criminal Justice Process*. London: Unwin Hyman.

Walklate, S. (1990) Researching victims of crime: critical victimology. *Social Justice*, 17(3): 25–42.

Walklate, S. (1997) Risk and criminal victimisation: a modernist dilemma? *British Journal of Criminology*, 37(3): 35–45.

Walklate, S. (1998a) Excavating the fear of crime: fear, anxiety or trust? *Theoretical Criminology*, 2(4): 403–18.

Walklate, S. (1998b) Crime and community: fear or trust? *British Journal of Sociology*, 49(4): 550–70.

Walklate, S. (2003a) Can there be a feminist victimology? In P. Davies, P. Francis and V. Jupp (eds) *Victimisation: Theory, Research and Policy*. London: Palgrave.

Walklate, S. (2003b) Local contexts and globalised knowledges: what can international criminal victimisation surveys tell us about women's diverse lives? Paper presented to the Women, Crime and Globalisation Workshop, Onati, Spain, September.

Walklate, S. (2004) *Gender, Crime and Criminal Justice*. Cullompton: Willan.

Walklate, S (2005a) Imagining the crime victim: the rhetoric of victimhood as a source of oppression. *Social Justice*, 32(1): 89–99.

Walklate, S. (2005b) *Criminology: The Basics*. London: Taylor and Francis.

Walklate, S. (2006a) Changing boundaries of the 'victim' in restorative justice: so who is the victim now? In D. Sullivan and L. Tifft (eds) *Handbook of Restorative Justice*. London: Routledge.

Walklate, S. (2006b) Community safety and victims: who is the victim of community safety? In P. Squires (ed.) *Community Safety: Critical Perspectives on Policy and Practice*. Bristol: Policy Press.

Walklate, S. and Evans, K. (1999) *Zero Tolerance or Community Tolerance? Managing Crime in High Crime Areas*. Aldershot: Ashgate.

Waller, I. (1988) International standards, national trail blazing and the nest steps. In M. Maguire and J. Pointing (eds) *Victims of Crime: A New Deal?* Milton Keynes: Open University Press.

Warr, M. (1985) Fear of rape among urban women. *Social Problems*, 32(3).

Warr, M. (2000) Fear of crime in the United States: avenues for research and policy. In *Criminal Justice 2000 Vol. 4: Measurement and Analysis of Crime and Justice*. Washington, DC: US Department of Justice.

Weaver, K., Carter, C. and Stanko, E.A. (2000) The female body at risk. In S. Allan, B. Adam and C. Carter (eds) *Environmental Risks and the Media*. London: Routledge.

Welchman, S. and Hossain, S. (eds) (2005) *Honour Crimes*. London: Zed Books.

Wemmers, J. (2005) Victim policy transfer: learning from each other. *European Journal on Criminal Policy and Research*, 11(1): 121–33.

Wertham, F. (1949) *The Show of Violence*. New York: Doubleday.

Whyte, D. (2004) All that glitters is not gold: environmental crimes and the production of local criminological knowledge. *Crime Prevention and Community Safety: An International Journal*, 6(1): 53–64.

Williams, B. (1999) *Working with Victims of Crime: Policies, Politics and Practice*. London: Jessica Kingsley.

Williams, B. (2003) Community justice, victims and social justice. Professorial inaugural lecture, De Montfort University.

Williams, B. (2005) *Victims of Crime and Community Justice*. London: Jessica Kingsley.

Williams, B. and Canton, R. (2005) Editorial: Victims of crime, offenders and communities. *British Journal of Community Justice*, 3(2): 1–8.

Wilson, M. and Daly, M. (1998) Sexual rivalry and sexual conflict; recurring themes in fatal conflicts. *Theoretical Criminology*, 2(3): 291–310.

Winter, J. (2002) The trial of Rose West: contesting notions of victimhood. In C. Hoyle and R. Young (eds) *New Visions of Crime Victims*. Oxford: Hart.

Women's National Commission (2003) *Seen But Not Heard: Women's Experiences of the Police*. London: Women's National Commission.

Wood, M. (2005) *The Victimisation of Young People: Results from the Crime and Justice Survey 2003*. London: Stationery Office.

Worcester, R. (2001) The world will never be the same again: British hopes and fears after September 11th 2001. *International Journal of Public Opinion Research*. http://www.mori.com

Wright, G. and Hall, J. (2004) Victims, crime and criminal justice. In J. Muncie and D. Wilson (eds) *Student Handbook of Criminal Justice and Criminology*. London: Cavendish.

Young, A. (1996) *Imagining Crime*. London: Sage.

Young, J. (1986) The failure of criminology: the need for a radical realism. In R. Matthews and J. Young (eds) *Confronting Crime*. London: Sage.

Young, J. (1999) *The Exclusive Society*. London: Sage.

Young, J. (2001) Identity, community and social exclusion. In R. Matthews and J. Pitts (eds) *Crime, Disorder and Community Safety*. London: Routledge.

Young, J. (2003a) Merton with energy, Katz with structure: the sociology of vindictiveness and the criminology of transgression. *Theoretical Criminology*, 7(3): 389–414.

Young, J. (2003b) Searching for a new criminology of everyday life: a review of 'The Culture of Control' by D. Garland. *British Journal of Criminology*, 43(1): 228–43.

Young, M., Byles, J. and Dobson, A. (2000) *The Effectiveness of Legal Protection in the Prevention of Domestic Violence in the Lives of Young Australian Women*, Trends and Issues in Crime and Criminal Justice No. 148. Canberra: Australian Institute of Criminology.

Young, R. (2002) Testing the limits of restorative justice: the case of corporate victims. In C. Hoyle and R. Young (eds) *New Visions of Crime Victims*. Portland, OR: Hart.

Youth Justice Board (2002) *Building on Success: Youth Justice Board review 2001/ 2002*. London: Youth Justice Board.

Zedner, L. (2002) Victims. In M. Maguire, R. Morgan and R. Reiner (eds) The *Oxford Handbook of Criminology* (3rd edition). Oxford: Oxford University Press.

Zedner, L. and Lacey, N. (2000) 'Community' and governance: a cultural comparison. In S. Karstedt and K.D. Bussmann (eds) *Social Dynamics of Crime and Control*. Oxford: Hart.

Index

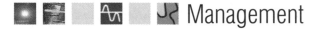